Following the Ball

Ohio University Research in International Studies

This series of publications on Africa, Latin America, Southeast Asia, and Global and Comparative Studies is designed to present significant research, translation, and opinion to area specialists and to a wide community of persons interested in world affairs. The series is distributed worldwide. For more information, consult the Ohio University Press website, ohioswallow.com.

Books in the Ohio University Research in International Studies series are published by Ohio University Press in association with the Center for International Studies. The views expressed in individual volumes are those of the authors and should not be considered to represent the policies or beliefs of the Center for International Studies, Ohio University Press, or Ohio University.

Executive Editor: Gillian Berchowitz

Following the Ball

THE MIGRATION OF AFRICAN SOCCER PLAYERS
ACROSS THE PORTUGUESE COLONIAL EMPIRE,
1949‒1975

Todd Cleveland

Ohio University Research in International Studies
Global and Comparative Studies Series No. 16
Ohio University Press
Athens

Ohio University Press, Athens, Ohio 45701
ohioswallow.com
© 2017 by Ohio University Press

To obtain permission to quote, reprint, or otherwise reproduce or distribute material from
Ohio University Press publications, please contact our rights and permissions department at
(740) 593-1154 or (740) 593-4536 (fax).

Printed in the United States of America
The books in the Ohio University Research in International Studies Series
are printed on acid-free paper ∞ ™

27 26 25 24 23 22 21 20 19 18 17   5 4 3 2 1

Hardcover ISBN 978-0-89680-313-8
Paperback ISBN 978-0-89680-314-5
Electronic ISBN 978-0-89680-499-9

Library of Congress Cataloging-in-Publication Data is available

To footballers everywhere, especially my two favorite players: Lucas and Byers

Contents

CHAPTER 5

Calculated Conciliation

Apoliticism in a Politically Charged Context

Illustrations

Acknowledgments

The process of researching and writing this book was extremely enjoyable, at times exciting, and, most importantly, it generated opportunities to interact with athletes, scholars, and others from across the globe. The research commenced in Portugal, and the first stops were, as is often the case, the Biblioteca Nacional and the Torre do Tombo. Staff at both repositories were, as always, professional and helpful. I also conducted research, for the first time, at Portugal's Ministério da Educação, where the staff were both patient and supportive, as were staff members at the Biblioteca Municipal de Coimbra. While I was based in Portugal, Adriano Cardoso and Luis Fazendeiro proved to be excellent research assistants, and even better travel companions, as we engaged in the process of tracking down, contacting, and journeying—via rental car, ferry, train, taxi, bus, metro, and, of course, on foot—to interview former players and coaches throughout Portugal. My great friend Jorge Varanda participated in this manner as well, and in so many other ways. At various times during my series of research trips to Portugal, Nina Tiesler and Cláudia Castelo provided key insights into various aspects of this history and were otherwise generous with their time and levels of assistance. I was also fortunate to have met Nuno Domingos and Rahul Kumar. Experts in Portuguese football—past and present—they patiently assisted as I slowly grasped the major developments and contours of this fascinating history and provided the type of support that would have suggested we had been lifelong friends. Even as this project concludes, I look forward to ongoing interactions with Nuno and Rahul.

As the research transitioned to Africa, Gil Filipe and Hélio Maúngue played roles similar to those of Adriano and Luis in Portugal; I am grateful to have worked with both of them. In Maputo, Moira Forjaz introduced me to Paola Rolletta—author of *Finta finta*—whose knowledge of Mozambican football far outpaces mine, but who demonstrated the same type of patience and assistance that Nuno and Rahul had back in Portugal. While in Mozambique, Dave Morton made a series of key introductions and greatly enhanced the time I spent there, while also making ongoing contributions to the project.

Others provided support away from my fieldwork sites, including Tom Paradise, who generated the two maps that appear in the book; and Marlino Mubai, who transcribed most of the interviews—a demanding endeavor, as anyone who has engaged in this undertaking knows well. Davi Rufino also transcribed some of the testimony, and Szymon Ligas offered research support at the onset of this project.

Funding for the project was primarily provided by different entities at Augustana College and, in particular, by a series of grants awarded by the Freistat Center. The Center for Lusophone Research (CLR) / Council of American Overseas Research Centers (CAORC) also provided funding at a crucial stage of the research process, as did the University of Arkansas as I was completing the manuscript.

Gill Berchowitz at Ohio University Press deserves special mention for the central role she played in bringing this book to publication. She believed in the project from the moment she perused a draft book proposal I had crafted that was undeniably short on refinement, even if it was, it seems, long on potential. Next, the anonymous readers of the manuscript identified important issues that, without their close readings, would most likely remain unrectified. And, as always, the staff at Ohio University Press were wonderful, helping me through the various production tasks and politely declining to comment even as I repeatedly fumbled many of them.

As I mentioned in the opening passage of this section, the project has unexpectedly taken me to a variety of places, generating innumerable introductions to individuals from across the globe, many of whom have made key contributions to this text. Often, this crucial input came in the form of comments offered at academic conferences. In the United States, soccer is still not a popular—or, in some cases, even a viable—topic of study. And African soccer even less so. But beyond our borders, there is a vibrant community of scholars, from across the disciplines, engaged in remarkably insightful and useful research related to the sport. Via this project, I've been fortunate to have met many members of this ever-expanding group. Their contributions may ultimately be individually immeasurable, but, collectively, their feedback and suggestions have undoubtedly greatly enhanced the book.

I am also extremely grateful to my informants, who took the time to sit down with me and discuss at length their experiences. Their testimony breathes life into the narrative, and their generosity and candidness form the backbone of this book. Sadly, at least three of the former players I interviewed have since passed away. I will be eternally grateful that they spent some of the precious time that remained to sit patiently with me and recount aspects of their lives that often took them far afield from the stadiums, fans, and sporting limelight.

Finally, I am grateful for the unwavering support that my family has provided throughout this process. When I began this project, our oldest son, Lucas, was only two years old; and his younger brother, Byers, was still two years away from joining us. Between then and now, they have grown into wonderful children as well as enthusiastic soccer players and fans. Throughout the summer of 2016, we faithfully gathered around the television in our apartment in Lisbon to tune in to each of Portugal's Euro 2016 matches. An uninspiring start to the tournament did nothing to suggest that we'd all be screaming with joy—along with the rest of the country—when Eder's shot eluded Hugo Lloris in the 109th minute of the championship game, and then again when the final whistle blew. In this manner, and in myriad other ways, soccer has deepened our familial unity and commitment to one another. As always, my wonderful wife, Julianna, is at the center of the family, relentlessly propelling it forward each day, even as her "three boys" constantly generate impediments to this advance. If my name on the cover of the book is equivalent to a striker enjoying all the glory immediately after scoring a goal, it was Julianna who delivered the probing pass that unlocked the defense and facilitated a simple tap into the back of the net. Quietly content, following the goal she unassumingly returns to her position on the pitch, waiting for the celebration to conclude and for play to resume; she deserves all the credit, but seeks none of it.

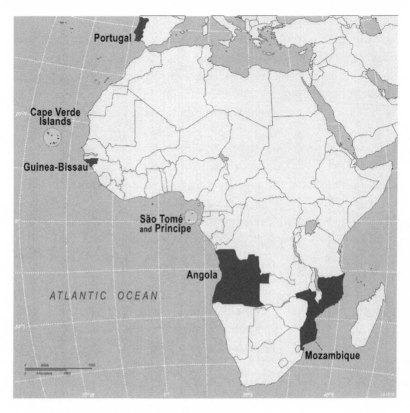

Portugal and its former colonies in Africa.

Introduction

I remember speaking to a Portuguese colleague of mine at work in Mozambique about my impending departure to play for Sporting Clube de Portugal [a major Lisbon-based squad] and he told me, "When you arrive there, you will be a man. A football player in Portugal is a very important person."

—Hilário da Conceição, 2013

In 1965 I was the first player from Africa and from Portugal to be awarded the World Player of the Year. For me it was an enormous responsibility. . . . I realized the enormity of winning [the award] because at that time I was twenty-three years old—old enough to understand what an honor, and a responsibility, it was. I represented Africa and Portugal, and there had never been a footballer from either to receive such an honor.

—Eusébio da Silva Ferreira, 2004

When superstar soccer[1] player Eusébio left the field following Portugal's 2–1 defeat at the hands of England in the 1966 World Cup semifinals, he was awash in tears, fiercely clutching his red and green jersey—the national colors of Portugal (see fig. I.1). Yet Eusébio da Silva Ferreira was neither born nor raised in the Iberian nation; instead, a Mozambican, he was one of the many Africans who made their way from Portugal's colonial territories to the metropole to ply their athletic skills from the late 1940s to the end of the colonial era in 1975. Like Eusébio, many of these African soccer players

Figure I.1. Eusébio leaving the pitch following the 1966 World Cup loss to England.

performed spectacularly on the field, significantly elevating the stature of their respective club teams and vaulting the Portuguese national team to unprecedented levels, and remain among the greatest footballers of all time.

While both Eusébio and Portuguese everywhere grieved following the squad's exit from the 1966 World Cup via the match that came to be known as the Jogo das Lágrimas (Game of Tears), the country was simultaneously engaged in far graver matters. Having disregarded the "winds of change" that had heralded European nations' abandonment of imperial territories in Africa beginning in the late 1950s, since the early 1960s Portugal had been actively attempting to suppress armed insurgencies in three of its five African colonies: Angola, Mozambique, and Guiné (the other two, Cape Verde and São Tomé, remained relatively quiet). Unlike other European colonizing nations, Portugal's dictatorial Estado Novo (New State) regime intransigently resisted mounting international pressure to decolonize, locking itself in a struggle to retain its African possessions. The government's insistence on the territorial—and, thus, racial—integration of Portugal and its African colonies was central to its public relations campaign intended to legitimize, and thereby maintain, the empire. As such, the reforms that facilitated the relocation of African players to the metropole were, at least in part, politically motivated, aimed to appease external critics of Lisbon rather than to genuinely loosen social restrictions and liberalize colonial society. The inclusion of African players, such as Eusébio, on Portugal's club and national soccer teams and their sustained continental and international success constituted valuable propaganda for the increasingly embattled Estado Novo regime, which was utilized to highlight the supposed unity of the metropole and the colonies, as well as the opportunities for social mobility that its African subjects allegedly enjoyed.

This book examines the experiences of these African athletes as they relocated to Portugal from 1949 until the conclusion of the colonial era in 1975, negotiated this politically charged environment, and consolidated their post-soccer futures.[2] Although always minorities on their Portuguese clubs, these players' sporting, social, and political impacts in the colonies, metropole, and, ultimately, globally, far outweigh their numerical modesty. Beyond their outsized sporting influence, they also instilled both racial and national pride among their African compatriots and concurrently generated esteem for an increasingly beleaguered Portugal. In reconstructing the players' transnational histories, the narrative traces their lives from the humble, informal soccer spaces in colonial Africa to the manicured pitches of Europe, while simultaneously focusing on their off-the-field challenges and successes. By examining this multicontinental space in a single analytical field, *Following the Ball* illuminates the structural and experiential consistencies and discrepancies across the constituent settings, and also considers the components and processes of empire. These athletes' experiences also serve to blur the lines between colonial and metropolitan milieus, as players, clubs, and sporting news and tactics increasingly circulated between these various nodes, reinvigorating their historical links and drawing them into closer dialogue, even as African liberation movements fought to sever these imperial connections. This book also engages with global processes by exploring not only how external political and sporting developments shaped these Lusophone histories, but also how players and clubs across the Portuguese empire articulated them locally.

Although this study features football and its practitioners as its central topics, it also provides a window into social relations in colonial and metropolitan societies, embedding sport in these shifting historical contexts and elucidating the ways that African players forged cooperative, symbiotic relationships across seemingly unbridgeable divides. Institutionalized racism profoundly shaped social interactions in Portugal's colonies, yet the meaningful and durable bonds these players cultivated with teammates, fans, and club officials suggest a complexity in race relations in both the colonies and the metropole that belies reductive renderings. Within this relational spectrum, the players often assumed roles as social and cultural intermediaries, operating between an assortment of societal segments and strata in Africa and Europe. Ultimately, by exploring the ways these players creatively exploited opportunities generated by shifts in the political and occupational landscapes in the waning decades of Portugal's empire, the book aims to prompt reconsiderations of social relations and processes in late colonial Lusophone Africa, as well as in the metropolitan core, while also opening up new ways of thinking about sport, society, and power in this pivotal period in global history.

From Africa to Europe: Navigating the Metropole

Although the Portuguese regime sanctioned the relocation of African players due to their athletic skills, it also deemed them valuable resources in an increasingly fraught global-political scenario. As such, even as the regime progressively emphasized football's role as one of the three pillars of the nation, alongside *fado* music and Fátima (famed location of a shrine to Christianity)[3]—the so-called "three f's"—the state secret police closely monitored players' actions. Even the labor reforms that facilitated the players' migration to Portugal were, ultimately, similarly restrictive. For example, despite steady interest from clubs across Europe to secure the signatures of these African footballers, the regime refused to permit them to transfer abroad, even going so far as to classify Eusébio as a "national asset" to preclude his exit. This unwillingness to allow athletes to practice their trade elsewhere contradicted the Estado Novo's self-congratulatory propaganda regarding the expansion of freedoms within the empire that these soccer migrants supposedly epitomized.

In addition to geographical constraints, African players faced an array of challenges associated with their long-distance migration. Having endured protracted journeys to Portugal, newly removed from friends and family members, and thrust into a climate that most of the athletes found disagreeable, many initially longed for their homelands. For example, as José Maria, who hailed from Angola and first traveled to Portugal in December 1962 to play for Vitória de Setúbal, explained, "I knew it was going to be colder . . . but I never imagined it would be that much colder. . . . That negatively affected my career when I first arrived. I wanted to run the field but I couldn't because I could feel the cold wind touching my skin like razor blades. . . . I thought I was going to die."[4] Notwithstanding the formidable climatic acclimation obstacles that migrant athletes faced, the vast majority eventually settled in well, adjusting to their new environs, succeeding both on and off the pitch, and often remaining in Portugal after their playing days concluded.

This transitional success was, however, predicated on more than just the players' sheer athleticism. Their typically steady integration into metropolitan society, their decisions to parlay their ability to migrate into a host of educational and remunerative opportunities—the benefits of which endured long after their athletic abilities faded—and their generation and sustenance of genuine adulation among a fan base that stretched from the metropole to the colonies (and beyond) required much more than simply excellent soccer skills. I argue that these players so adroitly navigated their new milieu owing to a series of strategies that they adopted, including: [1] cooperation across a range of social and racial divides; [2] the internalization of Portuguese customs prior to their arrival; [3] employment of labor tactics learned or observed in the colonies; and [4] an unflinching apoliticism, even as the wars for independence were raging in Portugal's African colonies—their homelands.

Most of the strategic behavior that underpinned players' social and athletic success in the metropole was formatively developed in the colonies, well before the migrants ever set foot in Portugal. As members of neighborhood (*bairro*) teams and underfunded clubs across an assortment of African municipalities, players began to forge the personal relationships that would assist them as they steadily ascended the successive layers of colonial and metropolitan soccerdom. Although social relations were initially cultivated among neighborhood friends, as the players moved up the levels, their clubs' rosters increasingly featured racial, religious, and geographical diversity.

These new teammates provided indispensable support as players transitioned from casual practitioners to professional athletes, committing increasing amounts of time to improving their soccer skills. Although football in Portugal's colonies had initially developed strictly along racial lines, and thus in parallel, after World War II the sport newly began to constitute a more diverse, inclusive space. Experiences on integrated squads in the colonies would serve African players well following their relocation to metropolitan outfits, as, despite their growing ranks, they never outnumbered their white teammates on any of the Portuguese clubs.

If participation on squads in Africa that featured demographical diversity helped these footballers integrate socially upon reaching the metropole, meaningful exposure to Portuguese culture in the colonies was similarly vital. Indeed, virtually all the African clubs with which these players were affiliated before being "discovered" featured Portuguese coaches and were invariably located in urban centers, the loci of European colonization. Consequently, every one of these future migrants spent time in intensely colonized spaces and was, therefore, exposed to Portuguese customs and values prior to leaving the continent.

Additionally, many of the players were members of an extremely small, semiprivileged minority in Portugal's colonies, known as *assimilados*, or "assimilateds." Until 1961, when the Estado Novo regime abandoned this classification, Africans whom the state deemed sufficiently Portuguese in regard to language, culture, religion, and so on could apply for this designation, which, in turn, afforded them a special, intermediate legal status. Assimilados typically benefited from otherwise-rare educational opportunities and were often the offspring of Portuguese fathers and African mothers, known as *mestiços* (mulattoes). In 1950, although less than 1 percent of the colonial subjects in Portugal's empire were officially "assimilated," almost 90 percent of mestiços were.[5] It's not a coincidence that many of the African footballers who relocated to Portugal derived from the mixed-race population; for these players, the process of cultural integration had begun even earlier and was inherently deeper.

Immigrant athletes also actively facilitated their success in the metropole by pursuing a variety of occupational strategies. If African players largely adapted—or integrated—culturally and socially with few difficulties, a series of creative, short- and long-term labor strategies that they had either previously employed in the colonies or simply observed and internalized helped them capitalize to the fullest extent possible on their new opportunities. In some ways, the superstar status that many players enjoyed helps to obscure both their fundamental existence as wage laborers and their reliance on strategies that were derivative, or even imitative, of those that African workers in Portugal's colonies had been employing for decades, if not longer. For example, prior to leaving Africa, many soccer prospects sought advice from players who had already migrated to Portugal, typically inquiring about which clubs offered the best working and living conditions. Armed with this knowledge, many followed in the footsteps of the athletes who had preceded them, roughly analogous to one of the countless Mozambicans and Angolans who worked in South Africa's mines during the colonial period soliciting occupational information from a returning migrant laborer, and then accordingly targeting a specific operation for employment. Once established in the metropole, these footballers also sought advice from more experienced coworkers (i.e., teammates) when renegotiating their contracts. Many players also engaged in secondary migration, subsequently affiliating with a series of different Portuguese clubs, just as migrant mine laborers deliberately switched employers in an effort to improve their working conditions. Thus, even as these African footballers navigated drastically different professional terrain, they fell back on well-established tactics. Indigenous laborers throughout Portugal's African empire would find neither the basic occupational nor the migratory strategies that these soccer migrants employed wholly unfamiliar.

The secondary migration paths that these athletes traversed didn't always entail simply swapping one club for another. Instead, many of the footballers parlayed their ability to travel to Portugal to continue their studies in the hopes of receiving an education that would, in turn, serve them well long after their athleticism withered. The pursuit of a degree in higher education was primarily accomplished by playing for Académica, located in the central Portuguese city of Coimbra. This football club was associated with the country's premier university, the Universidade de Coimbra, and during the colonial era the squad was composed solely of matriculating students. Mário Wilson, who arrived in Portugal from Mozambique in 1949, was one of many soccer migrants from Africa who acknowledged having strategically pursued this educational option: "I came to play for Sporting [Clube de Portugal]. But I only played there for one year even though I was the top scorer that season. I felt that football wasn't the solution; no one achieved financial independence from [just] playing soccer. . . . So I went to school in Coimbra and also played for many years for Académica in the first division."[6]

Other African footballers pursued postsoccer security by attaining long-term employment with CUF (Companhia União Fabril), an industrial conglomerate located near Lisbon that required members of the first division team it sponsored to be company employees, and also guaranteed them jobs following their playing days. Although neither Académica nor CUF were particularly competitive on the pitch, in both these scenarios the secondary migration strategies that players employed in order to secure academic and employment opportunities constituted foresighted thinking that sacrificed (potential) short-term athletic glory for long-term financial security.

Just as these players strategically seized educational and remunerative opportunities in Portugal, they also deftly navigated the politically charged environments in both the metropole and the colonies that the wars for independence were fueling. Consequently, they were viewed neither as subversives in Portugal nor as political stooges by their African brothers who were fighting—and literally dying—for independence. Although often internally conflicted, the athletes' professionalism and determination to improve their lives underpinned their conspicuous apoliticism throughout this turbulent period. As such, despite their allure as potential nationalist symbols for the various African independence movements and the Portuguese regime, they failed to serve either the insurgencies or the counterinsurgency well, while remaining widely respected and admired in both the colonies and the metropole.

Historiographical Significance

Scholars are increasingly engaging with topics related to soccer and Africa, generating a nascent yet growing body of literature.[7] This trend is also evident in the Lusophone context, with this project contributing to the emerging corpus.[8] Although the on-the-field accomplishments of African players who migrated to Portugal during the colonial era have previously appeared in a number of homages—virtual hagiographies—this study is the first to consider these athletes' daily experiences beyond the stadium walls, far from the droves of cheering spectators and laudatory biographers.[9] In fact, *Following the Ball* constitutes the initial academic engagement with this otherwise-renowned stream of migrant athletes who ushered in the golden era of Portuguese soccer, while also helping to shape an evolving system of global football in which national borders are increasingly immaterial.[10] This belated scholarly consideration stands in sharp contrast to the considerable attention that African footballers who played in France during the colonial period and, in particular, their radical political activity, have received.[11] While my study is informed by this scholarship, I link the Lusophone migrants' destination and places of origin not through revolutionary politics, but via durable occupational strategies and the extended process of cultural integration.

In the following section, I outline the broader historiographical, analytical, and epistemological utility of five aspects of these African footballers' histories, including their strategic apolitical disposition and comportment; their social engagement across an array of well-established divides; their role as cultural intermediaries; their importation and application of labor strategies in the metropole, which facilitated success both on and away from the pitch; and their self-improvement objectives vis-à-vis colonial and, ultimately, neocolonial exploitation. Through an analysis of these distinguishing features, this book moves soccer studies in novel directions, while also making utile contributions across a number of scholarly fields well beyond the realm of African football.

I. Scholars of the history of soccer in Africa have cogently established that although Europeans introduced the game, indigenous practitioners were hardly passive consumers, contesting various aspects and fashioning new meanings of the sport.[12] Pioneering work by Fair and Martin, among others, astutely identified the nationalist and proto-nationalist dimensions of soccer in British and French colonial Africa; insightfully reconstructed the contention over leisure time and the limits of European control; and rightfully analyzed football as a "terrain of struggle." More recently, Alegi, Bittencourt, and others have built upon these foundational studies.[13] In much more hyperbolic fashion, Goldblatt has claimed that "all across the continent, Africans turned the colonists' game against them," and that "lessons learned on and off the pitch were [newly] turned against colonialism."[14] And, in perhaps the most extreme examples of the politicization of football, Lanfranchi, Taylor, Wahl, and others have considered the Francophone African players who fled France to overtly support the struggle for Algerian independence.[15]

In continuing to highlight Africans' active, if less confrontational, engagement with the sport, Domingos and others have demonstrated that indigenous practitioners essentially appropriated the game, attributing meanings to it unintended by those who had originally introduced it. As part of this process, African players produced unique, often "creolized" styles that reflected local aesthetic values and typically featured a performative "flair" largely absent in European versions of this activity.[16] Beyond such patterns of amendment and transmutation, Fair, Alegi, and Moorman, among others, have shown that when banned from white clubs and associations in the colonies, African players and coordinators formed teams and leagues of their own that helped foster the development of distinct (local and national) oppositional identities and, concomitantly, political consciousness.[17] In certain cases, this autonomous endeavor of sporting organization simulated the process of institution building in an imagined postcolonial state.

This book builds upon the aforementioned landmark scholarship, but instead of highlighting appropriation, contestation, or even liberation politics, it explores the ways African soccer players adopted European styles and conventions and, microcosmic of the broader colonial populations—settler and indigenous alike—embraced Portuguese football clubs and their local affiliates. This amenability constituted neither a Gramscian, hegemonically induced capitulation to cultural power, nor a Fanonesque, reverential, if perverse and subconscious, emulation of the dominant community; rather, Lusophone African footballers pragmatically pursued opportunities to improve their lives and, by extension, those of their families, while still retaining indigenous identities that were, of course, never static in their composition.[18] Throughout these processes of engagement, players remained strategically apolitical as they transitioned from Africa to the metropole, even as their sporting success provided political cover, confidence, and a semblance of legitimacy—no matter how spurious—to the increasingly besieged Portuguese colonial project. While acknowledging the asymmetrical power relations that existed between African athletes and club, colonial, and metropolitan officials, the analytical salience of the former's deliberate, willful cooperation significantly outweighs the much less frequent instances of discontentment or confrontation. By unconditionally applying their athletic acumen to this erstwhile foreign leisure activity, the footballers generated opportunities for social mobility and, ultimately, a ticket to, and (for some, permanent) placement in, metropolitan society.

II. If these players increasingly began to join the traditionally whites-only clubs in the colonies, at a more personal level they also cooperated in both Africa and Europe across a range of social and racial divides with teammates, supporters, and, in many cases, women-cum-wives. As these players ascended the different tiers of colonial soccerdom—in the process moving spatially from the largely black suburbs to the predominantly white city centers for their "home" matches—they experienced greater diversity among their teammates, who derived from different neighborhoods or even provinces. Indeed, over the course of the colonial period, football became a more integrative than divisive endeavor. Although players' divergent backgrounds and the resultant unfamiliarity, or even rivalry, may have generated hostility in other scenarios, as teammates any identity politics dissipated in the face of common goals and cultivated camaraderie. At the top levels in colonial leagues and even more profoundly once in Portugal, African players on racially integrated clubs forged meaningful, reciprocal relationships with players of European descent that problematize purely antagonistic understandings of race relations in these settings.

In fact, once in the metropole, provenance served as a durable social bond, transcending, eroding, or at least tempering racial divides. It also generated a type of resilient solidarity, as black and mestiço players shared a series of formative experiences with white players from the colonies—many of whom also traveled to Portugal to play and, like their African counterparts, were permitted to do so only after formal policy adjustments. Indeed, the Portuguese had been active in, for example, Angola and Mozambique for centuries; and, thus, the many white migrant footballers that these settler communities produced felt stronger connections to Africa than to the imagined *patria* (homeland), a place many of them had never previously visited. Testimony from Hilário, a mestiço footballer who first arrived in Lisbon in 1958, captures these social dynamics and the experiential importance of (African and, more specifically, Mozambican) provenance:

> Players from Africa—black or white—who were already in Portugal always helped a lot because they wanted to see the new African players succeed and triumph. The players from Africa had a deep connection with the continent and most would have rather stayed in Africa than have traveled to Portugal, but we had to come to play soccer. Therefore, we would support everyone who came from Africa, giving advice or anything else they needed. We liked helping one another. We didn't care about the color difference. . . . Normally, whoever was from Mozambique was proud of being born in that country. . . . Wherever we were in the world, if there was someone from Mozambique there, we would be supported; the "Mozambique nation" will always be there to help.[19]

Although scholars have considered the implications of provenance among immigrant communities elsewhere, examples of interracial cooperation in these reconstituted communities are rare, as diasporic populations often reflect and actively maintain preexisting social divides.[20] My emphasis on the experiential importance of provenance and, in particular, its transcendent role in helping to facilitate and deepen intercultural amity among these migrant athletes builds upon work by scholars who have examined the development of genuine interracial, intergender relations in colonial Africa.[21] However, this book extends the analytical and geographical scopes of such work by adding intragender examples that featured on the continent, but also persisted into the diaspora. Although scholars have rightfully debunked Lusotropicalism—the notion that the Portuguese were uniquely predisposed to interact with their colonized subjects in a more congenial, less exploitative manner—these players' engagement in a multitude of cooperative and conciliatory relationships with Portuguese in both the metropole and the empire to enhance their lives suggests that a more complex rendering of race relations in both settings be perpended.[22]

III. By considering the ways high-profile immigrant athletes occupied liminal spaces and, thereby, bridged gaps in colonial and metropolitan society, this book also engages with the extensive literature regarding African intermediaries. Heretofore, scholars have reserved this category for indigenous clerks, soldiers, and police, and, at times, traditional authorities—in short, those who assisted with the delivery or facilitation of colonial projects.[23] The inclusion of African soccer migrants broadens this collection of historical actors. In the colonies, the migrant footballers increasingly operated in an intermediary manner as they ascended to play for predominantly white clubs in the urban centers, while continuing to reside in the largely black suburbs. And, in the metropole, as successful indigenous practitioners of a European game and tangible manifestations of Africa at a time when few individuals from the continent were present in Portugal, they routinely functioned as social and cultural intermediaries. Their ability to navigate, straddle, and increasingly move fluidly between African and European circles helped to erode some of the perceived cultural distinctions between these communities.

Analogous to African clerks, soldiers, and police "delivering" colonial control, these players' success with Portuguese affiliate clubs in the colonies, with the parent clubs in the metropole, and, for some of them, with Portugal's national team, transmitted Portuguese culture as sport and greatly intensified the (Lusophone) African consumption of it. Indeed, Africans in the colonies increasingly, and enthusiastically, engaged with this dimension of Portuguese culture, listening to broadcasts of their favorite metropolitan clubs, reading about these squads in the newspapers, attending matches that Portuguese teams played in the colonies as part of extremely popular summer tours, and, in particular, closely following African footballers who were playing in Europe.[24] In practice, these players constituted the palpable go-betweens of the distant metropole and African stops, familiar vessels through which well-received entertainment, rather than exploitative colonial policy, was conveyed to the indigenous subjects of empire.

Although scholars have traditionally characterized African intermediaries as having wittingly bolstered colonial projects, thereby prejudicing their fellow imperial subordinates, these soccer players engaged in neither predominantly "collaborative" nor resistive behavior. While acknowledging the difficult roles the footballers were forced into as individuals who were conversant in multiple cultures, compelled to navigate a collection of settings that featured varying degrees of racial hostility, and simultaneously exalted by a wide range of supporters from all backgrounds, their experiences as social intermediaries evince a pattern of multidirectional strategic engagement. Ultimately, by highlighting these athletic intermediaries' recurring expressions of cooperation and conciliation, this study further problematizes the "interpretive dichotomy of resistance and collaboration" that reductively construes Africans' actions as either assistive of or obstructive to the colonial process.[25]

IV. Through an examination of the ways these African migrants drew upon occupational skills in the metropole that had been learned in their homelands, this book also engages with the extensive literature that traces the application of indigenous knowledge and techniques in the diaspora. Studies by Carney and Knight, for example, demonstrate how Africans in the Americas employed assorted techniques and skills to enhance their lives or simply to mitigate the hardships that many of these marginalized, or even enslaved, individuals faced.[26] This study extends the area of investigation to include not only particular proficiencies, but also a series of operative labor tactics to which emigrant athletes had been exposed or had practiced themselves while still in Africa, typically during nonsoccer employment arranged for them by their colonial football clubs. Following their arrival in Europe, players applied these tactics in creative ways or drew upon them to inspire new occupational strategies.

African footballers also displayed a type of professionalism in the metropole that they had cultivated and internalized while playing in the colonies and, thus, even before they became remunerated practitioners. This approach included adherence to strict practice schedules and cooperation with coaches, teammates, and club officials. Yet this ethic also extended to life away from the pitch, including players' commitment to lifestyles that wouldn't undermine or compromise their athletic abilities or capabilities.[27] In most cases, the Portuguese coaches active in the colonies were responsible for instilling this approach to the game among aspiring talents. As former players in Portugal, these overseers introduced the tactics, strategies, and, perhaps most importantly, training regimens that African players would need to adopt if they were to succeed in the elite echelons of the Portuguese, European, and, eventually, global soccer firmaments.

If indigenous practitioners had infused the game with theater and artifice—supposed constituents of the "flair" that the African-appropriated game came to feature—aspiring players had to temper these tendencies and demonstrate the type of athletic discipline and tactical approach demanded at the highest levels of the sport. In these contentions, my analysis diverges from conclusions drawn by, for example, Lanfranchi and Taylor, who have argued that "the particular skills required have allowed African [footballers] with relatively low levels of 'Westernization' to become successful on both continents. . . . Like music, football has created popular figures . . . who have progressed without . . . requiring training to adapt to Western standards."[28] In the Lusophone context, players' occupational "Westernization" was absolutely vital to their success in Portugal. Former player Hilário, who hailed from Mozambique and starred on Portugal's 1966 World Cup squad, confirmed this assertion in testimony he offered during our interview: "On almost all of the teams in Mozambique, the coaches were Portuguese. . . . When I left Mozambique at the age of nineteen, I was already able to play for Sporting [Lisbon] and the [Portuguese] national team. . . . In the colonial time, the soccer formation was better, the Portuguese coaches maximized our skills. When we got to Portugal, we could play for [the best teams], and now if the best player from Mozambique comes here [Portugal], he would have to play in the second or third division."[29]

V. Finally, a substantive examination of these Lusophone players also helps to shift scholarly focus away from "exploitative colonial and neo-imperial states" and "predatory clubs"—recurrent themes in African football scholarship—to the athletes themselves.[30] By listening to these migrant footballers' motivations and objectives, by considering their social origins, and by examining their strategic actions, it's clear that their experiences not only reflected but also actively shaped colonial and metropolitan interactions and policies. Furthermore, the salaries they earned from their clubs were commensurate with their experience; meritocratic (Eusébio, appropriately, eventually became the highest-earning footballer in the country); and largely consistent with Portuguese players' wages, while many African-born footballers also captained their squads and even the national team. Similarly, their relationship with the Portuguese regime was functional for both entities, rather than purely exploitative for either, and even its political dimensions remained largely undeveloped.[31] Throughout their careers, these athletes exhibited both highly pragmatic and calculated behavior, belying a passivity and victimization that "predatory" relationships inherently feature.

In this contention, my study echoes the work of scholars who have dismissed reductive characterizations of African migrant footballers in Europe as "merely tools of European club owners," thereby dispelling notions of these athletes as casualties of alleged exploitation.[32] Instead, I analyze them as emigrant workers—professionals—who, with an eye to their postathletic lives, strategically offered their labor to those employers in both the colonies and the metropole that provided the most appealing working conditions. As Eusébio's mother candidly proclaimed after being asked why her son chose Benfica, a celebrated Lisbon-based outfit, over other metropolitan clubs who were also aggressively courting him: "Benfica gave 'big money.'" Studies that sound the alarm regarding the historical (and contemporary) exodus of African footballers thereby risk ignoring these migrants' aspirations to improve their lives, and those of family members, just as millions of Africans did throughout the colonial era and continue to do today.

Methodology and Sources

This book draws upon archival materials, popular media sources, and interviews with former players and coaches in order to reconstruct the experiences of these African athletes and the multitude of settings in which they operated. Portugal's Ministry of Education houses the most useful and insightful archival sources, namely, the colonial-era records associated with player transfers from Africa. This trail of documentation is particularly illuminative of the period covering the buildup in the 1940s to the initial relocation of African footballers to Portugal, as it features debates between metropolitan and colonial officials and representatives from the most powerful Portuguese clubs, including Benfica, Sporting, Porto, and Belenenses, which coveted the star prospects. Sensing that the Estado Novo government might be amenable to these athletic imports, during the 1940s metropolitan clubs began submitting formal appeals to the administration to permit their relocation. Although each of the eventual player transfers to the metropole prompted a clutch of accompanying paperwork, these sources are most revealing when problems arose during the transferal processes. Recurrent issues included disputes over fees, competition among clubs for a particular player, and the accommodation of players' requests to relocate to a specific location, often to live with relatives or to continue their studies. In these situations, the paper trail features a range of contributing entities and offers considerable detail, which proved extremely useful to reconstructions of the players' lives.

Popular media similarly constituted extremely illuminative source material. Portuguese newspapers from the period provide not only social and sports commentary, but also interviews with the footballers, even if these players' statements primarily relate to on-the-pitch events. Much more insightful was the extended run of *Ídolos* (Idols) pamphlets, published as a series in Portugal during the 1950s, '60s, and '70s, each issue of which featured a particular athlete from one of an array of sports, including soccer. These booklets include biographical information, personal histories, interviews, and photos. And although many of these "idols" were white Portuguese athletes, a number of African-born players were included in the collection as well. Although the tenor of *Ídolos* is light and naturally celebratory, the African footballers offered candid answers to questions that probed their "likes" and "dislikes" about life in Portugal and how they spent time away from the pitch in their daily lives—the fodder of social history.

For all the insights these sources provide, however, they remain limited in several important ways. First, although many of the popular media sources feature African voices, forthright expression of political opinions or other "topics of national safety and security" was impossible during the reign of the dictatorial Estado Novo regime. As such, the commentary provided by players in newspapers was typically highly guarded and concentrated around "safe" matters, namely, their sporting exploits. Similarly, mention of political matters in the *Ídolos* pamphlets is conspicuously, if predictably, absent. Second, written materials offer only very brief and often superficial glimpses into players' broader lives. Such limitations hinder a reconstruction of their experiences away from the pitch, including virtually the entirety of their time in the colonies prior to relocating to

Portugal, as well as their daily existence once in the metropole, beyond the few hours a week they spent in the public eye during matches.

As such, oral testimony constitutes essential evidentiary material for this study. I gathered these articulations from a number of different sources, including recent interviews given by the players that appear in newspapers, videos, and in published form. Even more useful was the recently released book *Finta finta*, which offers brief biographical sketches of the thirty-one greatest Mozambican footballers of all time (a list that includes a number of players from the colonial period). As part of this endeavor, author Paola Rolletta interviewed some of the footballers profiled in *Finta finta* and periodically incorporates excerpts from their testimonies in the text.[33]

Much more insightful than any of the aforementioned sources, though, were the interviews that I conducted in Africa and Europe with former players, their Portuguese teammates and coaches, and members of the, albeit extremely small, nonfootballing African community resident in Portugal during the colonial period. These indispensable sessions enabled me to reconstruct these African athletes' lives in the colonies, including: their social origins, their ascension through the various leagues in their respective settings and across different eras, the assorted challenges they faced as they were enjoying this athletic success, and the eventual attention that metropolitan clubs paid them. Further, their testimonies illuminated their understandably anxious departures from the colonies, the often weeks-long voyages to Portugal, the important social insights they gleaned during the journeys, and the ways travel experiences solidified bonds among migrants, irrespective of race, who shared common points of departure. Finally, this testimony proved equally crucial in attempting to understand footballers' social experiences in the metropole and to better comprehend the role(s) they wanted soccer to play in their lives, especially for those players who sought to consolidate their postathletic lives by strategically seeking educational or long-term employment opportunities. In fact, most of my informants, accustomed to fielding countless, virtually identical questions about their footballing feats in Portugal, were pleasantly surprised, arguably even bemused, when I inquired about their experiences—both quotidian and significant— *away* from the pitch.[34]

Organization

Over a series of loosely chronological chapters, I consider the development of football in the colonies and thereafter trace these athletes' histories as they enjoyed initial success in Africa and subsequently relocated to Portugal, negotiating a metropolitan environment that was, at once, both vaguely familiar and unsettlingly unfamiliar. Utilizing the aforementioned archival and oral evidence, I highlight change over time within each thematic chapter in order to provide a diachronic understanding of the various settings and the changing ways the footballers navigated these milieus.

Chapter 1 offers a foundational overview of the Portuguese empire in Africa, including the shifting environments that indigenous residents daily negotiated. To illuminate these contexts, I consider the social backgrounds of the emigrant footballers, many of whom were mestiços or were otherwise intermediate members of colonial society. This chapter also explores the introduction of football into Portugal's African empire by a variety of agents, whose interests often overlapped, and the role that newspapers and radio played in the sport's popularization. Both practitioners and fans catalyzed this growth, eagerly consuming soccer developments from the metropole and around the world, and rapidly forming allegiances to Portuguese clubs.

Chapter 2 examines the various ways Africans began to play the sport, including by forming "native" clubs and associations (leagues). Initially barred from participation in associations reserved for white practitioners, Africans gradually began to organize their own versions. Over time, mestiço and black players were invited to play in the formerly whites-only leagues in the colonies, and eventually this racial barrier was dissolved, the first step toward the very best players—irrespective of race—showcasing their skills in the metropole. The chapter further examines the social backgrounds of these footballers and also plumbs the process of cultural exposure and adjustment that commenced in the colonies—in mixed-race households, on racially integrated clubs while playing for Portuguese coaches, and at workplaces—which collectively played a key role in the migrant athletes' success in the metropole, both on and off the pitch.

Chapter 3 explores the regime's motivations to permit these footballers to relocate to Portugal, as well as the scouting and signing processes that advanced and facilitated the outflows. The chapter explicitly links Africa and Europe, following the athletes as they undertook long journeys from the colonies to the metropole, during which they often established or deepened relations with fellow migrant athletes—white, black, and mestiço—as well as with Portuguese copassengers. Upon arrival, these players remained under the custody of their new clubs, which supported the footballers materially and helped them adjust to their new environments. Although many of the African migrants would be based in or around the capital city of Lisbon, many others headed north, some south, and a few into the eastern interior of the country.

Chapter 4 examines the range of challenges players faced as they attempted to settle into life in Portugal. Most of their tribulations were attributable not only to separation from friends and family, but also to the rigors of professional football in Europe. The footballers also faced other impediments, including the inability to transfer to clubs beyond Portugal's borders owing to their propagandistic value and the regime's political insecurities, as well as to the considerable competitiveness and attendant fame they generated for Portugal's club and national teams. In response to these constraints, players drew from a set of labor strategies to capitalize upon opportunities available *within* the metropole. Although the athletes relied on their prodigious soccer skills to succeed on the pitch, the labor tactics they applied away from it constituted vital methods for those footballers who farsightedly sought to exploit their situations before their athleticism faded.

Chapter 5 explores the ways players navigated the politically charged environments in both the colonies and the metropole, especially following the outbreak of the wars for independence in the African territories in the early 1960s. Most of the players eschewed politics, at least overtly, strategically cooperating with an assortment of entities, as manifested in recurring, eventually normative, displays of social conciliation and professional focus. This approach was at times difficult to maintain, however, namely, during moments of political unrest in Portugal, in which football was used as a vehicle for both popular protest and statutory repression. Although the regime tried to exploit the players for political ends, they generally maintained their distance from the dictatorship in an attempt to dispassionately avoid co-option. Nor did most of these Lusophone athletes engage in revolutionary politics and, thus, none of the nationalist movements operating in Portugal's colonies actively sought their support.

Finally, an epilogue considers both the immediate plights and the enduring legacies of these African athletes in the years and decades following their playing days. Many of the retired footballers remained in Portugal, while others returned to their respective homelands or relocated elsewhere in the world, forming a global diaspora of former athletes. It would be difficult to overemphasize the effects these players had on their Portuguese club teams and, perhaps more visibly, on a national team that had been in shambles prior to their arrival. Yet their impact wasn't limited to the period in which they were engaged in athletic careers. These "Jackie Robinsons" of global soccer were among the first African players who collectively precipitated waves of aspirant athletes to trace their footsteps from the innumerable pitches and endeavoring associations on the continent to the various leagues in Europe and beyond.[35] Had these Lusophone footballers not been so effective on and off the pitch, this form of athletic emigration may well not have developed so rapidly, or spawned so many imitators.

1

Foundations

The Introduction and Consumption of Soccer in Lusophone Africa

In Mozambique, I saw Belenenses [a Lisbon-based club] when they came. I also saw Académica [a Coimbra-based club] when they came to play in the Portuguese Cup. . . . In Africa, we saw Portuguese football as something from another world. We didn't have TV; we relied on radio. But the following day at school, or at work, when we discussed the result of the match we often said: "Did you see that play? Did you see that cross?" Others would say, "He was offside." But we had only heard the match on the radio! We had passion for metropolitan football. . . . It was always a frenetic environment when Benfica, Porto, or Sporting [Portuguese clubs] came to Mozambique or Angola. . . . Angola had . . . better conditions, but the enthusiasm was great everywhere.

—Shéu Han, a Mozambican player who traveled to Portugal in 1970 to launch a career with Benfica and also participated on tours of the African colonies while a member of the club, 2014

Few Mozambican youth would go on to enjoy the type of decorated soccer career that Shéu did, but virtually all of them followed metropolitan football growing up in the colony, enthusiastically and imaginatively envisioning events unfolding on the distant pitches. The seeds of this durable sporting enthusiasm had been planted decades previously by an array of individuals wielding a range of motives, many of which overlapped. This mélange of football advocates included missionaries, soldiers, sailors, colonial administrators, corporate officials, and merchants. In the aftermath of Portugal's consolidation of formal colonial control at the end of the nineteenth century, soccer was introduced into the series of oppressive, exploitative environments that made up the country's African empire. These constituent settings featured institutionalized racism, segregation, and pervasive inequity. Yet, even in these unlikely sporting incubators, the game steadily took hold. Subsequently, newspapers, radio, and, eventually, television would transmit the latest metropolitan soccer developments to colonial populations—both African and European—who eagerly consumed this news and, just as Shéu and his colleagues did, endlessly discussed it. The sizable Portuguese settler populations in Angola and Mozambique fed this soccer fervor. Beyond rooting for their favorite clubs, colonists shared their soccer allegiances with indigenous residents, cultivating and influencing the latter's loyalties. As African footballers began playing for Portuguese clubs, the dialectical connection between colonized subjects of empire and metropolitan football only intensified. These passions were periodically stoked when Portuguese clubs toured the colonies during the summer months, with both settler and indigenous fans flocking to watch their footballing heroes—especially those players who had been locally produced.

This chapter examines the introduction of football into Portugal's African territories, its growing popularity in these stops, and the myriad ways that metropolitan football both deepened and broadened consumption of the sport in the empire. I begin with an overview of Portuguese imperialism in Africa, including consideration of the shifting colonial environments that indigenous residents daily negotiated. It was in these milieus that football would come to flourish, with local practitioners and fans responsible for the sport's explosive growth. Finally, I examine the ways that various forms of popular media in Africa facilitated local allegiances to metropolitan clubs and, in general, heightened interest in the game in the colonies; the profound impact that African footballers who joined these squads had on local consumption; and the sporting, social, and political dimensions of Portuguese teams' soccer tours to the African colonies.

The History of the Portuguese (Empire) in Africa

The Portuguese first reached the areas in Africa that would eventually constitute its empire on the continent in the 1400s. In many places on Africa's western, southern, and eastern shores, the Portuguese were the first Europeans to arrive and would subsequently parlay their navigational precocity to generate considerable wealth via a flourishing trade in gold and slaves, among other items. The waves of European commercial imitators that followed in Portugal's footsteps quickly outpaced the Iberian originators of the commerce between Europeans and sub-Saharan Africans. Yet the various Portuguese outposts along Africa's coasts endured, primarily as embarkation points for slaves headed across the Atlantic and also as dumping grounds for metropolitan exiles, known as *degradados*. Otherwise, these stations waned in importance and influence over time, languishing for centuries and yielding few tangible rewards for Lisbon.

As European nations contemplated and subsequently engaged in the violent invasion of Africa during the second half of the nineteenth century, Portugal was compelled to claim imperial space on the continent in order to preserve its overseas interests. Reflective of its severely eroded standing in Europe, Portugal predicated these territorial assertions on its history of commercial interaction in sub-Saharan Africa dating back to its initial forays some centuries earlier. Ultimately, internecine power politics and rivalries among the European heavyweights facilitated Portugal's otherwise unlikely establishment of an empire in Africa. Consequently, the diminutive nation departed from the 1884–1885 conference in Berlin, at which the European imperial powers carved up Africa into colonial domains, with geographically incommensurate, yet formally recognized, claims to five territories: Angola, Mozambique, Guiné, Cape Verde, and São Tomé and Príncipe.

In the aftermath of Berlin, Portugal strove to subjugate the indigenous populations resident within its imperial claims. Lisbon also began to actively colonize these territories, though primarily only in and around the torpid urban spaces that Portuguese merchants and a handful of intrepid settlers had established centuries earlier. It took the underfunded Portuguese military significantly longer to satisfy the requisite "pacification" of local populations that the Berlin accord stipulated than it did the more powerful European nations. Yet Portugal was eventually able to establish control, often relying on high-profile acts of terror to maintain order, which, in turn, facilitated the exploitation of local human and natural resources.

In order to justify the initial conquest and ensuing overrule, the Portuguese state fostered powerful notions of European cultural superiority and, correspondingly, African inferiority. These increasingly accepted "truths" were reinforced at every turn, thereby influencing racial sentiments and, attendantly, interracial interactions in both the metropole and the colonies. Isabel Castro Henriques has described this specious position as pure "mythology," which not only condescended to Africans, but also portrayed Portugal as a victim of the other European imperial nations. Rival continental powers allegedly "had 'illegitimate' African appetites," since, after all, the Portuguese had been the first Europeans to arrive in sub-Saharan Africa.[1] Henriques further contends that "this situation led to the reinforcement of ideas and prejudices that had already taken root in Portuguese society, in which the somatic, the Negro, and social, the slave, were articulated together to define the African."[2]

Another measure that Lisbon took to legitimate and consolidate control in its African empire was to encourage metropolitan citizens to relocate to the colonies. Influxes of these (often destitute) settlers in the early twentieth century significantly altered the demographic and economic landscapes in the two colonies that received the overwhelming majority of these individuals: Angola and Mozambique. In the former, for example, the white population more than doubled from 1900 to 1920, from 9,198 to 20,700.[3]

In both of these settings, waves of incoming Portuguese rapidly displaced long-standing *mestiço* (mulatto) populations, newly occupying low-level positions in the colonial bureaucracies that members of the mixed-race communities had previously held. Prior to these Portuguese arrivals, mestiços had provided invaluable service in the strapped administrative apparatuses that featured in the empire. With Lisbon unable to allocate sufficient human resources to African outposts, Portuguese men had long miscegenated with local women—a combination of libido, human nature, and administrative necessity. As such, Lisbon tolerated this form of intercultural interaction, even if it didn't actively encourage it. The case of former footballer Hilário, who was born in 1939 in Lourenço Marques to an ethnic Chopi mother and a Portuguese father, is exemplary of these types of scenarios. He explained that his mother "was one of those who have tattoos on the face and on the belly. It was a style that was very beautiful and she had luck with boyfriends. . . . My mother came from Manhiça to the city [roughly 100 kilometers separate Manhiça and Lourenço Marques]. . . . She was a very beautiful girl."[4] Indeed, it was from these mixed-race communities that many of the most prominent members of the community of footballing migrants, Hilário included, emerged.

With the overthrow in 1926 of the Republic of Portugal, a short-lived government that itself had come to power only after toppling the Portuguese monarchy in 1910, the colonies were increasingly eyed as sources of revenue rather than as spaces to develop. With the emergence of the corporatist, authoritarian Estado Novo in 1933, expenditures for the empire were slashed while Lisbon continued to squeeze whatever revenues it could from the territories. With the advent of the new regime, the relative fiscal and political autonomy that the colonies had enjoyed under the republic came to an abrupt end; power was increasingly centralized. As part of the broader political and economic calculus of the Estado Novo (1933–1974), the regime facilitated the relocation of thousands of Portuguese to the colonies, in part to rid the metropole of under- or unemployed members of the population, but also to stimulate the colonial economies, such that the settler communities in both Angola and Mozambique grew more than tenfold between 1930 and 1970.[5]

Providing a complementary ideophilosophical justification for overseas Portuguese settlement, in the early 1950s the Estado Novo regime formally embraced the Brazilian sociologist Gilberto Freyre's concept of Lusotropicalism to further explicate the relationship between the Portuguese and the constituent peoples of the empire. Freyre theorized that the prevalence of mixed-race individuals in areas Portugal had colonized was attributable to a form of inherent racial and cultural tolerance that the Portuguese, as a people, uniquely embodied and exhibited. After initially distancing the Estado Novo from *Lusotropicalismo* on racialist grounds following its promulgation in the 1930s, António de Oliveira Salazar, the dictator who durably ruled Portugal from 1932 to 1968, eventually adopted it as official state ideology. Salazar invoked the theory to justify empire, even if the exploitative treatment of both blacks and mestiços in the colonies experientially undermined any veracity that the dubious concept might have contained.

Even as the regime self-righteously promoted Lusotropicalism to defend its perpetuation of empire, Portugal couldn't prevent the "winds of change" from blowing across the continent, inaugurated by England's decolonization of its Gold Coast colony (Ghana) in 1957. By the 1960s, these breezes had turned to gusts, with a steady succession of colonies transitioning to independent states. Yet, while the British, French, and Belgians all abandoned their African colonial projects, Portugal's dictatorship clung ever more tightly to empire. In a bid to stress the indivisibility of the colonies and the metropole, in 1951 the regime recast these possessions as "overseas provinces," signifying that they were as integral to Portugal as were the various regions of the metropole. This obstinacy and artifice did not, however, come without cost. With colonial empires rapidly disappearing, Portugal's political stance was becoming increasingly anachronistic. Moreover, the global left, which by the 1960s also featured a large number of newly independent African states, was openly condemning Portugal for its resolute preservation of the empire and, more specifically, the racist policies in force in its colonies. Even staunch allies of Portugal, such as the United States, were privately imploring Lisbon to relax statutory controls in the empire. In another blow to the regime, the Indian army forcibly annexed the historic Portuguese colony of Goa on the western coast of the subcontinent in 1961; protestations were all the enfeebled Iberian state could muster.

The early 1960s constituted an ominous time for Portugal and its empire. In February 1961, the Angolan war for independence commenced, followed shortly thereafter by nationalist eruptions in Guiné (1963) and Mozambique (1964). These three conflicts would each rage for over a decade, with the Portuguese conceding the most territory in Guiné. With mounting numbers of Portuguese conscripts losing life or limb while fighting in the African bush, the increasingly unpopular wars were crippling

an already teetering state. Finally, in 1974, a group of mid-level army officers, tapping the sentiments of the war-weary Portuguese citizenry, staged
a largely bloodless coup that toppled the Estado Novo state and thereby
ended the colonial conflicts almost immediately, paving the way for the independence of the African territories. Portugal's colonial adventure on the
continent had finally come to an end.

Daily Life in Portugal's African Colonies

Following the consolidation of control in Portugal's imperial claims in Africa at the end of the nineteenth century and, in more resistive, "trouble-
some" spots in these territories in the early twentieth century, indigenous
residents newly operated in environments marked by racial violence and
exploitation. Consistent with other imperial European nations active in
Africa, Portugal's colonial project was predicated on racial and cultural superiority, cloaked in an altruistic "civilizing mission." For African subjects,
the key elements of this "mission" included the imposition of taxes, the
implementation of forced labor schemes, and the daily threat of violence
for any actual or perceived incompliance. Africans' labor was vital for the
generation of revenues, but the local populations otherwise constituted
nothing more than burdens for a metropole that lacked the resources to
develop its colonial possessions, though the realization of widespread social improvements was never a genuine objective for the regime anyway.

Over time, influxes of Portuguese settlers saw sleepy colonial outposts
transformed into vibrant urban destinations, most profoundly in Angola
and Mozambique. Consequently, the capital cities of Luanda and Lourenço Marques (Maputo), respectively, eventually featured "concrete" city
centers populated exclusively by settlers, and concentric rings of suburbs
in which black Africans, mestiços, and, complicating this otherwise stead-
fast racial configuration, poor white settlers resided, though the latter's
numbers were comparatively small. The residents of these hardscrabble
suburban or peri-urban areas were typically impoverished and vulnerable,
but far from destitute. Testimony from Hilário captures both the tenuous-
ness and the resilience of life in the (Lourenço Marques) suburbs: "Poverty
was normal. We had our houses of wood and zinc, we fed ourselves with

flour and rice and fish and prawns. . . . There wasn't so much misery that we would go hungry. No, we lived well within the possibilities that we had."[6] Urban centers in Portugal's other African colonies, such as Bissau (the capital of Guinea-Bissau) and Praia (Cape Verde's capital city), featured degrees of social and economic variance due to their smaller settler populations, but the racial conventions that prevailed in Angola and Mozambique similarly applied in these settings.

Following the overthrow of the Portuguese republic in 1926 and the implementation of Salazar's authoritarian Estado Novo regime soon thereafter, the colonies became even more commercially friendly. Owing to a spate of new policies that reduced Africans to legally marginalized and (violently) exploitable colonial subjects, in rural areas settlers and private enterprises could newly access cheap, bound indigenous labor. Only by achieving *assimilado* (assimilated) status could Africans in the colonies escape existence as *indígenas*, a legal and social designation that rendered them extremely vulnerable. Yet the passage to formal assimilation was open to only a scant few. In 1950 in Angola, for example, only 1.38 percent of the over four million Africans and mestiços enjoyed this status, and if the latter are removed from the equation, that figure sinks to just 0.7 percent.[7] The Estado Novo regime did little, if anything, to alter this social configuration until newly independent African nations elsewhere on the continent began to utilize the international bodies at their disposal, such as the United Nations and the International Labor Organization, to malign, disgrace, and increasingly isolate the resolute Portuguese state.

Begrudgingly, Lisbon reactively began revising its colonial policies. In the early 1960s, with the wars for independence under way, the regime dismantled the forced labor schemes in place and began allocating additional funds to extend (albeit skeletal) education and health-care infrastructures. Even if these decisions were politically motivated—calculated, though belated, efforts to win the "hearts and minds" of indigenous residents—Africans did, nonetheless, benefit. Indeed, as Domingos has argued, "The toning down of the social segregation mechanisms, especially after . . . 1961, created the conditions to speed up the dynamics of mobility that were already in place. The need for economic mobility demanded the end of political obstacles."[8] Yet Marcelo Bittencourt reminds us that despite these concessions, the politico-martial events of the 1960s "radicalized the

Portuguese colonial authorities; the eyes and ears of the government agencies came to suspect any type of association . . . in which black and *mestiços* congregated."[9] As such, even as whites, blacks, and mestiços began mixing with greater fluidity, often within formerly segregated spaces, pervasive suspicion and tension engendered by the wars for independence marked the various colonial settings.

The Social Backgrounds of Footballers as Windows into Colonial Contexts

As the denouement of the Portuguese empire approached, the African footballers who would eventually relocate to the metropole were humbly being born and sired on soccer. Notwithstanding the divergent social and economic circumstances in which individual players were raised and the different decades in which they reached their formative footballing years, their experiences exemplarily illuminate daily life in an array of Portuguese colonial settings.

The majority of these future soccer stars grew up reasonably poor, even if some—and, in particular, mestiço players, owing to their Portuguese fathers—had somewhat more comfortable upbringings. Many mestiço footballers' settler parents were employed in the colonial bureaucracies, which afforded them decent livings, though none of these families would have been considered elite. For example, Miguel Arcanjo, who grew up in Angola in the 1940s and would go on to play for FC Porto, had a Portuguese father who was employed in the colonial treasury, where he was apparently both "distinguished and admired."[10] Many of Arcanjo's siblings would also go on to serve as public functionaries. Although being an assimilado or mestiço in the colonies did not preclude significant social and economic challenges, the social strata from which many of these players derived rendered their migration to Portugal more a form of geographical rather than social mobility, as they were moving from one reasonably advantaged environment to another.

Elsewhere on the socioeconomic spectrum, Armando Manhiça, who was raised in the suburbs of Lourenço Marques in the 1950s and would eventually play in Portugal for Sporting Lisbon and FC Porto, had a much more modest upbringing. The sixth child in his family, his father worked in a factory, earning a salary that was "not large," while from the age of four Manhiça helped his mother carry, deliver, and sell fish in the city's popular Xipamanine market.[11]

Irrespective of the divergences in the socioeconomic statuses of players' families, virtually all of these future footballers attended school for at least some period of time. Enrollment was at the insistence of their parents, who deemed formal education the key to future success. In fact, no matter how personally enamored the guardians may have been with football, most considered the game a threat to their sons' studies and, therefore, an endeavor that could potentially derail the professional trajectories they envisioned for their children—a sentiment that was especially pronounced in relatively well-off families. For example, Shéu Han recalled that his father did not want him to "dribble away his life" playing soccer, and, as such, "it was very difficult to convince him to permit the aspiring footballer to pursue his ambitions."[12] Shéu's father, who was Chinese, instead wanted him to study to become an engineer. To this end, he sent Shéu to live with his maternal uncle and attend school in Beira, the second-largest city in Mozambique, hundreds of miles north of the small fishing village of Inhassoro, where the future Benfica star had been born.

Despite these parents' best intentions for their children's educations, familial financial expediencies could trump and, thus, truncate schooling careers, as was the case with Joaquim Adriano José da Conceição, who would go on to star for Portugal's Vitória de Setúbal football club in the 1960s. Well before those later, more comfortable years, Conceição grew up in a Luanda *bairro* (neighborhood) in the 1950s, and the meager salaries his painter father and sewer mother earned, coupled with the presence of eleven children to feed, forced him to abandon his studies upon completing elementary school to take up work at a carpenter's shop.[13] For players raised in single-parent homes, this eventuality was even more unavoidable. As Vicente Lucas, who grew up in Lourenço Marques and lost his father when he was fourteen years old, explained, "We were semi-poor. My mother even sold rope. . . . I walked to school, but eventually stopped attending and went to work for a blacksmith. . . . We weren't really happy in Mozambique because there were many children—four boys and four girls—and we had difficulties of various types."[14] For players like Lucas, continued schooling simply wasn't economically viable.

Unfortunately, for players such as Lucas and Conceição, the intellectual and intercultural competency facilitated by extended schooling in the colonies helped migrant footballers integrate once in the metropole. Indeed, those players, typically from more privileged families, who were able to complete secondary school while in the colonies, and, even more significantly, those who opted to play their football for Académica, typically experienced even more facile transitions into metropolitan life. Of course, neither these scholar-athletes nor the parents who had mandated schooling in the colonies realistically envisioned this eventual social-athletic outcome. Nor did a parental emphasis on education necessarily generate enthusiasm for academics among these budding football stars; for most of the athletes, soccer, rather than school, motivated them.

For those players who were thrust into remunerative activities in the colonies, employment often featured a soccer connection, just as it would for those who opted to sign for CUF (Companhia União Fabril) once in the metropole. Oftentimes, clubs in the colonies were operated by, or at least had meaningful links to, commercial interests and would arrange employment with a private or state entity (e.g., the railroad) to attract talented footballers to their squads and, subsequently, to retain them. For example, Augusto Matine, who grew up in Lourenço Marques in the 1960s and played locally for Clube Central before going on to play for Benfica in Lisbon, recalled:

Sr. António, Central's leader, came to me and asked me what I did. . . . I learned the trade of surveyor of measures in gas stations and of agrarian measures and taxi meters. . . . There were others who were placed elsewhere and learned to be mechanics. After one year, a year and a half, two years, we really started to earn some money in the places where we worked. We became part of the staff. I remember that I made 400 escudos a month and I could use this money to feed my family.

One of Central's directors had a factory called the Companhia Industrial da Matola, which made various types of pasta and cookies. At the end of the month, he gave me a *rancho*: ten kilograms of sugar, ten kilograms of rice, two soap bars, milk, butter, cookies, and some money for my mother. If I received 400 [escudos], I would give 300 to my mother and keep 100. That was to protect myself. If my brothers asked me for something, they wouldn't lack anything. This was how I lived. I grew as a man and as a respected football player because I worked for it.[15]

Footballers of European descent who made the jump from the colonies to the metropole typically enjoyed more comfortable, if still modest, upbringings. For example, Alberto da Costa Pereira, who grew up in the 1940s in Nacala and Nampula, in the far northern reaches of Mozambique, before going on to star as a goalkeeper for Benfica and the Portuguese national team, was a "total sportsman"—a basketball player, an accomplished sailor, and a record holder in the shot put. He also, in his free time, hunted rabbits, impalas, and other antelopes.[16] As a child, Pereira was inspired by magazines such as *Stadium*, which arrived in Mozambique from Portugal, Brazil, and the United Kingdom, and occasionally featured African track stars, including Tomás Paquete, Matos Fernandes, and Espírito Santo, each of whom hailed from the Lusophone territories.[17] His father worked for the railroad, so the family didn't figure among the colonial elites. Yet the nature and wide range of leisure activities in which he engaged certainly differentiated his childhood experiences from those of the majority of African and mestiço players during their formative years in the colonies.

The Introduction of Football in the Colonies

It was into the colonial environments outlined above that a variety of individuals, including soldiers, missionaries, merchants, administrators, educators, corporate officials, and, eventually, settlers (especially as their numbers increased over time) introduced the game of football. This process of dissemination was highly uneven but generally commenced in port cities, such as Bissau, Luanda, and Lourenço Marques, in the late nineteenth century. The game subsequently traveled along overland routes and, eventually, railroads and other thoroughfares, such that it had widely penetrated the interior by the 1920s. Despite the game's notable diffusion, though, the process of introducing it was largely unsystematic, lacking any type of formality or organization. Only much later would colonial authorities deem the sport useful to maintaining control and, thus, try to supervise this process of propagation. In the meantime, the game was introduced wherever and whenever European practitioners were active and felt compelled to share the rules, conventions, and strategies of the sport with Africans.

Scholars have debated to what ends Europeans introduced football to local residents and, attendantly, the efficacy of their designs. Some have examined the hegemonic motivations behind the introduction of soccer, while others, conversely, have considered how Africans frustrated these intentions, embracing the game but actively rejecting the elements of inculcation hidden in this alleged sporting "Trojan horse." Irrespective of the divergent interpretive angles, it's important to note that not all Europeans shared the same objectives related to the introduction of football to Africans. For example, unlike Portuguese soldiers who may have introduced soccer simply to generate indigenous competitors, missionaries championed the sport as part of a broader emphasis on "muscular" Christianity. Meanwhile, the colonial state was more interested in the game's potential to subdue, distract, reinforce racial hierarchy, generate respect for authority, and minimize what colonial social engineers perceived to be an unproductive use of leisure time by indigenous residents. As such, the state encouraged soccer as a "civilizing" endeavor for African populations as part of its wider efforts to use physical education to control the bodies of the colonized masses. As Domingos has argued regarding soccer in the Lusophone African context, the games themselves were "instruments of socialization, infusing discipline . . . respect for hierarchies and rituals."[18] In this capacity, football was undoubtedly more than just a game. And the associated methods and intended lessons were far more important than the game itself.[19] Although football's efficacy as a tool to maintain social control is disputable, the sport unquestionably constituted a key component in Portugal's cultural imperialism campaign, an important pillar in the broader process of empire.

Finally, it is important to note that in many instances, and especially in the early decades of colonial control in Portugal's territories, Africans themselves were responsible for introducing the game. This phenomenon was most frequently associated with Mozambique and, to a lesser extent, Angola, due to their proximity to and economic links with South Africa, the site of the first recorded football matches on the continent. Regarding Mozambique, the incessant streams of migrant laborers were exposed to the game, and subsequently brought that knowledge back with them following stints in the South African mines. As Patrick Harries and others have argued, strong cultural, social, and economic connections existed between urban South Africa and Lourenço Marques, as well as along the overland routes to and from the mines.[20] Migrant Mozambican mine workers cultivated and daily reinforced these links, with football figuring centrally in this transnational exchange of leisure habits.

The Consumption of Football in the Colonies: "Diseased" for Portuguese Clubs

Shortly after the introduction of football in the colonies, Africans began dribbling, passing, and shooting just about any spherical object they could fashion or find. Yet the engagement with the sport was not limited to practicing and playing. Both practitioners and fans contributed to the popularity of the sport by eagerly consuming soccer developments from the metropole and rapidly forming allegiances to—or, as some avid followers referred to this phenomenon: "becoming _diseased_ for"—the major Portuguese clubs. Indeed, while the distance between the dusty pitches in Africa and the verdant fields in the metropole was both literally and figuratively immense, newspapers, radio, and, eventually, television daily delivered Portuguese soccer matches and news to the continent, effectively reducing the expanse.

Initially, the media accounts were primarily consumed by European colonists, who had packed up their metropolitan club loyalties and brought them to the colonies. This sporting fealty enabled settlers to retain important cultural connections to the metropole and also facilitated entry into social networks in the colonies that revolved around football fandom. The example of the family of José Águas, who grew up in colonial Angola and would eventually go on to star for Benfica, is illustrative of the durability and pervasiveness of sporting devotions within Portuguese settler communities.

According to his profile in a 1956 issue of *Ídolos,* "He was always a Benfica supporter, as he came from a family of 'benfiquistas' [ardent Benfica supporters]. He knew the names and the characteristics of all the players, heard the reports, clipped the photos. When Benfica won the Taça Latina [in 1950], he was delirious with enthusiasm."[21] This type of football fidelity reigned in mixed-race households as well, given that virtually all of these domiciles featured Portuguese patriarchs. For example, the father of mestiço player Mário Torres was an avid supporter of Sporting Lisboa and tangibly expressed this allegiance in colonial Angola by founding two local affiliates of the metropolitan powerhouse: Sporting do Huambo, based in the colony's second largest city; and Sporting de Vila Nova, located nearby.

If Portuguese settlers were the original consumers of metropolitan football in the colonies, Africans also began to develop metropolitan sporting allegiances, similarly gravitating toward the "big clubs"—the same outfits that most colonists supported. In fact, Africans' club loyalties were often influenced by the Portuguese with whom they interacted, typically at their respective places of employment. An account by Ângelo Gomes da Silva, who played locally in Mozambique, is exemplary of the transference of footballing loyalties from Portuguese to African laborers. According to Silva, Africans and mestiços conversed with "co-workers who had come from the metropole and who supported particular clubs. So, when a Portuguese would ask which club an African supported and he didn't have a response, the inquirer would retort, for example, 'You don't have a club? Then you have to support Sporting.... You are a man, why don't you support a club? It must be Portugal's Sporting.'"[22] These implorations explicitly imposed Portuguese notions of masculinity upon local populations, either encouraging or even shaming Africans and mestiços into footballing allegiances.

Adherences of this nature also provided Africans a topic that they could safely discuss with Portuguese coworkers, transcending the racial divides that pervaded every colonial setting. Domingos has convincingly argued that at a range of worksites in the colonies, "football, acting as a repertoire of interaction, guaranteed a minimum common denominator for interactions between colonizers and colonized and served as a way to start conversation."[23] Indeed, Augusto Matine recalled that he used to discuss football with coworkers during breaks and that Portuguese soccer news and events dominated these conversations: "People talked more about metropolitan football than our own. We started to have all kinds of information about football. As I read Benfica's newspaper, I knew more about the club than some guys who were there [Portugal]. I devoured that newspaper to learn more about Benfica, about every sport. If I saw a magazine with things about Sporting I would also grab it and would not pass it to anyone before I finished it. Only then would I pass it to the next guy."[24] Matine's account underscores both the personal and the social importance of this type of sporting knowledge.

Regardless of the influence that some Portuguese exerted on indigenous residents as the latter formed their club loyalties, most Africans developed their particular soccer allegiances organically. Most often, these fidelities developed for the same reasons they always have: sporting success. As such, young boys in the colonies formed allegiances to the best Portuguese clubs, namely Sporting, FC Porto, Benfica, and Belenenses. Fans of all ages would often gather around to listen to someone read the latest news regarding the clubs, or, from the mid-1930s on, radio broadcasts in the colonies of metropolitan matches, which both facilitated and hastened this affective process.[25] Supporters often listened to games on transistor radios powered by car batteries—events that drew clusters of people huddled around the set, alternately elated or deflated according to the unfolding events. Matine, a Mozambican who would eventually play for Benfica in the 1960s, indicated:

Growing up, I wanted to be like Travassos, like Coluna. They were my idols. I saw them in the newspapers. . . . I was "diseased" for Benfica: I did not miss a single report in which Benfica appeared. My dad had a little radio, always tuned to Emissora Nacional, the metropolitan national radio. It was three o'clock in Portugal, five o'clock in Mozambique. We had finished everything, I had played in the morning in my district, had played on Saturday, and on Sunday I would listen to my club play. We lived as if we were watching the game. That disease still exists today. I knew every single Benfica player, the entire team, managers and all that. I was fortunate enough to have access to the club newspaper. There was a Portuguese man in Mozambique who owned a photography company and subscribed to Benfica's newspaper. After reading it, he passed it on to me. Even if it was last week's, I wanted to know everything that was going on with my club. There was that disease.[26]

In response to newspaper accounts, radio broadcasts, and other sources of football information, countless neighborhood kids latched on to one of the major Portuguese clubs and imaginatively closed the space between them and the distant squads to which they had pledged their allegiance. For example, António Brassard, who would play for Académica in the 1960s, recalled that as a child, his bairro team was called the Águias Dourados, or Golden Eagles—the nickname of Benfica: "We even made the emblem with the eagle. Benfica really was the club of our dreams! We used to listen to the radio commentaries and we imagined we were playing with the stars of the team."[27] By engaging with the major metropolitan clubs in a variety of creative ways, African fans were embracing a topic that could be endlessly discussed and debated among family, friends, coworkers, and even strangers.

Despite the demonstrated alacrity that characterized Africans' engagement with metropolitan soccer, some scholars have questioned the organicity or benignity associated with the development of this keenness. For example, Paul Darby argues that "the extent to which Portuguese football was promoted by the Portuguese colonial authorities as culturally superior to the local game was further exemplified through the provision of radio broadcasts of Portuguese football. . . . These practices had resonance beyond football and they can be read as part of the broader drive to promote colonial hegemony."[28] Yet, upon closer examination, Darby's binary appears experientially spurious: colonial officials also "culturally" enjoyed "the local game," which similarly featured a preponderance of Portuguese players. Moreover, as Domingos reminds us, settlers also had loyalties to local clubs, which were "axes of urban sociabilities, and identification with these clubs became a means of individual and collective recognition."[29] Further, the football played in Portugal was of an indisputably higher quality, which itself offers an explanation for its popularity that is both plausible and innocuous. Former Rádio Clube de Moçambique announcer João de Sousa affirmed that when a metropolitan match began at the same time as a local game, the former was the one that was transmitted. This option, he indicated, was "justified on commercial grounds. This was the game more people wanted to hear."[30] Finally, by failing to plumb Africans' sporting sentiments, scholars risk ignoring the tastes, desires, and predilections of these football consumers; instead, indigenous fans are cast as unknowing, helpless victims of hegemonic pressures exerted by anonymous colonial officials such as those invoked above by Darby, or of some type of "false consciousness." As Allen Guttmann has cogently argued, this dismissive conclusion related to culturally dominated groups' enthusiastic engagement with sports is quite simply "not persuasive."[31]

As outlined above, the local affiliate squads were, for a variety of reasons, less popular than their Portuguese parent clubs. Yet, by often featuring the same, or very similar, team names and virtually identical uniforms, local clubs provided Africans and Europeans a more proximate means of connecting with their more famous parent teams—a type of association by proxy. As Gary Armstrong has contended, the supporters of these local affiliates had "an implicit loyalty to their Portuguese namesakes."[32] However, for all of this local support and the umbilical links that many colonial clubs featured, as de Sousa indicated above, it was the parent clubs that consistently captured the auditory devotions and most stoked the sporting passions of both settlers and Africans alike in the Lusophone colonies.

Following the initial transfers of players from the colonies to the metropole in the 1940s, interest in Portuguese soccer enjoyed even greater support in Lusophone African stops. As African players began relocating to the metropole, news about Portugal's Primeira Divisão (First Division) was of increasing interest to fans throughout the empire. For example, according to Ângelo Gomes da Silva, who played locally in Mozambique but never made the leap to Portugal, "Matateu's transfer to Belenenses [a club located in greater Lisbon] in 1951 was the defining moment. . . . When the players started moving to Portugal and began to succeed there, we became really interested in Portuguese football."[33] Matateu's brother Vicente Lucas, who would himself go on to star for both Belenenses and the Portuguese national team, confirmed the enormity of his older brother's relocation to and subsequent footballing success in Portugal: "When we came to know, through the newspapers, the extent of the success that he was having in Portugal it generated enormous happiness for everyone. I cut out the newspapers . . . with all of the commentary on the goals that he scored. There was much praise for him."[34] Moreover, Augusto Matine indicated that because African footballers who transitioned to Portugal were newly seen as paragons by locals, the resultant adulation further intensified the consumption of metropolitan soccer in the colonies: "When I was playing in Portugal I was a role model for my friends here in Mozambique. All of them wanted to know what was happening with me, and I became a reference for them. But I said Matateu, Coluna, Eusébio, Manhiça, Valdmar, Rui Rodrigues, Mário Wilson; all these guys were references—not me. Everyone in Lourenço Marques knew that we [Africans] were in professional football. In every bairro there was an interest in knowing more about the Portuguese clubs where we were playing."[35]

So deep was the interest in, and affinity toward, the metropolitan clubs that the renowned Portuguese author António Lobo Antunes has revealed that these loyalties even generated empathy, if only temporarily, between otherwise mortal enemies. In describing his combat experiences in Angola as a conscript fighting for Portugal against the nationalist Movimento Popular de Libertação de Angola (MPLA; People's Movement for the Liberation of Angola) guerrillas, he candidly admitted:

When Benfica was playing, we would aim our rotating rifles toward the bush and, consequently, there were no attacks. The war stopped. Even the MPLA was for Benfica. It was an extremely strange situation because it didn't make sense that we were angry at people who were pulling for the same club as us. Benfica was, in fact, the best protector of [combatants during] the war. And nothing like this happened when Sporting or Porto were playing, which annoyed the more well-born captain and some junior officers. I even understand how you could shoot a supporter of Porto, but one from Benfica?[36]

Summer Projects: Metropolitan Clubs' African Tours

As early as the 1930s, and increasingly commonly from the 1940s on, metropolitan clubs toured the Portuguese colonies during the summer, following the conclusion of their domestic seasons. These tours were extremely popular, drawing both European and African fans to a series of exhibition matches. Although residents in the colonies could connect with their favorite metropolitan teams through local affiliate clubs and popular media, neither form of engagement rivaled witnessing "the real thing." Eventually, African migrant footballers themselves served as promotional agents of the sport in the colonies, returning home with their respective touring metropolitan clubs to play in the matches against local squads.

Notwithstanding the eventual success and popularity of the tours, they began rather inauspiciously and not without a host of associated obstacles, many logistical. Indeed, prior to widespread air travel, these forays to the colonies necessitated maritime travel, which entailed weeks at sea just to reach, for example, Luanda from Lisbon, and additional time to circumnavigate the Cape of Good Hope to arrive at Lourenço Marques. With limited time for players to rest and rejuvenate during the summer months, this type of elongated travel was particularly onerous. Upon arrival in the colonies, metropolitan-based footballers also voiced their grievances related to the rudimentary playing conditions, namely the dirt pitches. The disagreeable nature of the tour experience at times colored the competitors' interactions as well. As Bittencourt reveals, "Some of these sporting encounters in Angola (and presumably elsewhere, as well) were marked by altercations between players from Portuguese clubs and those from Angola, as happened with Acadêmica in 1938, Benfica in 1949, and C.U.F. in 1954."[37] And it wasn't always the African-based players who instigated these fisticuffs. According to Bittencourt, CUF players sparked the 1954 incident as, having just won the second division in Portugal, they were "bitter" after losing 6–1 to a team of Luanda-based footballers.[38]

Although metropolitan clubs were always favored to triumph in these matches, they occasionally failed to play their part, as supposedly inferior, yet manifestly plucky, teams from the colonies periodically won and, just as CUF discovered, sometimes by wide margins. Metropolitan clubs were most vulnerable when they were matched up against teams composed of the most talented footballers from the colonial capitals, essentially local "all-star" squads, and especially when those squads featured players who would later go on to star in Portugal. Even when the typically racially diverse colonial teams didn't win, though, they instilled local pride among both indigenous residents and settlers.[39] Indeed, Domingos has argued that these sporting visits constituted "instances in which the settler could demonstrate his vitality in front of a representative of the empire's ruling center."[40]

The impetuses for these footballing jaunts varied, changed over time, and are still debated. What is irrefutable is that the tours were lucrative for the participating clubs, with the revenues on offer providing ample motivation (and explanation) for their realization. But the tours also appear to have featured a patriotic/political dimension, a way to reaffirm the links between the metropole and the empire, which collectively composed the multisited *mundo português*, or Portuguese world. Ana Santos, writing about Benfica's tours throughout the empire, indicates that metropolitan media traveled with the club and filed multiple daily reports, thereby reinforcing the regime's emphasis on political union. Santos further explains that upon arrival in the capitals of Angola and Mozambique, the club was regaled with the same honors that visiting heads of state received.[41] The regime's official recognition of such sporting forays was seemingly intended to confirm its mantra, and associated propaganda, that "Portugal is not a small country" (see fig. 1.1). Indeed, even if the Estado Novo neither engineered nor mandated the tours, Lisbon certainly condoned these constitutive examples of what Michael Billig has called "banal nationalism"—the seemingly insignificant, yet highly efficacious, everyday representations of the state that collectively cultivate a national, imagined sense of community.[42]

Elsewhere, Lanfranchi and Taylor have unambiguously referred to these trips as "propaganda tours," while Marcos Cardão has written extensively about their explicitly political objectives.[43] For example, in addition to providing local entertainment, Benfica's tour of Portuguese Goa in 1960 was seemingly intended to remind indigenous subjects of their imperial connections and responsibilities. The presence of General Vassalo e Silva, the governor-general of the colony, at the associated events was undoubtedly intended to reinforce this message and to signal to neighboring India that Goa remained Portuguese territory. Yet, while the Indian brass may have been impressed by the football on display, they patently ignored the political overtones: just one year later, the Indian army successfully invaded Goa, quickly removing what Jawaharlal Nehru had described as "a pimple on the face of India."

Following the outbreak of the struggles for independence in the African colonies, beginning in Angola in the initial months of 1961, the tours became undeniably political, with the participating clubs requiring no patriotic prodding. For example, in May 1961, less than five months after the

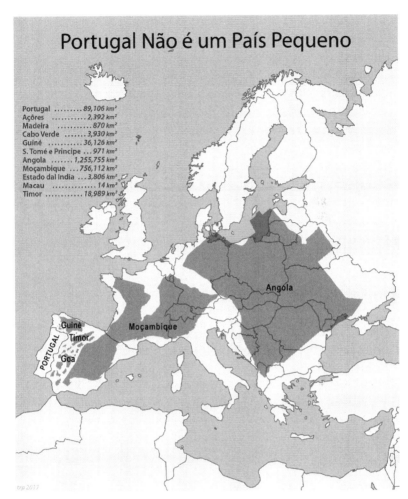

Portugal Não é um País Pequeno

Portugal .... 89,106 km²
Açôres .... 2,392 km²
Madeira .... 870 km²
Cabo Verde .... 3,930 km²
Guiné .... 36,126 km²
S. Tomé e Principe ... 971 km²
Angola .... 1,255,755 km²
Moçambique ... 756,112 km²
Estado dal India ... 3,806 km²
Macau .... 14 km²
Timor .... 18,989 km²

Figure 1.1. Replica propaganda map of the type regularly generated by the Portuguese regime during its reign.

outbreak of violence in Angola, Benfica offered to play a match in Luanda against a team of Angolans, with the receipts from the game going to "the victims of terrorism" in the colony.[44] Shortly thereafter, Benfica threw its support behind not only the civilian victims of the Angolan nationalists, but also the Portuguese armed forces, who had, in the meantime, commenced a brutal counterinsurgency campaign. The following summer, in

1962, Benfica toured both Angola and Mozambique, declaring in its official organ, O Benfica, that the club was bringing "the brilliance of its prestige and its metropolitan friendship to the Portuguese, who are fighting
in Africa for the integrity and the continuation of the Pátria."[45] As Cardão
registers, "One of the stated objectives of this tour was to raise funds for
the construction of a hospital for the recuperation of the soldiers of the
Forças Armadas [Portuguese armed forces] who were engaged in combat
in the African colonies."[46]

Notwithstanding this political overtness, it is important to note
that Portuguese clubs also traveled to other places in Africa (and South
America), belying contentions that these tours were *exclusively* intended
to deepen colonial control. Furthermore, clubs from all over Europe (as
well as some from South America—most notably, Brazilian squads—and
others from South Africa) also toured the Portuguese colonies, underscoring the fact that not every visit by a foreign club was intended to reinforce
the links between the metropole and the empire.[47]

Once Portuguese clubs began utilizing players from the colonies, the
tours also provided opportunities for metropolitan team officials to identify, scout, and, in some cases, sign talented African-based footballers. For
African hopefuls, the matches constituted occasions to showcase their
skills in the hopes of making lasting impressions on prospective employers. One rather extraordinary example of this phenomenon occurred in
Angola during Benfica's summer 1960 tour. Already aware of the prodigious talents of José Águas, who played for Lusitano Lobito, Benfica officials indicated that they would be assessing the footballer's skills during
the scheduled matches, one of which was surprisingly won, 3–1, by a team
of Lobito-based "all-stars," with Águas tallying a brace against the famous
Lisbon club. Exceptionally, the nineteen-year-old striker signed for and
immediately joined Benfica as they proceeded onward to other stops on
their African tour, and he would eventually go on to play thirteen more
seasons for the club.

Irrespective of the particular motivations for these tours, or even the
final scores of the constituent matches, they were immensely popular,
granting adoring, football-frenzied fans in the colonies opportunities to
witness their heroes perform at close range. For example, responding to
my question regarding the turnouts for matches involving touring metro-

politan clubs, Augusto Matine responded: "The stadiums were full. There was no [empty] space," and, to a follow-up inquiry regarding the affordability of attending, Matine explained: "For the cost of living at the time, it was expensive. But, even though it was, people made sacrifices. . . . Normally, the people who used to go to football matches were those with good jobs, but even the poor would pay 20 escudos for a ticket."[48] Similarly, Miguel Arcanjo, who grew up in Angola and would go on to become a fixture in central defense for FC Porto throughout the 1950s and into the first half of the 1960s, recalled that when the club toured the colony in the late 1940s (a tour that also included a visit to the neighboring Belgian Congo), throngs of local kids, including himself, chased after the vehicles that were carrying the visiting players, hoping to catch a glimpse of their sporting idols.[49] And in no way were the scenes that Arcanjo described anomalous. In the summer of 1955, for example, when Belenenses arrived in Luanda as part of a tour of Angola, residents flooded a neighborhood of the colonial capital to present the great Mozambican player Matateu with presents and even constructed a throne upon which they insisted the footballer sit.

The individuals who introduced football to the indigenous residents of Portugal's African territories could not have foreseen how immensely popular the game would become. Beyond generating countless practitioners, the sport also attracted legions of fans. Over time, the ability to converse knowledgeably about local, metropolitan, and even global football developments facilitated entry into social networks in the colonies and constituted an important component of masculine identity. Newspapers, radio, and, later on, television catalyzed and both broadened and deepened the consumption of local and distant soccer-related events. Eventually, African emigrant footballers themselves helped to popularize the metropolitan version of the sport in the colonies not only via their athletic success, but also by returning to the continent on summer tours as sporting heroes—embodiments of African capability.

Long before some of these Lusophone African players became international footballing idols, indigenous engagement with the game in the colonies began much more discreetly, though with a mounting fervor that presaged future success. In the ensuing chapter, I explore this unassuming process as Africans began to practice and play the sport in settings throughout Portugal's colonial empire. Shortly after they began kicking around a ball, Africans formed "native" clubs and leagues and developed new styles and approaches that substantively transformed the activity to which they had originally been exposed. With time, the skills of talented mestiço and black players were too great for organized clubs to forgo, even in the highly racialized colonial settings. Consequently, these talented footballers were invited to play in formerly whites-only leagues in Africa before eventually going on to play in the metropole and, for some, on the world's grandest and most revered soccer stages.

2

Engaging with the Game

African Practitioners in the Colonies

He used to play football with his many brothers on the sandy grounds of the suburbs, from dawn until dusk. He reached the football fields at a run, running like someone fleeing from the police or from the misery snapping at his heels.
—Eduardo Galeano, celebrated Uruguayan journalist and writer, describing Eusébio's childhood

The football of my time was played with a joy and a desire to show our skills as players. Today, this football doesn't exist because economic interests come first.
—Abel Miglietti, who was born in Mozambique in 1946 and would eventually go on to play for a series of clubs in Portugal, including Benfica and Porto

Although it is, of course, impossible to pinpoint the first time an African in what would become Portuguese imperial territory kicked a soccer ball, or even something approximating one, it's quite possible that she or he enjoyed it. If Africans in the colonies eagerly consumed metropolitan soccer happenings, they just as zealously played the sport, increasingly generating their own noteworthy footballing developments. Africans' enthusiastic engagement with the game grew largely in parallel to the expansion of soccer within the European settler communities: these two groups of practitioners were segregated by the administrative policies that demarcated colonial spaces along racial lines. Following the introduction of soccer in Portugal's African empire, decades would pass before the racial boundaries that divided these footballing worlds dissipated, enabling blacks and whites in the colonies to play against and with one another.

Well before this integrative process eroded these sporting barriers, Africans resourcefully formed their own clubs and associations, organizationally mimicking the Europeans-only leagues and adhering to the rules and regulations of the game as initially conveyed to them. However, they also developed their own "creolized" styles and dynamics of play. In this manner, and in many other ways, Africans appropriated the game—making it their own, filling it with new meanings, and infusing it with a performative dimension devoid of the European version of the sport. Later, though, as talented African players began to join traditionally whites-only clubs, to achieve success they would have to conform to the prevailing tactics and approaches advocated by the array of Portuguese coaches in the colonies. Local observers bemoaned the resultant disappearance of indigenous styles of play, as footballing panache became one of many casualties of the mounting emphasis on victory above all else.

In response to a range of external pressures and administrative calculations, the various governments in the Portuguese colonies eventually incorporated the African associations into the longer-established European leagues. In turn, the elite colonial clubs newly began recruiting large numbers of talented black and *mestiço* (mulatto) players. On these racially integrated squads, African footballers forged meaningful friendships across racial lines, united by their athletic acumen and common sporting cause. Yet, for all of their social and sporting success, players' salaries remained nominal. In the absence of living wages for squad members, colonial soccer teams attracted skilled footballers by arranging for employment either directly with club patrons or through associated commercial networks. By engaging in remunerative work in mixed-race environments, players both contributed to household finances and sharpened their social integration skills. And, perhaps most importantly, they also developed labor strategies that many of them would subsequently apply in the metropole in creative and innovative ways to facilitate their long-term success, both on and away from the pitch.

This chapter examines the various ways that, over time, Africans in the colonies played the game—from the dusty neighborhood matches to the downtown leagues—and traces the social and economic impacts of this evolving engagement. Although indigenous practitioners formed "native" clubs and associations and some of these footballers eventually joined formerly Europeans-only clubs, Africans never stopped playing informally in seemingly every available space, reflecting the game's steadily expanding popularity. In these modest sites, local cultural emphases and creativity blended with a rejective spirit to produce novel playing styles and approaches that proved remarkably durable in the *bairros* (neighborhoods) in which they were conceived and cultivated. Conversely, African players who ascended the tiers of colonial soccerdom were forced to abandon former modes in order to continue to realize footballing and, ultimately, financial success. This chapter examines their shifting engagement with the sport as soccer in the colonies steadily became something much more than just a game.

Playing the Game: Informal Engagements

It appears that football was initially introduced in Portugal's African colonies sometime during the end of the nineteenth century. Regardless of the exact date, by the early twentieth century, the sport had gained significant traction. In Mozambique, for example, by 1904 matches were already being organized, while local teams were apparently challenging the crews of ships docked at Lourenço Marques.[1] In explaining Africans' initial receptiveness toward the game, scholars have emphasized the strong relationships and linkages between soccer and precolonial martial and athletic traditions, especially those that featured a ritualized space in which to perform.[2] John Bale and Joe Sang have argued that these indigenous customs and associated notions of masculinity constituted the "soil into which the seeds of European sport would later be planted."[3] In the Lusophone African context, precolonial traditions and competitions of this nature helped fuel soccer's initial appeal, as well as its eventual widespread popularity. In the following section, I examine the ways that African practitioners began engaging with the sport and trace these fundamental, often rudimentary, forms of participation over time.

Peladas *and Makeshift Balls*

In the Global North, images abound of barefoot Africans kicking around improvised spherical objects on uneven patches of dusty land bookended by makeshift goals. Although these images are somewhat misleading—formal soccer venues of all sizes can be found throughout the continent—virtually every one of today's elite African footballers learned the sport by playing on exactly the types of scruffy pitches that fill Western imaginations. Not surprisingly, African practitioners in Portugal's colonies commenced their engagement with the sport in similar fashion, often playing without a proper ball, or even shoes, as they partook in pickup games, or *peladas*.[4] Into the waning decades of Portugal's empire, these austere conditions persisted; indeed, each and every footballer who was talented enough to play in the metropole initially developed his skills in these humble spaces.

Unable to afford proper soccer balls, participants in neighborhood peladas instead fashioned makeshift balls from whatever materials were available: rags, socks, women's stockings, and even the innards of animals. According to Calton Banze, who grew up in the Chamanculo neighborhood of Lourenço Marques in the 1960s, "We had to make the balls. Socks, rags, plastic, elastic—these were the materials we used. And I shouldn't forget the stomach of an ox, which was already a ball. I also remember a tennis ball that somebody brought, already too old to use for tennis any longer. We also used inner tubes stolen from bicycles."[5] Although players continued to craft these improvised balls through the end of the colonial period, and beyond, in the 1960s, a rubber company headquartered in the Mozambican capital introduced the Facobol. This development improved the quality of innumerable neighborhood contests; yet, for most practitioners, the cost, though minimal, of the revolutionary ball rendered it out of reach. As such, the rubber Facobol quickly became a status symbol, separating those players with sufficient means, however limited, from those for whom the purchase of even this reasonably priced item was cost-prohibitive.

If African footballers weren't discouraged by the lack of a proper ball, the absence of athletic footwear—or shoes of any sort—similarly did little to temper their enthusiasm. Because footwear was not historically customary in many African communities, this apparent problem was, in fact, not an issue at all. But over time, as colonial fashion influenced local sartorial styles, the practice of wearing shoes became increasingly widespread, especially in cities, the loci of soccer engagement and development. Still, neighborhood football remained an almost universally shoeless endeavor. Even when games in the bairros were better organized and local teams were formed, players rarely donned footwear. As Eusébio recalled in 2004: "It is normal in Africa, even today, for the kids to play barefoot in their neighborhood teams. When we played for our local team, we never had boots or shoes."[6]

White players who lived and played in the neighborhoods similarly participated in these sans-shoes affairs, though not always for exactly the same reasons. According to Ernesto Baltazar, a white Mozambican hailing from a poor family who grew up playing alongside Eusébio and other future talents deriving from the colony, "We [Eusébio and I] played soccer barefoot. I had sneakers, but if I arrived home with dirty sneakers, I was in trouble. In the beginning, I removed the sneakers and played with socks. My socks were dirty and pierced; my mother ordered me to wash them. After that she would beat me. After that I realized that there was no chance; otherwise, I would have been beaten every day. So I played barefoot, too."[7]

Playing Spaces: "Infinite Horizons"

If proper balls and shoes of any type constituted lavish accessories, space in which to play was much more essential. Consequently, committed players found space wherever they could, even in the tightest areas. For example, according to Calton Banze regarding 1960s Lourenço Marques, "With the tennis ball and other balls, we played on the verandas of the houses. The verandas were about two meters wide and seven or eight meters long. We played two-versus-two or one-versus-one. . . . How many windows were broken! How many times we raced away to avoid being caught! And how many balls were ripped to shreds because they landed in the backyard of somebody who didn't like football!"[8] Of course, the greater the number of players, the larger the requisite space. Thankfully, for these enthusiastic youth, even the steady population growth that the colonial capitals and secondary cities experienced didn't deprive practitioners of ample room for matches of all varieties. As António Joaquim Dinis, an Angolan who would eventually play for Sporting Lisboa, conveyed during a 1972 interview regarding this available recreational space: "Empty, wide lots, which we could use as our field, we had plenty of those. In this aspect, the kids of Luanda are happier than those in the metropole, because there are several empty spaces where they can entertain each other without the risk of breaking windows or suddenly having the police showing up."[9] Reminiscing about these open spaces, Shéu Han, who used to play on the beaches of Inhassora, on the Mozambican coast, before he began suiting up for Benfica in the 1970s, declared, "That's where great champions such as Matateu, Eusébio, Mário Coluna, came from. They were all shaped by these infinite horizons, by the fascination for those great spaces."[10]

Although African players nostalgically remembered the "infinite horizons," many of them also soberly lamented the gradual disappearance of at least some of these spaces. Over time, urban development encroached upon many formally open plots. And later, the influxes of rural refugees fleeing the fighting generated by the wars for independence and the ensuing civil conflicts, which engulfed the newly independent Lusophone African states, further filled what remained of these spaces. During our interview, Hilário explained that

in Mozambique and especially in Lourenço Marques there were a lot of abandoned lots, so growing up we would play on these lots all around. . . . Another thing that is a difficulty for the current players—and the opposite helped us—was the amount of free space we had to play and exercise, and when the colonial and civil wars were happening everyone who was in the provinces [countryside] fled to the capital and they would build their little houses in the free spaces, so the capital got overpopulated and the spaces in which we had to play and have fun don't exist anymore.[11]

Former players also often cite the deleterious contemporary footballing implications that stem from these demographic and geographic shifts. According to Matine, "During the colonial period in Lourenço Marques, in the suburbs, there were a lot of empty fields where people used to play soccer. That's not the reality nowadays, and that's the reason that there is not a lot of talent coming out of African countries like there used to be. . . . Some of those fields are now markets, among other things, so it becomes very hard to find talent because you don't teach soccer to an African; one just has to keep playing. We would play at school and then in those fields when we were out of school."[12]

Beyond serving as physical spaces in which to kick a ball around, neighborhood pitches, informal as they might have been, also became centers of entertainment and socialization. Further, they bestowed on the communities surrounding the spaces a sense of identity that grew out of, and was shaped by, the action on the field. As footballers from one neighborhood battled against a squad from another, spectators took pride in the players representing their locality. And, as these identities cohered and hardened over time, soccer helped to further demarcate and differentiate individual neighborhoods. According to Hilário, "Football was tough because there were many rivalries, between districts. . . . The districts were a boundary. In order to enter Chamanculo I had to know people there. This did not mean I couldn't go in, only that it was tougher. What defined the boundary was having been born there, having huts there, having a place to listen to music, talk about football, to form a team to play in another district."[13]

A Dangerous Pastime? Finding Time to Play

Finding space to play football was unquestionably important, but so was finding time. As mentioned above, many parents, especially during the sport's infancy in the colonies, saw little value in this activity and, thus, discouraged their sons from allocating too much time to play the game. However, as the sport gained both popularity and legitimacy, parents' tolerance for the endeavor gradually grew. But guardians still typically deemed whatever schooling might have been available for their sons to have been significantly more important; meanwhile, for those families unable to afford an education for their sons and daughters, contributing to the family finances remained paramount. As such, children often had to engage with the game discreetly. Yet, just as kids the world over have done and continue to do, African youth also found time, even at the expense of more productive undertakings, to play and have fun.

The histories of two players, João Santana and Armando Manhiça, illuminate particularly well the tension that a love for the game could generate between passionate children and unconvinced parents. The childhood and teen years in the 1940s and early 1950s of Santana, who grew up on Angola's central coast and would go on to play for Benfica, are exemplary in this respect. Keen on football, but not on the career that his father had envisioned for him, Santana's passion for the game generated friction between his parents and him. Eventually, he acquiesced and accepted a position at the nearby Cassequel sugar factory on the central Angolan coast. Predictably, relations with his parents improved almost immediately, and they, in turn, granted Santana permission to go to a local field after work to watch his football idols practicing and, every once in a while, to kick the ball around himself. Eventually, Santana caught the eye of the manager of the team sponsored by the sugar company, Sport Clube da Catumbela, and with his father's consent he joined the squad and was accordingly excused from work each afternoon.

Meanwhile, in Mozambique, the case of Armando, who was born in 1943 in Chamanculo, a Maputo suburb, and who would eventually go on to play for Sporting Lisboa, similarly highlights this footballing passion and the attendant tension it could generate. Growing up in a poor family, at a young age he began helping his mother sell fish, but by as early as eight years old he had already begun stealing away to play soccer with other kids in an open space in front of the market. Moreover, on the way to or from a customer's dwelling, he regularly snuck in some football; oftentimes, he utilized the basket he ought to have been using to deliver the fish as a goalpost! His passion for the game unfaltering, upon eventually starting school at age twelve Armando often skipped out on his education to play soccer, unbeknownst to his parents. Once caught, he was roundly punished and told he could never play football again. Chastened, he was never truant again, or even tardy. Nor, however, did he lose his passion for the game, and he quickly found ways to reincorporate soccer into his life, eventually playing each day after school, from 4:00 p.m. until the sun set.[14]

Football as Facilitator: Connections and Transcensions

The growth of neighborhood soccer produced novel ways for African players to interact and connect with one another. Players of different ages mixed, individuals with different professions and means battled with and against one another, younger siblings found even more ways to idolize their talented older siblings, status was generated and lost, and in some, albeit rare, cases, the sons of settler families would play alongside or against Africans. Commenting on this sporting and social miscellany, Matine recalled that these neighborhood matches featured, among others, "carpenters, masons, and various apprentices, some who ironed clothes in a family's house, some who washed clothes in the suburb, in the river . . . some who were cotton pickers."[15] At other times, age rather than occupational discrepancies generated otherwise uncommon social/sporting partnerships. In the case of Matateu, it was during the 1930s in the streets of Minkadjuine, in Lourenço Marques, where he allegedly, "as a child, dreamed to be a player like Alberto, his older brother . . . and he always managed to enter the teams of the older boys during the lively and hotly disputed games along Zixaxa road."[16] Similarly, Matateu's younger sibling, Vicente Lucas, looked up to his gifted older brother and would eventually follow in his footsteps to Belenenses and, ultimately, the Portuguese national team.

Regardless of the informality of the matches, the competition was often fierce and the skill on display in certain neighborhoods would eventually be considered "world class." Commenting on the wealth of talent that derived from a single Maputo neighborhood, Vicente Lucas reminisced that "the neighborhood in Alto Mahé [in Maputo] could be considered a luxury [for us] at one time, because we were living at the feet of Coluna, Eusébio, and Hilário."[17] Abel Miglietti echoed Lucas's sentiments: "I remember that when I was thirteen years old I played for a neighborhood team and I had as opponents Armando Manhiça, Eusébio, Carlitos, and my brother Justino, and many more who became famous because of football."[18] Apparently, this talent manifested itself at even earlier ages than thirteen. Indeed, according to a 1959 issue of *Ídolos*, "At the age of seven, barefoot, with sewn up shorts and ripped shirts, Hilário was the little idol of the group of his street. . . . Others always wanted him on their team."[19]

If local practitioners connected with other players through neighborhood matches, their limitless imaginations and aspirations connected them to global soccerdom, thereby linking what Domingos has described as otherwise disparate "football narratives."[20] The names of the local teams that young players formed evinced these creative connections. For example, Hilário started out playing for a neighborhood team named Arsenal, in obvious imitation of the famous London-based club. Apparently, one of the local club's founders had seen a clip of an Arsenal match during the intermission of a film at a local cinema; the neighborhood team even did the best they could to don red jerseys for matches so as to dutifully maintain tonal consistency with the English outfit. Hilário rendered plausibility to the alleged origins of this appellative replication: "In Mafalala, news from Europe arrived to us, in the bairro. . . . There was news. In the intervals of films, for example, there were bulletins . . . and information circulated."[21] But these emulative connections weren't limited to European football teams. For example, clubs featuring the names Botafogo, Vasco da Gama, and Flamengo were also formed in the Portuguese colonies, in reverence to these three renowned Brazilian squads. And, perhaps most famously in this bilateral vein, in the 1950s Eusébio and a collection of other teenage players from his neighborhood formed Os Brasileiros de Mafalala (the Brazilians of Mafalala). According to Baltazar, a Mozambican footballer of Portuguese descent who played with Eusébio on Os Brasileiros, the inspiration for the formation of the club was as follows: "In that time, many Brazilian teams came to play in Lourenço Marques. Teams like Portuguesa de Santos, Portuguesa de Desportos, and Ferroviário. They had artistic football. We liked that type of football, and that was why our team became 'Os Brasileiros de Mafalala.'"[22] Individual Brazilian soccer stars also impressed young African players in Portugal's colonies. For example, Nuro Americano recalled, "We received news about Brazil[ian] football via the radio. In fact, my idol was Gilmar, the Brazilian goalkeeper."[23] Brazil's triumph at the 1958 World Cup in Sweden, which marked the debut of a seventeen-year-old Pelé on the world stage, further extended the legendary status and popularity of that footballing nation and its assortment of superstar players.

If neighborhood practitioners dreamed about foreign clubs in distant lands capturing the world's most prestigious soccer trophies, the prizes on offer for winning local matches were much more modest and mundane. Although a great deal was at stake in these contests—reputation, pride, identity, and, eventually, an opportunity to showcase one's talents for metropolitan football scouts—prizes reflected indigenous residents' limited resources in these colonial milieus. The most common spoils was a can of cashew nuts or, later, as the cash economy took hold, small pots of money, which players collectively generated prior to kickoff. Mário Coluna, who spent his childhood in the 1940s playing in the Chamanculo district of Maputo, recalled, "When local teams challenged groups from other districts, we bet cans of cashew nuts and whoever won took the whole lot. In those times, there was no clock and whoever scored four goals first won."[24] Rewards could, however, be more significant, or at least more varied. For example, Nuro Americano, who grew up playing on the island of Pemba off Mozambique's northern coast, indicated that a bottle of rose syrup and five sardines were on offer for the victors of at least one match in which he participated.[25]

African Organization: Leagues of Their Own

Although neighborhood matches were a mainstay of suburban life throughout the colonial period, African players and spectators also organized formal leagues of their own, modeled on the Europeans-only squads and leagues that Portuguese settlers had formed. Initially denied access to these associations, such as the Associação de Futebol Lourenço Marques (AFLM) in Mozambique, due to racially segregative policies in the colonies, Africans formed their own squads and leagues, thereby democratizing organized football. In Mozambique, beginning in the 1920s and ultimately formalized in 1934, African players organized (and were confined to) the Associação Africana de Futebol (AFA), composed of more than ten participating clubs. In Angola, a similar initiative gave birth to that colony's African league, though the association in that setting featured only roughly half as many clubs, while the association in Portuguese Guiné was even more modest.[26]

Portuguese colonial officials, unlike their French counterparts elsewhere in Africa, condoned these imitative leagues, deeming them innocuous and potentially even constructive. This type of replicative sporting development has prompted Richard Cashman to ask elsewhere, in regard to the growth of cricket in the West Indies: "Where does the promoting hand of the colonial master stop and where does the adapting and assimilating indigenous tradition start?"[27] In the Lusophone African context, it would be difficult to discern an exact transitional point between these two processes, as, in practice, they were complementary, overlapping, and flowed seamlessly into one another.

In an effort to analyze this dynamic in the realm of cricket, scholars of the sport, including Fahad Mustafa and, perhaps most famously, C. L. R. James, as well as scholars of soccer, such as David Goldblatt, have interpreted the formation of indigenous associations—and, more abstractly, "traditions"—as "resistance" and "platforms for political struggle."[28] Yet, in practice, there was no political struggle, explicitly or otherwise, that flowed out of this sporting process in the various Lusophone African settings, even if nationalist leaders, such as Amílcar Cabral in Guiné, recognized that sport could be used to mobilize his countrymen for the struggle against colonialism and even formed a club with this aim in mind in 1954 in the capital city of Bissau.[29] Regardless, it's difficult to identify any tangible "platforms," or roots, of contestation in these initiatives in the Lusophone colonies. Although many Africans who would go on to join the various nationalist movements initially played for the teams that composed these leagues and political discourse certainly circulated within these clubs, it would be misleading to characterize the squads or, more broadly, the associations, as loci of anticolonial sentiment. Eschewing the tendency among scholars of Africa's past to locate "resistance" in seemingly every aspect of colonized life, I instead consider the indigenous leagues as intermediate stops at which African practitioners enjoyed the game and forged meaningful relationships with teammates, while the most gifted among them honed their skills to facilitate further sporting ascension. Indeed, it was to the constituent clubs of "native" associations that talented African players from neighborhoods throughout the colonies graduated. And it was at these same clubs that they would subsequently showcase their skills for scouts from the superior colonial leagues and, eventually, from the metropolitan teams.

The clubs that composed the African leagues in the colonies required from their players a level of commitment, a sporting discipline, and a sense of European-influenced formality, including mandatory jerseys and shoes, that were absent in the bairro peladas. In turn, these new behavioral and athletic emphases would serve players well as they continued to ascend the ranks of colonial soccerdom. But despite some novel elements of decorum, the football played in these leagues by and large continued to feature the improvisation and "creolization" that had been devised in neighborhood contests. Many European observers praised this indigenous approach to the game, while the oft-dancing, -drumming, and -singing African spectators both reveled in and further encouraged this style of play. Conversely, football traditionalists rejected this performative flair, deeming indigenous players to be, first and foremost, entertainers, rather than faithful disciples of the game. Ultimately, African players would have to curb these crowd-pleasing displays in favor of a more subdued, disciplined approach in order to continue their footballing ascension.

Imitative Leagues

The leagues formed by African patrons, coaches, and players resembled the Europeans-only leagues in their organizational structure but were, divergently, very poorly funded. Local elites, who were often, though not exclusively, *assimilados* (assimilateds), generally bankrolled the clubs and covered the leagues' administrative expenses, though the players themselves typically derived from lower social strata.[30] Alegi has attributed the development of these leagues elsewhere in Africa to "wage-earning urban workers with some Western education—men with discretionary income and leisure time." But his profile of these individuals as "dressed in jackets and trousers . . . secretarial workers . . . situated in a position of intermediary ambivalence," would overstate the economic means and cultural outlook of many of the footballing entrepreneurs in the Lusophone African settings.[31] For example, Hilário characterized these individuals in Mozambique as "guys who lived in the districts, in huts, shall we say, wooden and zinc houses, and worked in factories or petrol stations, in the quay or the railway."[32] Even if these players enjoyed only basic accommodations, though, they typically did have steady, if modestly compensated, employment in much-needed lines of work. For example, the founding members of Grupo Desportivo Beirense, a Mozambican AFA club, included a fish trader, two shopworkers, three drivers, seven attendants, one lifeguard, one dockworker, a collector, and five servants—each occupation important, but all poorly compensated.[33]

Unlike the exclusive, Europeans-only leagues in the colonies, the African associations accepted all comers; securing talented players was the sole objective for the constituent clubs. Yet, even in the absence of racial exclusion, owing to the African leagues' attempts to be taken seriously, they did institute what amounted to de facto exclusionary policies. For example, the AFA required players to furnish their own footwear and coordinated socks and shorts, and, as club owners generally provided only a team jersey and covered players' registration fees, these league mandates effectively limited participation.[34] Consequently, footballers in these associations typically enjoyed at least moderate, if still quite modest, levels of income, which enabled these "weekend footballers" to procure the requisite equipment and attire.

Conversely, in other imperial settings in Africa, European authorities banned indigenous players from wearing soccer boots as a way to reinforce cultural-racial divides. For example, a decree of this nature was in place in the Belgian Congo, yet this type of restriction was arguably most stringent and far-reaching in the French colony of Congo-Brazzaville. Reacting both to Africans' increasingly assertive approach to the game and, preemptively, to the potential for confidence in the sporting arena to mix explosively with proto-nationalist stirrings, in 1936 the colonial government banned footwear in the African leagues. Goldblatt explains, "The ban was ostensibly to limit on-field violence but in reality it was designed to demean their subjects the way the Belgians did in the Congo, where Africans were already forbidden from wearing shoes when they played."[35]

Unlike Belgian and French colonial administrators, Portuguese authorities mandated that shoes be worn on the pitch. Although these divergent policies were seemingly at odds, European racial superiority underpinned both approaches. In the Lusophone African context, colonial officials were attempting to keep the formal, organized version of the game beyond the financial reach of much of the African population, as soccer boots were cost-prohibitive for most indigenous residents. Regardless, talented African players typically found ways to procure the requisite footwear, oftentimes via the salaries they earned from the jobs that European-run clubs, eager to utilize their soccer talents, arranged for them. In this manner, these teams were, in effect, undermining this otherwise restrictive colonial contrivance.

The footwear policy did, however, generate numerous victims, as many players simply couldn't afford soccer boots—an accessory that essentially amounted to a luxury item for their impoverished families—thereby blocking their participation and possible ascension. Moreover, Augusto Matine, who grew up playing in the Chamanculo neighborhood of Maputo, cited an entirely unintended consequence of this policy that ironically impeded the progress of even those players who *could* secure a pair of boots: "It was a problem for some players, who were used to playing barefoot and never got used to wearing shoes. Many were lost in this manner. Great football players were lost."[36]

For those footballers who were able to both secure soccer shoes *and* excel once donning them, the African leagues provided opportunities to hone their skills against emerging domestic talent and, in some cases, even players and squads from beyond the borders of Portugal's African domains. For example, the AFA established relationships with black South African leagues, including the Transvaal African Football Association (TAFA) and the Johannesburg African Football Association, which produced visits by clubs from the respective associations. Products of this rudimentary networking among African associations included a trip by Beira-Mar, an AFA club, to South Africa in 1933, while three years later, Johannesburg's All-Blacks Football Club, composed entirely of African mine workers, suited up against an all-star selection of AFA players.[37] And it wasn't just the footballers themselves who traveled to the games. Fans and members of the press were also permitted to accompany the players on these regional journeys to watch their teams perform against "international" competition; victories in these matches naturally generated local pride among supporters.

Inimitable Styles

Although the African leagues resembled the European associations in their structure and organization, the styles that indigenous players exhibited on the pitch were substantively different. Reflecting local aesthetics and tropes, spectators exhorted and applauded trickery, deception, feigning, and, especially, creative dribbling. This approach to the game had originally been developed on neighborhood pitches, but even as players transitioned into more formal leagues, these styles persisted, encouraged by the even larger crowds that attended the matches. As Alegi has incisively contended, "This outcome frustrated colonial officers who believed that teaching Africans how to play the game was as important as getting them to accept football in the first place."[38] Rather than emphasizing subversion, contestation, or even intimations of political autonomy as embodied in the expressive moves of the aspiring footballers, though, I consider what participation in this more formal tier of colonial soccerdom meant in social and sporting terms for practitioners. Even if European evaluators of soccer talent often characterized this brand of play as "unstructured" or "undisciplined," it was undoubtedly entertaining, with the aesthetic of the performance typically trumping the final score in the eyes of the spectators.

Players who were particularly adept at this improvisational approach to the game acquired both status and prestige. According to Saide Mogne, who offers a fan's perspective stemming from his childhood experiences in colonial Mozambique during the 1960s, "The dribbler in AFA games was the public's hero, everyone's hero, the player who, when the games ended, was carried shoulder high."[39] The players themselves also appreciated the aesthetic appeal of the style for which they were being lauded. Issufo Batata, who played locally in Mozambique in the 1950s but never made the transition to the metropole, indicated that this approach was "defined by its 'sweetness,' the meanings produced by the gestures and movements of those who interpreted an improvisation executed to the rhythm of the local association."[40] And Angolan player António Fernandes, or "Yaúca," who would go on to play for Belenenses and Benfica in the 1950s and '60s, remarked upon settling into the metropolitan capital, "The players from Africa appear to have more flair and talent. I don't know what it is, but I like to watch them more."[41]

Beyond the pleasing aesthetic, Alegi suggests that this creative, deceptive style also captured Africans' adeptness in "getting around difficulties and dangerous situations in colonial societies."[42] If this style of play did, indeed, reflect Africans' adroitness in navigating colonial life, there were also risks associated with it—in particular, the humiliation it was capable of generating for opponents. Vicente Lucas explained that "[back] then, if you used your trickery, you'd pay for it. If you tried to pass the ball between the legs of other players, they would beat you senseless. I used to dribble by a guy once, and he would fall to the ground. I would wait for him to get up and dribble by him again, but if I did it a third time he might physically beat me."[43]

The celebrated Mozambican poet José Craveirinha provides some of the most vivid written descriptions of this freewheeling style of play. He penned the pieces while working as a journalist for *O Brado Africano*, a Lourenço Marques newspaper launched in 1918, which took a keen, almost singular interest in covering the AFA.[44] A January 1955 piece he crafted for the paper exemplifies the appreciation that spectators had for this style of play:

> The black player's predisposition to adopt football could be attributed not just to the merits of resistance and elasticity with which nature gifted the vast contingent of black races, but also to a strange and unusual power of assimilation and improvisation, in which the instinctive sense, less blunt than in the Western man, is revealed exuberantly in the Westernized African. The black man lives—and with what an ardor!—any given sport, surrendering himself to a sensorial vibration that is very rare in other racial groups.[45]

As Domingos has pointed out elsewhere, Craveirinha's suggestion that these athletic traits and proclivities were racially innate both lauds and essentializes in the same breath.[46]

Superstitions

Just as players brought the styles they had honed in neighborhood contests with them to their new leagues, they also imported local superstitions that were intended to prejudice their opponents and, concomitantly, propel them to victory. Young players observed older boys and adults engaging in these practices and, in turn, perpetuated them, just as footballers would continue to do throughout their ascension in colonial and, eventually, metropolitan soccer. In fact, these traditions persist in present-day African soccerdom, as well as in sites overseas, such as Lisbon, where large numbers of African footballers play and reside. Indeed, local advertisements for shamans in these settings offering to influence sporting affairs are readily encountered.

Well before players started employing supernatural tactics at the highest levels of world football, though, their application began much more humbly in countless Lusophone African neighborhoods. According to Daúto Faquirá, who was born in 1966 in the Mozambican coastal city of Inhambane, "We used to . . . reproduce those things we saw the adults do: sometimes we put down salt, sometimes we used chicken legs, copying the rituals of our elders, behind the net, in order to remove the bad luck of a defeat."[47] And, mirroring other scenarios in which healers and witch doctors were employed, when these measures proved ineffective or their divinations inaccurate, adherents cited a failure to properly follow instructions or procedures, rather than questioning the efficacy of the methodology.

Geographical and Cultural Transitions: To the Downtown Leagues

Responding in part to mounting international pressure to improve conditions for colonized subjects in the Portuguese empire, colonial officials eventually disbanded the African leagues by incorporating the constituent clubs into the lower tiers of the formerly whites-only associations. But prior to these sweeping changes, a handful of talented players—almost exclusively assimilated mestiços—had made the transition from the bairros to the city centers, the nuclei of colonial settlerdom. Instead of continuing to play their home games in the suburbs, these players newly suited up in front of large crowds in the downtowns, or *baixas*, of these urban settings.[48] On these clubs, players enjoyed superior facilities and coaching, and, in general, were subjected to strict training regimens, both on and away from the pitch, as well as much more structured playing environments. In fact, for most African players, participation in these leagues constituted their initial exposure to formal conditioning of any sort, as in the "native" leagues there were no practices, only games, while players, if they trained at all, did so on their own. Irrespective of the new training regimen, Craveirinha and other observers of the game in the colonies bemoaned, on a much more fundamental level, this shift of local talent to the formal leagues and the concomitant degradation and eventual dissolution of the African associations. Yet players from the bairros undoubtedly benefited—socially, athletically, and, if often only indirectly, economically—from the more rigorous sporting environments. And, by joining the clubs, the aspiring athletes were now closer to realizing their footballing dreams.

In the new squads, the social and cultural—including linguistic—proficiencies that players cultivated were arguably as important to their long-term success as the soccer skills they continued to develop and hone. Indeed, as Magode has contended, within the soccer clubs and associations in colonial Lourenço Marques, "command of Portuguese . . . [and] the adoption of a European lifestyle . . . were valued qualities."[49] This process of acculturation proved vital to the players' future success in the metropole, where the array of away-from-the-pitch challenges was just as formidable as the obstacles they encountered between the lines. Instrumental to this adjustive process were Portuguese coaches, who featured at nearly all of the colonial clubs with which African and mestiço players were newly affiliated. Regular exposure to these mentors, as well as to the players' new teammates, ensured that footballers from the bairros developed a level of familiarity with Portuguese culture prior to leaving the continent.

The game itself also contributed to this familiarization process. If, as outlined above, the introduction of football was a calculated endeavor, a component of the broader colonial project, it follows that Portuguese conventions, protocols, values, and beliefs were deliberately transmitted through the sport. Indeed, Stoddart has argued that the game was intended as an "instrument of socialization, infusing discipline . . . and respect for hierarchies."[50] Similarly, Mangan theorizes that sporting practices played a role in the creation of "cultural bonds" between the colonizer and the colonized, which prompted the latter to accept the former's practices and values.[51] With Portuguese coaches increasingly serving as the teachers/transmitters in colonial soccerdom, both Stoddart's "hierarchy" and Mangan's "bonds" developed over time and were subsequently reinforced. As players moved from African clubs and associations to traditionally Europeans-only equivalents, these interactional phenomena arguably smoothed their transitions; indeed, their entrance into these core colonial spaces newly required humility and, to a certain extent, reverence.

A Proximate, New World

As African and mestiço players began trickling into the world of downtown football, they joined long-standing clubs, many of which are extant. Some of these teams featured umbilical connections to their more famous metropolitan namesakes, such as Mozambique's Sporting de Lourenço Marques (Sporting Lisboa), created in 1920; and, in Angola, Sport Luanda e Benfica (Benfica), founded two years later; while in Guiné, Sporting Clube de Bissau was launched in 1936. Over time, consistent with prevailing football trends, the clubs also developed "juvenile" and "junior" squads for players who were under sixteen years old or who needed further seasoning before potentially joining the "senior" squad. However, with the new emphasis on talent above all else, age exceptions were often granted to allow skilled footballers to play at the highest levels, even before they would otherwise have been officially permitted to do so. For example, in 1954, José Ferreira Pinto, who would go on to play for both Sporting Lisboa and CUF (Companhia União Fabril) in Portugal, joined the Angolan club, Sporting Clube de Benguela, at fourteen years old, even though the minimum legal age was technically fifteen. The Provincial Sporting Board granted Pinto an exemption, the first such waiver issued in the colony, apparently because he was "so big and built for his age."[52] Similarly, in 1958 in Portuguese Guiné, the Associação da Guiné gave special dispensation to Bernardo da Velha, who would eventually go on to play for Sporting Lisboa and FC Porto in the metropole, to join the senior squad at FC de Teixeira Pinto, even though he was one year shy of the required age. To formalize the arrangement, the association directors needed his mother's signature (as his father had passed away), and although she was "scared that her 'little boy' could end up hurting himself in the midst of a man's game," she eventually consented.[53]

It was in the 1930s that the first players began transitioning from neighborhood teams to the topflight colonial clubs and leagues. In Mozambique in 1938, for example, Vicente, from Beira-Mar; and Américo, from João Albasini, accepted invitations to play for Desportivo, an AFLM club. The presence of even small numbers of African players in these premier leagues generated pride in the bairros as well as a newfound interest in the neighborhoods for so-called "downtown," or *baixa*, soccer. Most importantly, these footballers' success following their transitions confirmed that they possessed sufficient talent, even if it remained somewhat "raw."

It wasn't until the 1950s that African and mestiço players were permitted to participate in the elite colonial leagues in any appreciable numbers, and even then, the process was highly uneven. In Luanda, for example, certain teams, including Sport Luanda e Benfica and Sporting Clube de Luanda, were referred to as *clubes dos brancos*, or "clubs of the whites."[54] In some cases, these affiliate clubs were simply adhering to their parent clubs' practices. For example, for many years, Benfica of Lisbon exclusively utilized Portuguese-born players, refusing to tap foreign pools of talent—even from neighboring Spain—to enhance its squads. Conversely, some clubs in Mozambique, including Grupo Desportivo de Lourenço Marques (or, more commonly, just "Desportivo," founded in 1921) and Grupo Desportivo 1° de Maio (or "Primeiro de Maio," founded in 1917), abandoned racial exclusivity policies earlier than other squads, thereby paving the way for ever-greater numbers of neighborhood players to make the jump downtown in that setting. Meanwhile, in an associated development, in 1952, the AFLM incorporated the mestiço teams Vasco da Gama and Atlético de Lourenço Marques, apparently to "mollify the educated and assimilated local elites."[55] In other cases, the name of the particular colonial club revealed everything. As António Brassard explained, in Mozambique, "the Clube Primeiro de Maio was multiracial; as you know, May 1 is Workers' Day. Therefore, that team integrated people of all races. In that time, it was one of the teams where there were whites, Chinese, blacks, and, thus, it was racially diversified."[56] Spurred on by these and other integrative measures, by the end of the 1950s, all of the African associations had been folded wholesale into the topflight leagues, effectively desegregating the sport. In turn, the elite clubs began scouting Africans from local leagues scattered throughout the colonies, newly seeking talent from across the racial spectrum.[57]

Adaptation: New Styles and Approaches to the Game

In order to fashion more disciplined players out of these allegedly "unrefined" African and mestiço recruits, the Portuguese coaches of colonial clubs demanded that these footballers become more tactical, more calculated, and, thus, attendantly less spontaneous and creative on the pitch. They also insisted upon a more professional approach to the game, stressing practice, fitness, planning, and preparatory routines, even as players struggled to find time to train owing to their away-from-the-pitch occupational responsibilities. Many of the coaches had themselves played in Portugal, subsequently importing the latest approaches to the sport to the colonies, but they also borrowed and incorporated new trends that were circulating in an increasingly interconnected global soccer firmament. Exposure to progressive tactics, coupled with a more professional approach to the game, served well those African players who made it to the metropole, as the physical and mental demands in that setting were even more acute.

In his extensive work on the development of football in South Africa, Alegi has reconstructed the ways that the dynamics between black players and white coaches stunted rather than facilitated the athletes' development, reflective of the racial tension and distrust that permeated that society. In one instance, he quoted a discontented player who declared that "apart from ordinary physical training routines they [white coaches] don't seem to teach us much theory. I feel they are holding back on us," with Alegi reporting that "due to the difficulties in dealing with white coaches, black professionals said they 'usually learned more from football through reading overseas magazines.'"[58] Similarly, Laura Fair indicates that African players in Zanzibar harbored dissatisfaction toward their European coaches: "Many of the men who played for department teams [i.e., police and Department of Public Works] resented the fact that they were 'required' to play for a team managed by a European."[59] However, despite the institutionalized racism in the Lusophone African contexts, none of my informants begrudged their coaches at a personal level. Conversely, they valued the Portuguese managers' "knowledge of the game," their "helpful advice and instruction," and, in general, the professional approach to the game that they espoused.[60] Moreover, the former players often credited their managers in the colonies with playing key roles in their eventual success, suggesting a qualitatively different relationship between African players and European coaches in these contexts.

Training and Conditioning

Fundamental to the new footballing regime was an emphasis on training and conditioning. This novel physical dimension to the game challenged

African players, as it had been completely absent from their previous interaction with the sport. For them, soccer was traditionally something meant to be played, not practiced or prepared for via a formal training regimen. As Fernando Gomes, a Portuguese-born footballer who also played in colonial Angola, contended regarding his observations of Africans' engagement with the sport in the colony: "Things were really different in Angola. Some players only practiced when they wanted. The Africans didn't look at the sport in a serious way. They approached it with a lack of professionalism. So, it was very difficult [for them] to compete against a team that was extremely professional. . . . It was evident that there was a substantial difference in the level of play between the Portuguese league and the league in Angola."[61] Over time, however, the creeping professionalization of the game in the colonies would vanquish the customary, more casual approach to soccer. The new importance on substance over style (i.e., winning at all cost) was rapidly changing the very nature of the sport.

Even though rigorous and regimented training and instruction constituted a new imperative at this level, the footballers weren't always adequately prepared. And, in fact, some of their managers may not have been either. Indeed, just as in contemporary sporting contexts, not all ex-players make great coaches; the same held true in the colonies, and for many of the same reasons. According to António Brassard, who played for Primeiro de Maio at the junior level from 1960 to 1962 and for the senior team at the Mozambican club during the ensuing two years before moving on to the metropole in 1964 to play for Académica:

> At the junior level I had a Mozambican coach. At the senior level, I was coached by someone who had played in Portugal. He went to Mozambique to live and to work. The training was completely different in Mozambique [than it was at Académica]. We used to train only two times a week because we were really not professionals. We were amateurs; people had jobs. We trained after work, around 5:00 p.m. Our coaches were not prepared as coaches; they were ex-players, but did not have training as soccer coaches. They went to Mozambique to work and took the opportunity to coach football teams, but they were not well prepared.[62]

If some of Brassard's managers were ill-prepared, at least they had previously played the game at the highest levels. Nuro Americano, who grew up on Pemba, off the northeastern Mozambican coast, far from the soccer locus of Lourenço Marques, cited an even more profound problematic: "We had local coaches. Well, one could say they were coaches, but they were, in fact, Portuguese military officers. They were coming to serve in the military, but they liked the sport and, thus, became involved."[63] Americano did confess, however, that perhaps somewhat predictably, these military types stressed physical conditioning, explaining, "I had to double my efforts. I used to train in the mornings and evenings. In the morning, I was training by playing football and in the evening, basketball."[64]

Just as Americano was compelled to enhance his conditioning, so, too, were most African players who joined the topflight colonial clubs. Even in the second division of the AFLM, incoming players faced a challenging physical regimen. Augusto Matine's experience upon joining Clube Central in 1963 illustrates well the new training environment into which these players entered:

> When we [the new cohort of players] arrived at Central, it was a small club but with good leaders. They were white leaders, the owners of the club. . . . When the training began, the coach was Sr. Rebelo, a Portuguese . . . and the physical part we did not like. It was very intense. All we wanted was the ball so that we could demonstrate our abilities. The technical part would come later, but in those early days he was focused on the physical component [of the game]. . . . We used to train three days a week: on Mondays, Wednesdays, and Fridays. Once we started training regularly, he intensified the physical work.[65]

New Approaches: Tactics

Once players were exposed to heightened levels of conditioning and had committed themselves to the training regimen, the coaches deemed them ready for tactical indoctrination. In fact, one of the starkest differences between bairro and downtown football was the emphasis on tactics in the latter. Europeans had been experimenting for decades with a variety of tactics, often manifested in different formations, though rarely did they ever settle on a particular approach or configuration for very long.[66] Regardless of the scheme or strategy du jour, most of these methods were new to the African players, who had previously enjoyed a kind of unconstrained approach to the game, with little attention played to positional or tactical discipline. In general, players reluctantly engaged with the new practices, though they did comprehend that success at this level required a mastery of them. Indeed, those footballers who made it to the metropole often reflected on their learning experiences in the colonies as being instrumental to their success. Testimony from Hilário exemplifies the appreciation that players had for this type of instruction: "On almost all of the teams the coaches were Portuguese. . . . We had a good 'school' system for soccer. When I left Mozambique at the age of nineteen, I was already able to play for Sporting and the [Portuguese] national team. . . . In the colonial time, the soccer formation was better; the Portuguese coaches maximized our skills. When we got to Portugal, we could play for Porto, Benfica, Sporting."[67] Similarly, Yaúca, commenting on his experiences in colonial Angola while playing for Desportivo de Benguela and Sport Clube da Catumbela, remarked, "The coach is the theory; the player is the practicality. There are things that no one ever taught me, nor would I be able to teach. There are others that I would never have known if I didn't have a competent coach."[68]

Indicative of the emphasis on tactics in the colonies was the widespread implementation of the "WM" system, which George Chapman had developed as manager of the London-based Arsenal football club in the mid-1920s. In general, this formation and the associated movements were intended to limit an opponent's attacking options rather than to generate more scoring opportunities for the adherent, and, thus, the system was inherently defensive.[69] Due to its effectiveness, it quickly spread to Portugal; and, from the metropole, it inevitably flowed to the colonies. In Mozambique, the "WM" arrived in the person of Severiano Correia, a longtime club manager and head of the Portuguese national team in 1947. Correia's passage to the colonies in 1949 came at the invitation of Trindade Pinto, the president of Clube Ferroviário, who was himself "motivated by the importance of tactics."[70] As Domingos has contended, "Correia was the first manager who possessed the sufficient time and liberty necessary to apply the 'WM' system in the AFLM. And, in 1951, the club newspaper considered him responsible for 'a better adjustment of stones' to the 'WM' system, the placement of some players in their assigned places."[71]

It was precisely these "assigned places" and the dogmatic movement of players, as if they were chess pieces, that most perturbed the fans of the neighborhood game. Supporters drew distinctions between the aesthetically appealing fluidity and spontaneity of the suburban game and the stifling rigidity and inflexibility of the downtown game. This stylistic divergence is roughly analogous to the contemporary differences that exist between unscripted "street" or "playground" basketball and the hyper-tactical National Basketball Association (NBA) version of the sport. The loudest voice among these critics in the colonies was Craveirinha, who lamented these footballing developments as strongly as he had previously lauded the panache of the neighborhood game. In particular, he maligned the "tactical mentality" that had taken hold. In a 1959 piece, the poet/sports columnist declared, "Tactics destroy the characteristics of the local game and the 'elite abilities' of the African player. . . . The local style is overcome by tactics and more tactics . . . and kill much of the good things in our player."[72] He went on to specifically blame the Portuguese managers in Lourenço Marques, as well as "some metropolitan sporting newspapers [which are] passed from hand to hand, and have created in the suburban footballer a tactical mentality." Craveirinha was not alone in his criticism. According to Saide Mogne, when the tactical system became too rigid, "the WM ceased to have football in it. There was no football in the WM . . . no football as we knew it. . . . Football became a different game, filled with similar rules to those who defined 'labor time': the observance of the division of labor; the specialization of roles; and acceptance of a hierarchy headed by the manager."[73] Irrespective of local observers' lamentations, the trends were irreversible; spectators could censure the new order, but their vocalizations were steadily drowned out in successive waves of tactical innovation and footballing success.

Sporting Pinnacles in the Colonies: Local Selecções

Participation in the top colonial leagues afforded select African and mestiço players access to the most competitive squads on the continent: the colonial "all-star teams," or *selecções*.[74] As outlined in the previous chapter, these local squads typically lined up against touring metropolitan clubs. But participation on the elite teams also generated valuable, if still somewhat rare, opportunities for African players to travel internationally.[75] For example, a 1960 trip to Mauritius in the Indian Ocean constituted Eusébio's first trip abroad, which he undertook at seventeen years old. Eusébio prosaically explained this nonetheless significant experience as follows: "It was with the Mozambique national team, the first time I went there. I don't remember the final score, but I think I scored three goals and we won by four. . . . I am talking about the Mozambique national team and the Mauritian national team. The only reason I went to the Mauritius Islands was because of the Mozambique national team. . . . We got there, played, and then went out with the older players. We would go to different places and bars and the next day we would come back to Mozambique."[76] In Guiné, the regional success of the colony's selecção, a squad composed of white settlers, Guineans, and Cape Verdeans, in tournaments throughout West Africa in part prompted the construction of a new stadium in the capital, Bissau, inaugurated in 1948. And the squads themselves were considered expressions of "Lusitanian valor" and "Portuguese unity" by colonial officials.[77]

Much more commonly, these all-star squads played much closer to home. Domestically, players either participated on the national selecção or, more frequently, for a particular city's selecção, pitted against other local all-star teams or those deriving from municipalities elsewhere within the empire. Most players who were selected for these squads were affiliated with clubs in the top colonial leagues, but exceptional talent residing at lower levels was occasionally spotted and rewarded with a spot on the teams. Augusto Matine's case following the 1965–1966 campaign, in which his club earned promotion from the second to the first division, constitutes such an example. According to Matine: "It was a very competitive championship and there is no doubt that in that year Central was the best team in the second division; as such, I was selected for the Lourenço Marques Selecção. I believe that at that time it was a surprise for many people because I was playing for a second division team and I was selected for the Lourenço Marques team. The match against the Inhambane Selecção was my first game in the squad and I scored two goals . . . and Baltazar, who was regarded as the [football] idol of Mozambique, also scored two goals. . . . We won that match 4–2."[78] Regardless of whether these all-star squads squared off against domestic or international competition, they served as ideal places for African footballers to showcase their skills for the growing number of metropolitan clubs interested in signing talented players, irrespective of race.

Social Exposure and Integration

In addition to honing their soccer skills, African footballers also engaged in a number of social processes on their desegregated colonial clubs; for those players who would eventually reach the metropole, such endeavors helped them immensely following their relocation. Primary among the social activities was players' increasing interaction in genuine, meaningful ways with teammates of different races, religions, and provenances on these fully integrated colonial clubs. This camaraderie and mutual support did have limits, which generally mirrored the strict socioracial divides that Portuguese colonialism imposed and relentlessly reinforced. Indeed, Augusto Matine reminds us that even if interpersonal relations among players were generally excellent on the pitch and in the training rooms, white settlers in the colonies were often heavily invested in racial segregation, especially after the wars for independence began in the 1960s. According to the former Benfica player, "When the game was over, each one knew what his place was. It never crossed our minds to go out and dine in a restaurant with a white colleague or vice-versa. We knew precisely the unwritten rules! It's strange how in Portugal I didn't feel this when I arrived in 1966."[79] Yet cracks in these segregative racialist structures did exist, and teammates regularly transcended broader societal boundaries to forge friendships, or at least to engage in various forms of fellowship. As Jacinto Veloso, a Mozambican revolutionary of Portuguese descent who had successful trials with Benfica during his university years, remarked about football in Lourenço Marques during the colonial era, "Sociability on the sports field was an interesting feature of the colonial period. . . . It should be recalled that colonial society was clearly discriminatory and racist, but sport was where humiliation and racism were least felt. What counted most was sporting skill."[80]

In addition to cultivating friendships across racial divides with team-mates, players also established supportive relationships with Portuguese coaches, who functioned more as mentors, rather than simply as disciplinarians, for these emerging talents. As such, participation at this level often commenced a process of cultural exposure, comprehension, integration, and, for some players, assimilation. Indeed, Paola Rolletta has assertively claimed that in Mozambique, "sport contributed to the advance of the struggle against racism in the colonial period and was, in fact, the only field where the pretense of integration actually worked."[81]

Soccer players deriving from the suburbs generally transitioned well into the new footballing settings, interacting with their new teammates and coaches. For mestiço players with a Portuguese father present, this integrative process had naturally begun even earlier and was inherently deeper. Testimony from Mário Coluna, a mestiço footballer who played for Desportivo de Lourenço Marques in the early 1950s, highlights how the environment in which he was raised aided in his transition into the club: "I adapted easily because here [Mozambique], this was Portuguese land. My father was white. At Desportivo, there were white players as well: Fernando Lage, João Ribeiro, and Oliveira Dias."[82]

Yet even those players who were neither mestiço nor raised in white-headed households typically transitioned reasonably smoothly into the elite colonial squads. In practice, the first footballers to make the move downtown served as pioneers, their sporting success and model behavior, in turn, paving the way for subsequent players. Among the initial recruits to make this transition, Matateu is rightly identified as a trailblazing figure. According to his younger brother, Vicente Lucas, "Previously, blacks couldn't play on the same teams as whites and, as such, he [Matateu] joined a club where only Africans played. He began to stand out because he was scoring so many goals and so he went to play for Primeiro de Maio. . . . From there, things began to change and after Matateu, other blacks enrolled in the club, beginning the process of undoing the 'apartheid' that existed in football."[83]

Other footballers followed, traversing the paths downtown that Matateu and other players had forged. The sentiments expressed by Augusto Matine, who joined Clube Central in the 1960s, reflected this new multi-racial footballing landscape: "Central was a club with six whites and five mestiços; the rest were black. No racism was experienced, on the pitch or in the locker rooms."[84] Testimony from Fernando Gomes, a Portuguese player who played for Benfica de Luanda and a club associated with the Portuguese Air Force in the late 1960s during his roughly one and a half years in Angola, suggests that at least some white players harbored similar sentiments to Matine's. Responding to my question about relations with Africans in the squad, Gomes remarked:

> They were excellent; there was no racism or anything like that. There were only two white players: myself and another forward. We were the only white foreigners in the team. There were some other white boys who went there to play, but they couldn't make it. The connection among the players was great. . . . We had a guy in our team who eventually became the president of the Angolan Football Federation, Justino Fernandes, and he used to sell Cuca [an Angolan beer] in the sex establishments of Luanda. We used to buy some beers from him and drink with him. We used to go to a place near Luanda to buy lobsters, very cheaply, and beers and drink together. We didn't have to integrate or assimilate, because there was no difference, only the color of our skin. The relationship among us was great and I loved living there.[85]

It is difficult to reconcile testimony of this nature, which suggests a benignity or inertness regarding sporting endeavors and interactions in colonial Africa, with scholarly analyses of the politicization of organized sports and the roles they allegedly played in the demise of European imperialism on the continent. For example, regarding the sporting atmosphere in colonial settings, Allen Guttmann has declared that "beneath the cooperative multicultural surface lay the political differences of which everyone was keenly aware." And, quoting Ben Larbi Mohammed and Borhane Errais, he continues, "Every Tunisian sports victory against the European sports organizations contributed to the destruction of the myth of colonial power."[86] Conversely, I would contend that colonial power was, in practice, quite real and, thus, anything but "mythical," and that the African and mestiço footballers on racially mixed squads in colonial Lusophone Africa were much more focused on playing well and advancing their careers than on "the destruction of colonial power." In these players' lives, persistent and pervasive rac(ial)ism constituted the greater immediate challenges.

Although footballers from across the racial spectrum typically accepted one another in their newly integrated clubs, African and mestiço players could still face hostility in their home neighborhoods, to which they returned after each game and practice. For example, according to Hilário, when, in 1953, he became the first nonwhite player on Sporting de Lourenço Marques, his friends back in Mafalala accused him of "going to play for the jackals" and subsequently stopped speaking to him.[87] This form of ostracism was particularly difficult for African footballers, as their social identities remained rooted in their neighborhoods, where their friends and families continued to reside. Yet, even in Hilário's example, he managed to weather this social shunning: for a time, he continued to play for his local team on Saturdays, and on Sundays for Sporting de Lourenço Marques (his downtown club), thereby demonstrating a resolve that would serve him well as he continued to ascend the footballing ranks.

Employment: El Dorado within Their Reach

It was with the downtown clubs in the colonies that African players were first able to associate soccer with meaningful remuneration. This link was not, however, predicated upon drawing footballing salaries that constituted or even approximated a living wage. Rather, clubs typically arranged for jobs at either a public or a private entity with which they were affiliated, or facilitated employment elsewhere. Thus, even if only indirectly, soccer had finally become a viable livelihood option for those players talented enough to secure a spot on one of the clubs in the top colonial leagues. Indeed, although remunerative rewards for footballing acumen were still reasonably modest, they were no longer measured in cans of cashew nuts. Moreover, it was in these new places of employment, away from the pitch, that African players daily interacted with Portuguese coworkers, learning sociocultural values and behaviors that would serve them well in the metropole. Similarly, many of the players/employees observed and internalized labor strategies that they would subsequently redeploy in innovative and creative ways upon eventually reaching Portugal.

Some colonial teams were sponsored by large employers and could therefore easily "absorb" players into their broader commercial organizations, while other clubs had to look farther afield to arrange employment for soccer recruits. The most significant example of the former was Ferroviário, the state railroad agency, which fielded soccer and other sports teams beginning in 1915 in Angola, and nine years later in Mozambique, and even featured smaller branches/clubs in the provinces of these colonies (see fig. 2.1). Eusébio, whose father played for Ferroviário de Lourenço Marques, characterized the Mozambican version of this outfit as follows: "Ferroviário was the team of the railway company and was not linked to clubs in Portugal, although the Portuguese scouts watched them play. The company signed players—like my late father—and then arranged jobs on the railways for them, and paid them for their jobs while they played so that they could have a better life."[88] Some African athletes even played multiple sports for this sporting/transportation entity. For example, Costa Pereira, whose father also worked and played for Ferroviário, enjoyed stints at both Ferroviário de Nampula (a large city in northern Mozambique) and the main squad in Lourenço Marques, where he also played basketball. In fact, Pereira, who would go on to play for both Benfica and the Portuguese national team, left a main rival, Sporting de Lourenço Marques, to join Ferroviário in part because of the excellent employment opportunity on offer at the latter.[89] Ferroviário of Angola similarly served as a stepping-stone for players who would eventually go on to play in the metropole. For example, Carlos Duarte, prior to leaving the colony to join the metropolitan outfit FC Porto in 1952, moved from Atlético Clube de Nova Lisboa to Grupo Desportivo Ferroviário.

Not all clubs doubled as commercial employers, however. In these scenarios, employment for players had to be arranged elsewhere. This was the case for Matateu, one of the first suburban players to transfer downtown. Until he was twenty years old, he played for João Albasini, but was lured to Primeiro de Maio with the offer of a civil construction job, as his family desperately needed the money it would provide. From Primeiro de Maio, he was enticed to join Manjacaze, owing to an offer

Figure 2.1. Clube Ferroviário de Lourenço Marques headquarters, 2012.

of 1,000 escudos per month to work in a job stamping black Africans' passes. And it was at this club that he eventually caught the eye of the Lisbon-based squad Belenenses, which tendered a contract to the rising star.[90] Hilário's case is similarly illustrative of the important link between football and formal employment. According to testimony from the former Sporting Lisboa player regarding the employment landscape in the Mozambican capital:

There were no professionals, no one earned money by playing at that point. What was provided was a job. I went to Sporting de Lourenço Marques because they arranged a job for me at the Companhia das Águas [Public Water Company]. The director was Dr. Nunes Pantaleão, who was a Sportinguista [Sporting supporter]. They had money available for all those who wanted to work at the Companhia das Águas and play for Sporting. . . . I was playing for Atlético de Lourenço Marques, in the juniors. A man by the name of Camilo Antunes, a scout for Sporting . . . came to speak with me in order to inquire if I wanted to go to Sporting. I told him: "I'll go, but Sporting has to give me a job." Antunes agreed. . . . I went to the Companhia das Águas to work as a plumber, but, in Mafalala, my friends wouldn't forgive me, because Sporting was the club that didn't accept anyone of color . . . and I said: "But I need to live. . . . I need to eat, I need to support my mother, my brothers, because I don't have money, I am not rich. I signed a contract because they arranged a job for me." I continued to work in the Companhia das Águas until I left to play in Portugal.[91]

The association between soccer and formal, nonfootball employment was not limited to the Lusophone colonies. Similar arrangements also existed in the Francophone African colonies, and, as Alegi has indicated regarding colonial Nigeria, then a British territory, "employers aggressively recruited talented African players by offering them relatively secure and good-paying jobs."[92] Similarly, in her work on soccer in colonial Zanzibar, Laura Fair explains that "the European men who controlled the department teams (Police and DPW) of course wanted their team to be the best, and to this end many of the best footballers were 'encouraged' to join the department teams . . . where men were often given jobs because of their skill as footballers."[93] In both cases, though, racial animosity simmered just beneath the surface. Indeed, Alegi has identified the paradoxical practice of recruiting and offering solid jobs to African players in the colonies "while still treating them like second-class citizens."[94]

Even as black and mestiço players remained socially marginalized in colonial Lusophone Africa, formal employment opportunities did facilitate upward mobility, or at least stability, for the footballers and their families. Yet some observers of colonial football, including a series of *O Brado Africano* columnists, decried any type of income derived from the sport, arguing that it threatened the game's integrity. For example, a piece that appeared in 1941, penned in response to the news that an African player, Laquino, would be earning between 40 and 50 escudos per match, grumbled: "What has African football come to, when you play for money and not for the love of the sport?"[95]

These types of protestations notwithstanding, African footballers enthusiastically sought opportunities that enabled them both to play their beloved sport and, attendantly, to earn a living. To this end, from the 1950s onward, an increasing number of suburban players began to move to the downtown clubs, lured by the elevated level of play, but even more importantly, by the prospect of formal employment. Predictably, individuals such as Craveirinha rued the steadily receding "unadulterated" days of neighborhood football. In a piece from 1964, he commented on the economic and sporting repercussions of the deracialization of the leagues and consequent developments with a mix of lamentation, resignation, and candor:

> With the doors of Lourenço Marques' big teams wide open, the consequence was that the suburban fans became increasingly interested in the football movement of the so-called downtown clubs. There was a strong reason for such a change. Individuals from the most humble social milieus had become famous and improved their living conditions. The downtown clubs began to attract those who wanted to achieve some glory and enjoy better bread, who . . . on account of close affinities and other factors, would see their frustrated rosy dreams finally come true. This was an El Dorado within their reach, which could not be wasted. And this was not all. The downtown clubs were also the easier launch pad for a flight to Lisbon, Porto, or some other metropolitan city. And this was a tempting prize. . . . And the [suburban] clubs . . . presently have serious difficulties in presenting eleven players on the field, properly equipped and on time. Is this a passing crisis? Unfortunately not.[96]

Off-the-pitch remuneration was undoubtedly what attracted most players to these clubs, as financial rewards related to their on-the-pitch exploits remained nominal, though they did inch upward over time. Players' salaries remained small, couldn't be formally paid until Lisbon officially permitted the professionalization of the sport in 1960, and, even then, were often distributed irregularly. For example, Eusébio's salary at Sporting de Lourenço Marques was 500 escudos, but he allegedly was paid only "from time to time." And even if this amount had been reliably distributed, it remained incommensurate with his spectacular Sunday afternoon footballing performances.[97] Indeed, for virtually every player, even at the highest tiers of colonial soccerdom, the financial compensation remained minimal. Yet apparently even seemingly negligible awards could, at times, inspire. At Clube Central, for example, Augusto Matine indicated that "at the end of training, they used to give us one Coca-Cola, one sandwich, and some small change for transport. . . . We started to play naturally and to be dedicated to the club and the results followed; our performance kept improving."[98] Similarly, Baltazar, who played for Ferroviário in Lourenço Marques, indicated that nonmonetary compensation at that club, though equally modest, was also motivational: "We did not have wages at Ferroviário, but they did offer us some incentives. Initially, it was chocolate and a big cheese sandwich. Later on, they gave us a premium that was enough to buy dinner."[99]

From kicking around balled-up rags in narrow streets or on indeterminate fields to securing solid employment via their footballing skills, Africans' engagement with soccer in Portugal's colonial empire changed dramatically over time. Indigenous players appropriated the game, cultivating their own styles and artistry before eventually curbing some of their creative tendencies to conform with the more tactical approach to the sport that had taken hold. Irrespective, though, of how zealously African players embraced current footballing trends and strategies, over time, the skills and promise that many of these practitioners were displaying on pitches throughout colonial Lusophone Africa were too considerable for the talent-hungry metropolitan clubs to continue to forgo.

In the ensuing chapter, I follow the players as they engaged in the scouting and signing processes that formally linked them with metropolitan clubs, examine their experiences during the long journeys to Portugal, and consider the aftermaths of their arrival. Irrespective of the various levels of fanfare that accompanied particular players upon reaching the metropole, their new clubs insulated the recruits from many of the potentially disorienting and distracting aspects of metropolitan life until they were better adjusted. Despite the custodial efforts, some African footballers struggled to adapt to their new environments, thereby impeding their progress, though most of the migrant athletes transitioned reasonably smoothly. In either scenario, the players had formally commenced the overseas chapters of their personal and professional lives, ultimately generating experiential books of varying lengths.

3

Following the Ball, Realizing a Goal

From the Colonies to the Metropole

At that time [1958], I used to play at Sporting Lourenço Marques, which was affiliated with Sporting de Portugal. With all the hardship we had, when the opportunity to play in Portugal came we would have even come for free, because we knew our lives would get better. The clubs would negotiate amongst themselves because they would also receive money, and since I played for a [Mozambican] club that was affiliated with Sporting [de Portugal], they took care of everything.

—Hilário, 2010

My history is curious. . . . It was like a movie. My father had a fishery right on the beach. We had to go there, some 400 kilometers from Beira; it was far. Benfica arranged for me to fly home. I remember that I boarded a two-seated plane. It was only me and the pilot. We flew and landed in front of my father's house . . . it was out of a film. That made a huge impact at that time. We landed, and the plane left. I went to see my father to tell him that Benfica wanted me to play in Portugal. My father refused, because for him the most important thing was school. . . . I told him: "Father, I don't know whether you will allow this dream to materialize, but as your son I also don't know what will happen in the future." He eventually reached a point where he agreed. . . . I promised him that I would continue with my studies in Portugal. He said "Okay, you can go under these conditions." . . . After my father's "yes," there were negotiations between the Benfica of Beira and the Benfica of Portugal.

—Shéu Han, reflecting on the process in 1970
of signing with Benfica, 2014

Just as African players began reaching the pinnacles of colonial soccer-dom, opportunities to continue pursuing their athletic dreams on the biggest footballing stages were simultaneously materializing. With international sporting and political pressures progressively squeezing the regime in Lisbon, and domestic club teams eager to enlist the prodigious footballing talent that the colonies were generating, confining skilled African players to their home continent was increasingly untenable. Or at least imprudent. Following the regime's blessing in the late 1940s to permit the relocation of the footballers to Portugal, the next step was to locate players who would make the most significant impacts. In many cases, the athletes were readily identifiable—stars on their colonial club teams who already enjoyed large followings and well-deserved reputations as superb footballers. Meanwhile, other players were more appealing due to their potential, rather than demonstrated, performances. Before the establishment of formal scouting networks, these footballing "diamonds in the rough" were often identified by Portuguese settlers, who then relayed their "finds" to a series of friends and acquaintances who were in positions to pass along these tips to formal representatives of the various metropolitan clubs. Once the talent was confirmed, club officials would arrive at players' typically humble homes with contract offers that, even if reasonably modest, were irresistible to most footballers and their parents.

Contracts in hand, the African prospects next commenced the long journeys that would take them from the colonial capitals to the heart of the empire. Players traveled mostly by boat, which afforded them opportunities to intermingle with fellow soccer recruits, but also with a variety of Portuguese voyagers, traveling to the metropole from various imperial stations. Upon arrival, players officially opened the overseas chapters of their lives, thousands of miles removed from their friends and family members. African recruits whose soccer reputations preceded them often arrived to great media fanfare before being whisked away to their respective club-arranged accommodations. Although their new employers invariably assisted them throughout the initial adjustment period, players adapted to their new environs with varying degrees of success. Many of the new arrivals adjusted well, embracing their new sporting and living conditions, while others struggled under the weight of the distance from their friends and family. Throughout, provenance remained an important aspect of personal identity, with African footballers hailing from the same colonies enjoying a natural affinity predicated on shared experiences and points of reference.

This chapter examines migrant players' transnational experiences as they transitioned from their respective colonial stops to the metropole. Upon signing contracts with their new clubs, soccer formally transitioned from an instrument through which they could secure remunerative work to a viable livelihood in and of itself. Yet the geographic relocation that this economically beneficial endeavor required took its toll on many of the new arrivals, retarding their football progression or, for some, even derailing their careers. For many African players, though, only the limitations of their skill sets hindered their advance, while for the most talented footballers, there continued to be very few, if any, circumscriptions on their sporting ascension. From the modest pitches of Africa, these players had truly arrived.

Highly Motivated: The Portuguese Regime and the Metropolitan Football Clubs

Just as the regime in Lisbon identified minimal or no value in permitting African players to relocate to the metropole prior to the 1940s, neither did the metropolitan clubs that would eventually employ these talents exhibit any serious interest. Only as governmental and footballing sentiments changed over time would the door truly open for African soccer prospects. External political pressures motivated the regime to make the necessary policy adjustments—initially by bestowing *assimilado* (assimilated) status on any African player signing for a metropolitan club—to facilitate these soccer inflows. Indeed, both international political allies (e.g., the United States) and enemies (e.g., the USSR) alike exhorted Lisbon to expand opportunities for its colonized subjects of empire. Transforming this political pressure into opportunity, the Estado Novo recognized the substantiative value of the African players as the state actively promoted the myth of Lusotropicalism and, like the French government had done previously, attempted to "demonstrate the success of its 'civilizing mission' and the allegedly positive nature of colonial rule" via the relocation of footballers to Europe.[1]

The Portuguese state was also motivated by recurring on-the-pitch humiliations; the disgrace associated with bad losses to other European nations over an extended period of time proved to be a powerful stimulus for the prideful dictatorship. And, as these African players began arriving and succeeding, the regime's motivations shifted from reactionary to calculated, with Lisbon exploiting for political ends the footballers' ongoing presence in the metropole.

Meanwhile, Portuguese soccer clubs similarly wanted to improve their performance in international competitions, and as inexpensively as possible. Team officials were increasingly aware of the pools of talent that had been accumulating in the empire. In eyeing these skilled practitioners, the Portuguese clubs were belatedly emulating their French counterparts. Competitive matches and even occasional defeats at the hands of squads from the colonies during summer tours to Africa highlighted the local talent available, while also prompting the, at times, humbled metropolitan clubs to attempt to secure it for their own benefit. In short, a perfect combination of sporting and political impetuses prompted well-placed governmental and sporting power brokers in Lisbon in the late 1940s to declare the season of "fishing" for talented African players officially—and permanently—open.

Pride and Pressure: Governmental Motivations

As soccer's popularity in Europe steadily escalated following the conclusion of World War II, the sport became increasingly important as a means for the continent's various governments to generate national enthusiasm, pride, and, indirectly, political support. Yet, at least initially, Salazar, unlike other authoritarian rulers around the continent, was not prepared to bankroll the national team.[2] And it showed. Beginning play in 1921, seven years would pass before the Portuguese national squad, or *selecção*, was able to earn even a draw. The 1930s and '40s brought little salvation, including a 9–0 thumping by neighboring Spain, which sowed national humiliation, as did a 10–0 loss to England in 1947. Regardless, financial support for the squad remained scarce, as were positive results on the pitch. The late 1940s and early 1950s witnessed further losses for the selecção, with the national team winning only three times in twenty matches between May 1949 and May 1955.[3] Particularly embarrassing were hidings delivered by the Spanish and the Austrians, 5–1 and 9–1, respectively, during the first rounds of qualifying for the 1950 and 1954 World Cups. Both defeats were considered to be national "disgraces" and "humiliations" by the media and precipitated "enormous sarcasm."[4]

Grumblings in the 1940s over these mounting, sometimes spectacular, losses eventually precipitated a formal response. Pressed by the metropolitan clubs that newly sought to sign African talents, the state was compelled to act. In 1949, after much deliberation, lobbying, and some vacillation, the Portuguese regime formally declared, as spelled out in a letter from the Direcção Geral to the Portuguese Football Federation, that "players who want to transfer from clubs in the Overseas Provinces to clubs in the metropole . . . can be freely signed."[5] But even following this edict, caution and moderation reigned. Mindful of the racialist tenets that the regime propagated to justify the ongoing colonial project, and not yet feeling the full pressure that the international community would eventually bring to bear upon Lisbon, the door to the metropole was opened, but only slightly. Slipping through initially, in 1949, were two players from Mozambique who would go on to enjoy considerable success in the metropole: Júlio Cernadas Pereira, or "Juca," the son of Portuguese settlers; and the *mestiço* (mulatto) player Mário Wilson. Although a few footballers from Africa had made this journey previously, the relocation of Juca and Wilson marked the dawn of a new era in which footballers would increasingly flow from the Portuguese colonies to the metropole.[6] Or, as Domingos has characterized this footballing development: "An imperial job market was finally opened between Mozambique and the metropole."[7]

Going forward, shifts in the Portuguese regime's motivations reflected and were arguably precipitated by changes in the domestic and international economic and political landscapes. Elsewhere, Alegi has considered how the French government creatively facilitated the migration of African players to the metropole to reinforce notions of a "greater France," while Darby—neocolonial preoccupations notwithstanding—has suggested that France's practice of "expropriating African footballers" constituted an "extension of the country's policy of *Gallicalisation* or the assimilation of the local population into the citizenship of the motherland."[8] Similarly, Lisbon undoubtedly wanted to stress the indissolubility of the constituent pieces of a "greater Portugal." Yet the regime also sought to maintain strong connections with the Portuguese diaspora, members of whom had migrated in large numbers to various nations in western and central Europe owing to the lack of domestic economic opportunities. As international criticism of Portugal's empire mounted, Lisbon adopted a siege mentality, which, in turn, rendered the migrant African footballers increasingly important as the regime sought support—and confidence—from all corners of its multicontinental diaspora. As Lanfranchi and Taylor have incisively written regarding the central role that Eusébio played in these unifying impulses and efforts:

> In the context of 1960s Portugal, a closed society with little contact with the rest of Europe, Eusébio became the hope for a better future. The emigration of Portuguese workers to other European countries (particularly France) was rapidly on the increase. A living example of social mobility, success and integration in a Salazarist Portugal where opportunities were so limited that 100,000 workers left the country annually, Eusébio's popularity among Portuguese workers abroad was phenomenal. He personified a proud and confident Portugal, and his popularity in the country has not been matched since.[9]

Untapped Talent: Eager Clubs

Although a host of economic and sporting pressures and incentives compelled Lisbon to sanction the relocation of African footballers, the singular motivation for the metropolitan clubs was to improve their fortunes against domestic and international competition. By the 1940s, the desire to enhance their squads with the best players available—irrespective of race or provenance—trumped long-standing traditions of utilizing only players from Portugal and the "adjacent islands" of Madeira and the Azores. Although Benfica, the most stringent observer of these nativist policies, didn't immediately move to sign African footballers, it arguably benefited the most once it did internationalize its roster. By the mid- to late 1950s, all of the major metropolitan clubs, following Sporting Clube de Portugal's lead, were actively "holding their heads up" searching for new talent, while "any player who appeared in Africa with any ability was now 'getting fished.'"[10] The race for African soccer talent was now well and truly on.

Until the 1940s, very few foreign players competed for clubs in Portugal's domestic leagues. Although South American and Western and Eastern European players had trickled into the Iberian nation prior to the arrival of their African counterparts, the unhurried, and consequently late, professionalization of the sport in Portugal limited the country's appeal to prospective migrant footballers. Moreover, although foreign recruits would have been unaware, they each had to be approved by Portugal's secret police force, the PIDE, before being cleared to relocate to Portugal. But with a growing soccer fan base and the attendant pressure to succeed in both domestic and continental competitions, Portuguese clubs began to eye the colonies as a talent reservoir, to which they enjoyed exclusive access.

Sporting Clube de Portugal was the earliest and most aggressive in this respect. From at least as early as 1947, the team began submitting formal letters to various entities in the Portuguese regime inquiring about the possibility of utilizing players from the colonies. Presumably, these missives grew out of conversations among club officials and perhaps from informal discussions with government officials as well. In one particularly blunt correspondence from 1947, Sporting representatives argued that players in the colonies were, in effect, "prisoners of their clubs," if the metropolitan statutes requiring that they "sit out a year from the date of their last game played if they are unable to present a 'carta de desobrigação' [a document issued by a club sanctioning a player's release]" are maintained.[11] To highlight the applied inconsistency of this policy, Sporting officials cited the cases of a number of players, including Eliseu Cavaleiro and João Nascimento Dóres, who left the club without permission and were subsequently able to play in Angola (for Sporting Club de Luanda) without ever receiving a "carta." Appealing to government officials regarding the primacy of the metropole in a letter from 1949, Sporting's secretary general wrote:

> It seems then that athletes from the colonies ought to be able to enroll as players for this Club without any carta de desobrigação, as this requirement pertains to a domestic law that doesn't apply to our colonies. On the contrary, it would be absurd to require a carta de desobrigação to come to play in the Metropole; and in the Colonies, for such document to be available. Otherwise, there would be a subordination of the Metropole to the Portuguese Colonies and an inequality clearly contrary to the principles established, not only by not featuring metropolitan superiority or subordination of those parts of the Territory that ought not to be privileged, which in these present cases would be unjust.[12]

It seems that the arguments posited by the various club officials were sufficiently cogent (though, as outlined above, their successive pleas were falling on increasingly receptive ears). On September 15, 1949, state officials notified Sporting de Portugal that "Mário Wilson and Júlio Pereira [Juca] could freely sign with the club without any further formalities," reversing the decision it had rendered just two weeks previously, which had required that these two players receive "cartas" from their colonial teams: Desportivo de Lourenço Marques and Sporting de Lourenço Marques, respectively.[13] Just over two weeks later, an official decree, dated October 4, 1949, permitted any footballer coming from the overseas territories to play in Portugal without any regulatory impediments.[14]

If Sporting Clube de Portugal helped to open the door to recruitment in Africa, its rivals—further motivated by the abilities of Juca and Wilson—barely hesitated before rushing through. Perhaps most notably, Belenenses signed the superb Mozambican player Matateu in 1951, and his younger brother, Vicente Lucas, three years later, both of whom would go on to excel for club and country. Simultaneously, FC Porto, the so-called "club of the north" given its location in Portugal, was actively courting players from the colonies to help it end a trophy drought that stretched back to the 1939–1940 season. In 1950, the club signed Miguel Arcanjo from Angola's Sporting Clube de Benguela; the defender would go on to become a member of the national squad and arguably the best at his position in the country. Porto was quick to tap this reservoir of talent again, as from 1951 to 1954 the club was overseen by Urgel Horta, a doctor and deputy in Portugal's National Assembly, who "sought to exploit the country's colonial affiliation" for footballing ends.[15] In 1952, the Dragões (Dragons) of Porto brought in three more influential African players: Rodolfo Albasini, from Primeiro de Maio de Lourenço Marques; Fernando Perdigão, from Desportivo de Lourenço Marques; and the Angolan forward Carlos Duarte. In 1956, these players, along with the Argentines Porcel and José Valle, and the Italian Del Pinto, helped FC Porto return to glory, capturing its first league championship in sixteen years.[16]

For all of the success that African footballers generated for Sporting, Porto, Belenenses, and other squads, special mention should be made regarding Benfica, Portugal's most storied and decorated club. Founded in 1904, Benfica's co-originator, Cosme Damião, and, for the ensuing decades, his successors, insisted that the "Encarnados" rely solely on domestic talent.[17] This nativist policy persisted with little controversy until football became increasingly internationalized following World War II. With Benfica's main domestic rivals, namely, Sporting and FC Porto, eyeing talent in the colonies and the Encarnado fans demanding results, the club revised its operating policies. In 1950, Benfica signed future Angolan superstar José Águas, the son of settler parents. And in 1954, Mário Coluna and Costa Pereira arrived from Mozambique, along with the Angolan Joaquim Guimarães, all of whom would go on to have distinguished careers for the club.

In fact, Benfica's forays into the international market weren't limited to players. Although the club had previously employed English, Hungarian, and Argentine managers, the hiring of the Brazilian Otto Glória in 1954 saw the Águias (Eagles) of Benfica led by a manager eager to utilize African talent. Following Glória's replacement by the brilliant Hungarian coach Béla Guttmann in 1959, the club looked even more intently to Africa to augment its squad. As Darby has proclaimed, the innovative Guttmann "was a strong proponent of the footballing resources in the colonies and he was particularly proactive in drawing on the rich pool of talent that it provided in his pursuit of domestic and European honors."[18] Ironically, the person responsible for luring Guttmann away from FC Porto following that club's league championship in 1959 was Maurício Vieira de Brito, who had himself been born in Angola and was the scion of a family that had earned its fortune from the sale of coffee cultivated in the colony. Indeed, the colonial connections at Benfica newly ran deep, and ultimately the attendantly broadened perspectives and attentions at all levels of the organization would net the club its greatest African prize: Eusébio.

Finding the Talent: Formal and Informal Scouting in the Colonies

Identifying talented footballers in Portugal's African colonies was an undertaking performed by formal scouts and informal observers alike. Until the metropolitan clubs began building scouting networks, a range of individuals—including fans, teachers, and small business owners, among others—was vital to mining this sporting resource. At times, the talent of a particular African player was so obvious that he attracted the attention of all the major Portuguese clubs, especially if he was already toiling for one of the top colonial squads. Other times, however, and much more frequently when talented players were plying their skills for clubs based far from the colonial capitals or other major population centers, word of a prodigious talent traveled informally before it reached someone with an official connection to one of the Portuguese clubs. And if the information was credible and the metropolitan club was desperate enough, no distance was too great for team officials to traverse in order to observe, engage, and sign potential footballing gems.

Informal Observations

Although Portugal oversaw a far-flung empire during the twentieth century, it also featured a reasonably small, tight-knit population that stretched from the metropole to the colonies, ensuring that any knowledge concerning possible soccer talent didn't have to travel along an extended chain of parties before reaching a metropolitan club official. This intimacy was perhaps most evident when fans in the colonies of a particular Portuguese club were able to precipitate the eventual signing of an African player due to their sporting allegiances. It's unlikely that a nation with a larger population and, thus, more layers between soccer brass and the average fan—especially when these entities were thousands of miles removed—would have been able to mine talent in this manner as effectively.

The experience of José Águas captures perfectly the ways that supporters of a particular team could play a vital role in the identification of talented African footballers during the early days of player transfers from the colonies to the metropole. Playing for Lusitano Lobito, a club based in the eponymous city on Angola's central coast, as a member of the junior squad from 1944 until 1948 before moving up to the senior team, Águas was brought to the attention of Benfica officials by a group of "Benfiquistas" based in Lobito, apparently sending word to Portugal that "they had a striker there who was capable of reaching great heights."[19] Although Benfica officials (and even some locals) exhibited restraint, the club did agree to observe the player during an upcoming tour to the colonies. Ultimately, the local advocates were proved prescient, as Águas would go on to enjoy a remarkable career with the Lisbon outfit.

Schoolteachers, shop owners, and other individuals similarly unaffiliated with Portuguese clubs in any formal capacity also served as the "eyes" for the metropolitan squads. Responding to my question about how he was "discovered," Mário Wilson indicated that "there was a guy in Mozambique who owned a stationery store and saw us playing and could see that I had exceptional soccer skills. And this guy had connections with the Sporting club of Portugal."[20] Just like the local Benfica supporters who first identified Águas as a future star, so, too, did this paper shop proprietor have a keen eye for soccer talent.

Undoubtedly, though, the most famous case of a player coming to the attention of a metropolitan club in an informal manner was that of Eusébio. Although soccer observers in Lourenço Marques were well aware of this emerging talent, it was a chance encounter in a Lisbon barbershop that ultimately sealed the young player's move to Benfica. As legend has it, Béla Guttmann was seated next to Brazilian manager and former national team member José Carlos Bauer. In Portugal on a soccer tour, having just completed the Mozambican portion of the trip, Bauer recommended Eusébio to Benfica's Hungarian manager, who immediately moved to sign—or steal away from Sporting (Eusébio was, at the time, playing for Sporting's affiliate club in Lourenço Marques), depending on one's perspectives and club allegiances—the nineteen-year-old player. If not for the informal nature of this talent assessment, Eusébio almost certainly would have been forever associated with the green and white of Sporting, rather than the red and white of their crosstown archrival.

Formalizing the Identification Process of African Talent

If zealous fans and serendipitous encounters were responsible for the eventual signatures of a number of African players, the available talent in the colonies was too substantial for metropolitan clubs to rely entirely on informal methods. As these footballers began to make significant contributions upon reaching Portugal, the big clubs steadily assembled formal scouting networks in the colonies. The scouts, or *olheiros*, weren't always full-time employees, but they were rewarded for their efforts and proved to be quite adept at identifying talented players. Eventually the metropolitan clubs also sent their own representatives to the colonies to scout for skilled footballers, signaling their commitment to mining African talent pools.

Scouts and club officials sought gifted players in both European and African neighborhoods, unconcerned with the social origins of these prospective recruits. Hilário's account of the scouting networks that had been established in Lourenço Marques by the 1950s highlights how quickly the metropolitan clubs reacted to this new source of talent, and also their determination to identify and secure skilled players:

> In Mozambique, and especially in Lourenço Marques, there were a lot of abandoned lots, so growing up we would play on theses lots. . . . The official clubs in Mozambique, such as Desportivo [the Benfica affiliate] . . . and others, had managers who would come and watch us play, and if they saw a player who had good skills they would come up to him and tell him that, for example, three players could come and play for Benfica or Sporting . . . or somewhere else . . . and that's how me, Coluna, and Eusébio came to Portugal. Costa Pregas and others came through a different process because they lived in the city suburbs and the managers would go watch them there also. That's how we came to Portugal: managers would invite us to come play in Portugal and we would take the opportunity with the hopes of having a better life.[21]

Many scouts in the colonies were former footballers who had grown too old to play competitively but who still loved the game and wanted to remain involved in some capacity. Other times, metropolitan club managers and/or their assistants would travel to the African territories during the summer months to observe talent, either as part of organized soccer tours or, just as often, unrelated to those undertakings. The case of the Mozambican player Augusto Matine illustrates the seriousness with which metropolitan club officials were increasingly scouting the talent available in the colonies. According to the former Benfica and Vitória de Setúbal player regarding the events of 1966, while he was playing for Clube Central, just prior to signing with the Encarnados of Lisbon:

There was a Benfica coach who had come to observe other players, but he eventually watched my match. At the end of the match he asked about me, my age, and so on. . . . My club made an appointment with him to watch our upcoming training session. . . . I came to the training on Monday and he was there, seated. . . . I went through training and at the end, I saw the man approaching. I thought, *This face is familiar; I know this face from somewhere.* But then I realized, *Ahhhh, this man is Fernando, the assistant coach of Béla Guttmann of Benfica*, because I read a lot about Benfica. He approached me and . . . asked, "Do you want to go to Lisbon?" I replied, "I want to, but it is important to talk with the Central managers and then go to talk with my mother." He said "First, I want to know whether you want to go." I responded, "I want to," as the ambition of any young man in Mozambique was to go to Portugal. I also wanted to be like Matateu and Eusébio. And he replied, "Okay, there will be a match in Angola; it will be Angola versus Mozambique. First it will be here [Mozambique] and then there [Angola]. I want to see you and a player from Angola's team." . . .

But when the match here came, the coach did not select me and I stayed out. . . . But Sr. Fernando was still around; he continued to watch the matches and I continued to train. . . . We went ahead and then Sr. Fernando showed up and said, "I am going to see Angola versus Mozambique and I know that you will be called up [to play]." No one told me anything. . . . They organized the team, and, in fact, my name was called. The managers informed me and I stopped training with Central when we went to Angola. . . . In the selecção, I was the only member of a second division club. I was worried because I thought Central would be weak because I would not be there; I was the key player there. I even thought of injuring myself to avoid going, but Sr. Fernando indicated that "you must go [to Angola]. That is the match I want to watch." And then, I went. . . . When I arrived there, the coach started to focus on me: "Augusto, here you must play as you play at Central . . . play in the same way. They will kick you, but they kick you there as well; play freely without fear . . . play how you know how to play." Then, on match day, Sr. Fernando came to me and said, "Augusto, this is not an exam; you have already passed the exam for Benfica. So play as it pleases you; play freely, as you play at Central." Therefore, this was one more motivation. What the coach was telling me and what my colleagues were telling me, this Benfica coach was also telling me, so I was full of pride and brilliance. . . . The match began, we started playing, and there was an Angolan player whose coach had told him, "You must mark Matine because Benfica wants to take him." . . .

When we arrived in the dressing room at halftime [up 2–0], the Benfica coach requested to my coach that I be taken out. But my coach said, "I can't substitute the boy because he is the one controlling the game. . . . I can't take him out. It is better to leave him in to play, but when we are fifteen minutes from the end I can take him out." . . . In the end, we won the game. The Benfica coach then told me, "I have informed Benfica that from today, you are a Benfica player. When we arrive back in Mozambique, I will talk with your mother and I will deal with Central."[22]

Scouts in the colonies typically had employment outside of soccer, performing these sporting functions for a number of reasons, including to augment their income, to enhance their favorite club's chances of glory, to reconnect with the game they so admired, or simply some combination of these motivations. The case of Nuro Americano highlights some of these impetuses, while also illuminating how far away from colonial population centers metropolitan clubs were willing to search for African talent.

Growing up on the island of Pemba, off Mozambique's northern coast, Americano was far removed from the colonial football epicenter of Lourenço Marques. Notwithstanding this distance, Rolletta has indicated that "at the time, in the smaller cities, there were Portuguese soldiers, high-ranking staff members, who also worked as talent spotters for the major Portuguese football clubs. They were people well placed in the military machinery, and they did not find it beneath their status to go looking for young champions."[23] During my interview with Americano, he confirmed this method of identifying emerging talent: "I was discovered because in that time there were talent searchers for various Portuguese clubs, and Pemba was no exception. . . . When I was discovered, I came to Lourenço Marques in transit to Lisbon. During my stay there [the colonial capital], representatives of Benfica hosted me."[24]

In another, rather remarkable case, an aggressive scout helped facilitate the signing of a player in a fashion that can be characterized only as an ambush. Playing in the interior of Guiné in the late 1950s and early 1960s for FC de Teixeira Pinto, Bernardo da Velha eventually attracted the attention of metropolitan clubs, including CUF, Sporting, and FC Porto. Rather than being brought to Portugal by one of these squads, however, he was instead rewarded by his employer, a "shop" at which he worked, with a trip to the metropole. Yet even this nonsporting arrangement didn't dissuade the metropolitan clubs from pursuing his signature. A scout based in Guiné working for Sporting tipped off club officials prior to da Velha's departure, and when the unsuspecting player arrived in Lisbon, they were waiting for him. Following a tour of Sporting's Alvalade stadium, da Velha agreed to a one-year contract with the Leões (Lions) of Lisbon.[25]

An account from Eusébio regarding the growth and the determination of the clubs to identify talent in the colonies perhaps best highlights the pervasiveness of their scouting networks and the aggressive nature of the scouts, or *olheiros*, who made up those networks:

The big clubs would send scouts out to watch the children playing football in the streets. These scouts would stop their cars, watch the game, see if there were any good players, call them over to ask their names, where they lived, and then go with them to talk to their parents. . . . There were scouts of Benfica, Sporting, Porto, and Belenenses in Mozambique who represented the professional clubs of the same name in Portugal. . . . For example, the Benfica representatives lived and worked there [in the colony], watched the team and scouted for talented players to send to Portugal, receiving in return a commission from Benfica.[26]

Commodification

Signing for the Future

African footballers engaged in the process of pledging their prodigious talents to metropolitan clubs were influenced by an array of factors. Perhaps the most important one, though, was the sentiments of their parents, as virtually all of these signees were minors and, thus, couldn't legally enter into contracts with their prospective employers. These fathers and mothers were motivated by their allegiances to particular metropolitan clubs (and corresponding antipathy toward the main rivals of their favored squads), which was often influenced by the colonial club for which their sons played. But the financial package on offer was also majorly influential; players were typically tendered a multiyear contract that included a salary; a signing bonus, or *luva*; and, at times, round-trip travel to return home each off-season.[27]

The players and their parents hardly conducted themselves like starstruck, pliable rubes during the negotiatory processes in which they were engaged. Many played rival suitors off one another, declined clubs' initial approaches in the hopes of receiving improved offers, or simply rebuffed overtures. Moreover, many of the guardians of their talented sons foresightedly prioritized life beyond football, which prompted many African players to eschew the major clubs in favor of Académica de Coimbra, where they could continue pursuing both the sport and their studies. Although parents played a larger role than did their sons in deciding for which club the latter would sign, the young recruits did influence these decisions by articulating their own, occasionally dissenting preferences, and also by strategically soliciting information from fellow African footballers who were already members of Portuguese clubs about living and working conditions in the metropole. In this fashion, African prospects were actively shaping their own football and postfootball futures.

Motivations: When Club Allegiances Trumped Money

Given the significant financial hardships that African families faced during the colonial period, it's remarkable that an allegiance to a particular metropolitan club could outweigh the superior sum of money on offer from a rival club. Yet that this scenario regularly occurred is a powerful testament to the important roles that soccer and fandom played in colonial societies. In practice, a Benfica supporter, for example, would be loath to permit his son to sign and play for Sporting, and vice versa. And in the case of Eusébio, who played for Sporting's affiliate in Lourenço Marques, but who ultimately signed for Benfica, such was the depth of the rivalry between the clubs that kidnapping accusations were leveled at the Eagles and the player was whisked away to a "safe house" immediately after arriving in Portugal (explained in detail below). Although this scenario was rather aberrational, and Eusébio's so-called "defection" from Sporting had more to do with a range of other factors—though, primarily, the superior money on offer—sporting allegiances undeniably played a central role in determining to which metropolitan clubs talented African footballers committed their futures.

The signing of Mário Coluna in 1954 illustrates well the influence that parents' footballing allegiances had on their sons' athletic fates. During a 1954 tour of Mozambique, Sporting de Portugal squared off against the city selecção of Lourenço Marques, for which Coluna had been selected. The Sporting managers were clearly impressed by his play and indicated their desire to have Coluna play for the Lisbon club. As Coluna conveyed to me during our interview, "I played, and it seems that I played well. At the end of the match, the administrators of Sporting Club of Portugal contacted me and asked whether I wanted to play in Portugal for Sporting. I told them that 'I am a minor; talk with my father.' My father was a 'Benfiquista' [Benfica supporter] and a shareholder of Desportivo de Lourenço Marques [the Benfica affiliate in Mozambique and the colonial club team for which Coluna played]. I do not know exactly what he told them."[28] Given the outcome of these discussions, however, his father's response leaves little to the imagination. Apparently "terrified" by the idea that his son could possibly don the jersey of Sporting—the cross-city rivals of his beloved Benfica— Coluna's father alerted individuals affiliated with the Encarnados of his son's availability.[29] As Coluna explained, "There was a local military officer who was affiliated with Benfica. When he heard about Sporting's interest, he sent an SOS to Benfica in Portugal, and apparently club officials replied: 'Put that young man on the first airplane [to Lisbon].' "[30] As Rolletta has poetically written, Coluna "now wore the red jersey of his dreams, and those of his father's."[31]

The central role of club allegiances in the signing experience of José Ferreira Pinto is also clear, even if this process was marked by much more spectacle than was typical. Deriving from Benguela in Angola, the mestiço footballer was playing for the Sporting affiliate in Benguela, Sporting Clube de Benguela, in the mid-1950s when he was approached by José Valdivieso, then the coach of Benfica's junior squad. After inquiring with Pinto's club and learning of his availability, Valdivieso received a verbal commitment from the player.[32] However, upon Pinto's uncle learning that his nephew was poised to sign with the archrival of the parent club of the player's current squad, the former dramatically intervened and scuttled the deal. Consequently, Pinto spent the first four years of his metropolitan career with Sporting before moving on to CUF (Companhia União Fabril), though he did, ironically, eventually sign for Benfica in 1965.

Motivations: When Money Trumped Club Allegiances

If allegiances to particular metropolitan clubs kept certain players out of the grasp of "enemy" squads, at other times sporting affinities simply weren't enough. The money on offer constituted an influential factor in the decision of a player's family, most of whom were struggling to survive in the various colonial settings. Consequently, many African players transitioned from affiliate clubs in the colonies to the parent clubs of archrivals in the metropole—most (in)famously Eusébio, whose jump to Portugal took him from Sporting de Lourenço Marques to Lisbon's Benfica. Moreover, even when club allegiances remained paramount to recruits and their parents, they could still exact higher wages and signing bonuses from their preferred suitors by strategically demanding that these teams match, or even exceed, offers made by rival metropolitan outfits. While the money on offer wasn't always decisive, as in many areas of life it constituted a powerful motivator.

The example of the Angolan player António Joaquim Dinis illustrates the influence that money had on determining for which club a player would sign. After performing spectacularly for his colonial club, ASA of Luanda, during two matches against a touring Académica side in 1968, officials from Belenenses approached him. However, the player and the courting club couldn't settle on a salary acceptable to both parties. Subsequently, FC Porto failed to sign the Angolan prospect for the same reason. Unlike many players, Dinis had a respectable job in the colonies, working for the Air Transportation Directory (DTA), and he was also in the military. Remarkably, another nine offers followed, with Dinis declining them all. Apparently Benfica came closest, as Dinis reportedly was willing to sign only for a "first-scale club." Eventually, however, Sporting swept in with a substantial offer and secured the player's services. Dinis would go on to star for the "Lions of Lisbon" and was ultimately selected for the Portuguese national team as well.[33]

At other times, even when parents intervened to ensure their sons went to this or that metropolitan club, they didn't entirely disregard the financial dimensions of the process. For example, although Coluna's father engineered his son's move *away* from a possible engagement with Sporting *to* his cherished Benfica, compensation remained in the forefront of his mind and, therefore, in his interactions with club officials. Indeed, before he permitted his son to sign for Benfica, he insisted that the Encarnados match Sporting's offer of 120 contos for a two-year contract. Apparently, Benfica reluctantly agreed, but the bidding war continued, and by the time it concluded the package had reached 150 contos, with a monthly salary of 2,500 escudos.[34] As such, even in this case of extreme club loyalty, financial sense and objectives were maintained.

For Mozambican player Augusto Matine, although his mother participated in the initial negotiations with Benfica, representatives from his colonial club, Clube Central, were much more centrally involved during the negotiatory process. Of course, these local officials were poised to be rewarded via the sale of their player to the deep-pocketed Lisbon outfit in exchange for furnishing Matine's *carta de desobrigação* (formal release), but their concern for his well-being certainly doesn't appear to have been entirely self-serving. According to the player:

The Benfica representative went to talk with my mother and my club directors. I could not negotiate because I did not know anything, and I was a minor. The officials from Central negotiated, as they knew professional football because the majority of them had come from Portugal. They had an idea of Benfica's salaries for juniors . . . and for intermediate players. . . . The Central men negotiated a reasonable salary. They said, "He has to have a salary to support his family. You must pay him three times what he earns now per month." . . . This was how it was done. This was my first contract. . . . It was lots of money. . . . I was well paid. . . . I used to send money to my family. Every month, I was sending 1,000 escudos to my family; I was sustaining my family with this money. The Clube officials protected me throughout this process because I belonged to their club.[35]

Perhaps no case better illustrates the focus on compensation, though, than Eusébio's. This story has been told and retold, now possessing almost mythical qualities, but it warrants inclusion here as it powerfully underscores the motivational power of money for African players and their families. As a member of Sporting's affiliate club in Mozambique, the logical transition to the metropole would have had Eusébio join the Lisbon-based parent club. His good friend Hilário had already traversed this path, leaving for the metropole two years before Eusébio would, and encouraged his former neighborhood companion to join him at Sporting. As Hilário explained regarding the facility of the transfer, "Since I played for a club [in Mozambique] that was affiliated with Sporting, they took care of everything. . . . We couldn't come to play in Portugal without the authorization of the colonial club . . . and in my case since it was an affiliated club, it was much easier."[36] Yet Eusébio opted for a more challenging—albeit more lucrative—route.

Although Eusébio did, indeed, entertain the Sporting option, money ultimately dictated to which club he would commit his future. According to the player: "They [Benfica officials] went to speak with my mother and my brother and offered a sum equivalent to 1,000 euros in today's money for three seasons. My brother asked for twice as much, and they paid. They signed the contract with my mother and gave her the money."[37] In fact, the exact amount of this initial sum is widely debated, and even Eusébio himself has indicated different figures during interviews over the years—typically ranging from the €1,000 cited above to sums as high as £7,500. Irrespective of the exact amount, the figure was at least twice as high as any quantity previously offered to an African footballer.

In recalling these early days, Eusébio has often downplayed the importance of the money on offer. Indeed, it does appear, for example, that Benfica had more faith in his footballing potential than did its Lisbon rival, as Sporting wanted to bring Eusébio to Portugal and place him on its junior squad "for the experience with no [significant] monetary award," while Benfica was eyeing the player for its senior squad.[38] According to the Mozambican great, "There was a newspaper picture of [my mother] with all the money on the table with her arms round it. I had never seen such money in my life. Sporting tried to spread the story that I'd stitched them up, but it was the other way round, because they tried to take me for free while Benfica was willing to pay."[39]

Yet Eusébio's widowed mother, Elisa, made it perfectly clear that the money did matter. Upon immediately consenting to Benfica's offer (she had to consummate the agreement, as Eusébio was only eighteen at the time), Elisa apparently remarked: "The present situation is unbearable. My son sometimes gets 50 escudos given to him by Sporting de Lourenço Marques, but how far does that go? He is already a man and has to help in supporting and bringing up his younger brothers. So, my son will join Benfica. . . . [The club,] with its big money, has turned my head."[40] Elsewhere, she would confirm that the reason she agreed to the club's offer was that "Benfica gave big money."[41] The player himself would later defend Elisa's decision, echoing and elaborating upon his mother's sentiments: "A player will go to the club that pays more and offers a better contract; it has nothing to do with tradition. . . . It all depended on the terms and conditions offered by the clubs in Portugal. . . . I played for Sporting in Mozambique, and Sporting Lisbon wanted to bring me over to Portugal for a trial. But why should I have gone for a trial with Sporting, when Benfica had the contract and the money ready to give me?"[42]

Priorities beyond Club or Money: Other Motivating Factors

If club allegiances and compensation were the major factors in determining for which metropolitan club an African player would sign, there remained still other considerations. Just as in modern sports, sometimes the footballers simply got a "good feel" for a particular organization, connected personally with a team official, or appreciated the way that club representatives interacted with their families. Even Eusébio regularly praised the attentiveness that Benfica officials demonstrated toward his family. For those African footballers (and parents) who lacked strong club allegiances, or who were willing to accept a reduced wage package in order to enter a scenario that appeared more welcoming or in which they felt they'd have a better chance to receive playing time and, therefore, succeed, these types of intangible factors strongly influenced their ultimate metropolitan destinations. For example, as Shéu Han commented regarding his signing with Benfica from his club in Beira, Mozambique, in 1970, "There was a certain amount to receive for the transference. When they told my father about the money, he said, no, I don't want any money. . . . But I wasn't interested in money either. All I wanted was to play football."[43]

One such player motivated by factors that transcended club allegiance and financial compensation was the Angolan forward António Fernandes, or "Yaúca," who relocated to Portugal in 1958 to play for Belenenses. During the courting process, he was first approached by Sporting, which made a generous offer, with Benfica subsequently tendering an even better offer.[44] However, while Yaúca and his family contemplated these options, the president of Belenenses, Francisco Soares da Cunha, who had already been instrumental in bringing the Mozambican players Matateu and his younger brother, Vicente Lucas, to the club, arrived to encourage the prospect to join them at the newly inaugurated site of the team's home matches, the Restelo stadium, on the outskirts of Lisbon. During a 1959 interview, a year after he had arrived in Portugal, Yaúca declared: "If it wasn't for the rapid and decisive intervention of Soares da Cunha, who had come to Angola to convince me to sign with Belenenses, I would have signed with Benfica. Fortunately, I ended up going to Belenenses. I say *fortunately*, because I am proud of my club and I have encountered in it a camaraderie and spirit of solidarity that has deeply impressed me."[45] The goodwill that Soares da Cunha generated, and to which Yaúca responded so positively, served the player well, as he was selected for the national team in 1959, and for each of the ensuing six years. Ironically, in 1963, overtures from Benfica proved irresistible, and he would eventually retire in 1968 with Belenenses' crosstown rival, following five productive years with the Encarnados.

Meanwhile, in an unusual signing process in which the parents of a player were evidently not initially involved, matters became quite complicated. In the early 1950s, Carlos Duarte was a rising star, playing as a winger in the Angolan league in Nova Lisboa (now the city of Huambo) for the club associated with the railroad, Grupo Desportivo Ferroviário. Apparently, while his father was away on vacation in Portugal, representatives from Belenenses approached the prospect and came to an agreement that included a signing bonus and a ticket on a passenger boat headed to Lisbon to join the club. Yet when his father found out, "a wave of telephone calls, telegrams, orders, and anxiety began," appealing to authorities that his son was a minor, and, thus, whatever had been arranged was invalid.[46] Evidently, four days before his scheduled departure, colonial authorities appeared and prevented him from leaving, at which point he was required to forfeit both the money and the ticket. Heartbroken and most likely chastened, Duarte's metropolitan dreams were not, however, dashed. Unbeknownst to him, senior FC Porto official Dr. Saraiva Caldeira, who was an ardent supporter of utilizing African talent, was eyeing the player and made the necessary arrangements for his transfer to the Dragões. Although Duarte's father was not immediately supportive, he accepted a trip to Porto from the club and was duly impressed. During the visit, he received assurances that Carlos would be "well-treated," which paved the way for the player's relocation and eventual inclusion on the Portuguese national team.[47]

Direct familial connections to a particular club also proved decisive for certain players in determining for which metropolitan squad they would sign. Perhaps the most famous case relates to the Mozambican sibling duo Matateu and Vicente Lucas, the latter of whom followed his older brother to Belenenses in the 1950s. Elsewhere, for the Angolan brothers José Maria and Conceição, these sibling siren calls proved to be just as efficacious. Over a year older than his younger brother, Conceição arrived in the metropole to play for Vitória de Setúbal in October 1962, promising to do whatever he could to ensure that José Maria would join him at the club.[48] Consequently, upon arrival, Conceição informed Vitória officials of his younger brother's talent. In fact, club officials were already aware of his abilities and were actively scouting him. With all parties in agreeance that José Maria could make a significant contribution to the squad, his transfer proceeded without complication. According to Maria regarding his signing, "I can assure you that the biggest slice of the pie went to the Angolan club [Atlético de Luanda]. I had to be satisfied with 50 contos, which, at the time, without really knowing the ropes behind professional football, seemed like a generous amount to me. Regardless, I am able to say that I accepted with great contentment the idea of going to the metropole [to play]. I was coming to start playing serious football, for a great club and, regardless of all that, the fact that it was my brother's team was enough to make me feel happy."[49] By December 1962, Maria was en route to Portugal to reunite with his older sibling.

Finally, many African footballers prioritized the opportunity to play for a top metropolitan club and hone their skills alongside elite teammates. As Hilário indicated, "There were some players who lived well in Lourenço Marques, and primarily came to Portugal because they wanted to play for a club that mattered and for the recognition."[50] The experiences of Jacinto João illustrate this focus on playing at the highest level, at least initially. Born in Luanda in 1944, João would play for clubs in Angola and the neighboring Congo before being recruited by Benfica while playing for its affiliate team in the Angolan capital. Receiving his father's blessing to sign for the Lisbon outfit, he would later reflect that "loving the sport and knowing my abilities and possibilities, I felt I could go to a big club, directed by a great coach like Béla Guttmann, and surrounded by great players, among them some of my fellow friends from home. . . . I would be able to improve my skills and learn the hard task that is the life of a professional, and above all to serve a well-known club and therefore have enormous responsibilities."[51] Yet, despite João's fixation on playing for Benfica, these aspirations never came to fruition. Unable to make the squad following a ruinous audition, he returned to Angola to play for FC de Luanda. Again, however, the suitors came calling: first Porto, followed by Belenenses, Vitória de Guimarães, and Vitória de Setúbal. According to João, "For two years, though, I didn't want to hear talk about transfers. I preferred the calm and tranquility of my old neighborhood and of my city to the dynamic life of the big metropolitan cities."[52] In 1965, however, the former director of Vitória de Setúbal, Major Lemos, observed João playing and thought he'd make a wonderful addition to the club located in the city adjacent to the Sado River. Smarting from his failure to make the Benfica squad, and humiliated after being forced to return to Angola, João hesitated before eventually committing. His desire to play in Portugal, coupled with implorations by two teammates whom Lemos was also recruiting, prompted João to pledge his future to Setúbal, dramatically vowing to return to Luanda only for holidays! His confidence justified, João would go on to play sixteen seasons for Os Sadinos, and six for the Portuguese national team. Ironically, during the height of this success, Benfica repeatedly tried to sign him away from Setúbal, only to have the player reject their advances. In an interview from 1969, João remarked:

> Being honest about it, when I started to triumph at Vitória, I was quickly approached about changing clubs. And the most curious part is that the most insistent was Benfica. It is always an honor to play for Benfica, but I am well at Vitória, I have my life in Setúbal, and even though it is not too far from Lisbon [some thirty miles], I feel well here and I would hardly consider leaving Vitória. I am well-treated, I have many friends, and I like the air of the city.[53]

Like João following his initial disappointment, many African footballers weren't particular about which metropolitan squad they joined. Given these sentiments, many players found their way to clubs that, although competing in Portugal's first division, rarely troubled the squads perennially at the top of the table. And even when African players with this more grounded outlook did find their way to one of the elite clubs, they remained indifferent about their particular destination. They were simply happy to continue their soccer ascension.

Strategically Engaging with Metropolitan Football: Sport and Study

Although African footballers were motivated by various factors to sign with this or that Portuguese club, some players adopted a decidedly strategic approach to their new careers in metropolitan soccerdom. Forgoing money, disregarding club allegiances, and eschewing the opportunity to play for elite clubs, many African soccer prospects sought to continue their studies, which they had begun in the colonies, while still playing the sport they loved. For most of these athletes, that meant committing to Académica de Coimbra, the club affiliated with Portugal's most prestigious institution. Other recruits were able to juggle academics and soccer elsewhere in the country, but most players (and parents) who were focused on their postfootball lives opted for Académica. Although Shéu Han declared to me during our interview, "In that time [the colonial period], it was totally different; in the 1960s, football was for people who did not like to study," these Coimbra-bound footballers were also undeniably "studiers," as well as gifted soccer players. Han's comments may well reflect the ongoing backgrounding of these more studious footballers in popular memories of soccer during the colonial period, as virtually all the best players of this era wore Benfica, Sporting, Porto, or Belenenses—rather than Académica—jerseys.[54]

One African player who forwent potential trophies and titles to divide his time between soccer and studies was Rui Rodrigues. Initially recruited by both Benfica and Académica in the early 1960s, he pondered both options; during our interview, Rodrigues explained why he chose the latter: "I received invitations from Académica and Benfica. Académica gave me a chance to play and study. But at Benfica, it was only to play soccer. I chose to join Académica, thinking of my future. Remember that I was young. When my father died I was only eight years old."[55] Following a wait of three months for Académica to furnish his ticket to the metropole, the player was finally on his way to the club of Os Estudantes.

Although most African soccer players who were serious about their studies landed in Coimbra, on occasion these dual endeavors could be pursued elsewhere in Portugal. Such was the case of Augusto Araújo, an Angolan footballer who came to the metropole to play in 1956. While playing in Huíla, in southwestern Angola, his coach was a former Académica player, who recommended Araújo to the Coimbra outfit. However, Araújo was determined to become an engineer, and at that time the renowned university in the city did not offer training in this field. Araújo subsequently moved to Benguela, on the Angolan coast, and completed his schooling there, while also continuing to shine on the pitch. Scouts from Benfica recognized his talent and he was soon offered a contract. Knowing that there was an engineering school in the Portuguese capital at which Araújo could continue his studies, his father assented to this arrangement.[56] Yet it was, perhaps not surprisingly, to Coimbra that the player would ultimately commit; after only one full season in the capital, Araújo quit the famed Lisbon squad, going out on loan to Académica, where he would fulfill his educational aspirations.

Strategically Engaging with Metropolitan Football: Soliciting Advice

Other African soccer prospects proceeded just as calculatedly, even if they ultimately ended up signing for one of the big clubs, similarly gathering information and weighing factors that often transcended potential sporting glory. Before committing, recruits first consulted with players who had already made the move to Portugal, typically soliciting advice and insights about life in various metropolitan Portuguese cities and the playing and living conditions offered by particular clubs in an attempt to discern which outfit would offer the setting that was most agreeable and most conducive to their success. For example, prior to joining Sporting de Portugal in 1964, the Mozambican defender Armando Manhiça sought this type of counsel from his seniors. Following a series of initial overtures from the Lisbon club, the player approached the goalkeeper, Octávio de Sá, who also hailed from Lourenço Marques, and who had played for Sporting in Lisbon for roughly four seasons before returning to Mozambique.[57] Beyond strategically soliciting advice from de Sá regarding life in Lisbon and what it was like to play for Sporting, it is important to note that the goalkeeper was the son of Portuguese settlers while Manhiça was black, an example of interactional trust that underscores players' prioritization of provenance over potential racial divides. Ultimately, de Sá's testimony helped convince Manhiça and his parents that Lisbon and Sporting were ideal living and footballing settings, respectively. Content with his decision, Manhiça would go on to play six seasons for the Lions before switching to FC Porto in 1970 for four more campaigns before finally hanging up his boots; he also made two appearances for the Portuguese selecção.

Although familial connections virtually ensured that talented recruits would sign with the metropolitan clubs for which their relatives were already playing, before committing, prospects often solicited from their siblings the same types of information and advice outlined above. The case of Matateu and his younger brother, Vicente Lucas, is exemplary. With the older brother already in place at Belenenses, the two regularly corresponded, with Matateu consistently providing the type of insight and encouragement in his letters that would eventually convince his talented younger sibling to follow in his footsteps. Indeed, while it was certain that the skilled fullback Lucas would eventually play in Portugal, it was, at least initially, much less certain to which club he would ultimately commit.

Homebodies: Refusing to Sign

Finally, it's important to note that no matter how much courting by metropolitan clubs African prospects endured or enjoyed, some of these players chose to remain in the colonies. Although countless talented African footballers never had the chance to play in Portugal, owing to a variety of racist manifestations, as well as much less formidable obstacles, others forwent their opportunities, primarily due to familial commitments or an unwillingness to be separated from everything they found familiar and of which they were genuinely fond. Perhaps the most famous case of this type of "rejection" was that of Ernesto Baltazar, a Mozambican player in the 1960s and '70s. The "midfield magician" began playing for Ferroviário de Lourenço Marques in 1962 and shortly thereafter began to receive offers from the elite metropolitan clubs. In 1965, the contract from Benfica finally arrived. As Baltazar explained to me:

> In 1965, I was twenty years old. . . . Until the age of twenty-six, Benfica appeared every year with an offer. Sporting, Porto, Belenenses; they all came. Belenenses offered 1,300 contos. In that time, that was

a lot of money. . . . We [Ferroviário] used to come to Portugal to play in the Taça de Portugal [Portuguese Cup]. . . . They [the players from the metropolitan clubs] were professionals and we were amateurs. Those clubs tried to convince me to stay in Portugal to play. . . . But I loved that land [Mozambique], and I still love it. I loved that land and I loved Ferroviário.[58]

Paola Rolletta, who counted Baltazar among the top thirty Mozambican players of all time in her book *Finta finta*, added, "When his father signed the contract from Benfica, Baltazar's suitcase was already packed, and the contract was fantastic, the highest ever: 800 contos for the player and 750 contos for Ferroviário—in the middle of the 1960s!"[59] Yet Baltazar obviously underwent a rapid change of heart. According to the player, "I went home and I began to cry. I didn't want to go to the cold! Mozambique was my country! I didn't want to go."[60] Only following independence, in 1976, and for reasons primarily related to his children who had been born in the meantime, did he agree to go to Portugal to play. During our interview, even as Baltazar revealed his regret that he hadn't accepted one of the many offers that came his way during the colonial period, he also reiterated his affection for Mozambique: club and country.

Transformative Trips: The Voyage to the Metropole

For the many players who did agree to ply their skills in the metropole, the next task was to get there. For most, this journey required transport via passenger ships that lasted weeks and included stops at numerous ports of call. Even those players who flew from Africa to Lisbon endured a number of stops and layovers en route. Regardless of how the footballers made their way to the metropole, their journeys often constituted much more than simply travel from one place to another. Most newly signed recruits were still teenagers; leaving friends and family and, in some cases, fiancées behind for the first time in their lives, these journeys were invariably emotional endeavors.[61] Moreover, while at sea, the players were instantly thrust into Portuguese space, as virtually all the passengers on the oceangoing ships were either metropolitan Portuguese or Portuguese settlers, returning from the colonies or traveling to the metropole, respectively, and both the cuisine and the entertainment options on board were squarely aimed at this audience. As such, the journeys further helped players adjust to their new environs as they transitioned from African to European contexts, while also reminding them that although they were ascending in the world of soccer, they would continue to endure discriminatory treatment at the very hands of those by whom they were newly being paid to entertain.

Tearful Departures

The first steps of these long journeys were often the hardest. Young athletes everywhere struggle to adjust when their sporting careers take them away from friends and family, but for these African footballers the situation was arguably much more acute. Many of them had never left their respective colonies, let alone traveled thousands of miles away to a foreign land on a distant continent. At times, the resultant *saudades*, or feelings of loss and remorse, were tempered by fellow soccer recruits who traveled with them to the metropole. For example, Miguel Arcanjo, who traveled in July 1951 from Angola to Portugal to play for FC Porto, was accompanied by António Lara, who had signed with Benfica, and Fausto Matos, who was heading to the metropole to play for Juventude de Évora.

Unlike this fortunate trio, however, many other players traveled to the metropole without fellow footballing recruits, rendering the initial separations from their homelands extremely difficult. In an account of Vicente Lucas's 1954 departure that appeared in a 1956 issue of *Ídolos*, the new Belenenses signing supposedly engaged in the following exchange with his mother: "No, son. You go. That is an adventure for men. I will stay here with your sisters and older brother and my seven little grandchildren." The piece continued: "And the helpless mother hid her tears, surrounded by the little boys, sons of her daughter, Albertina."[62] While this version may well have been dramatized, it does highlight the emotional nature of players' departures, exacerbated by the fact that Lucas was the second son his mother had "lost" to football: his older brother Matateu had already left for Lisbon some three years earlier to play for

Belenenses. Like so many of these players, Eusébio also experienced this type of suffering as he separated from his family. "We were a very, very close family—always together and always gathering at my mother's house. Even my brothers who had left home always came back and we would be together for Christmas, birthdays, etc. This went on for 18 years, and then I left for Portugal. It was extremely difficult for me. . . . My problem was my family—we were very close. I was 18 years old, had lived all my life surrounded by family. It was a long way in those days—there were no jet planes—and it used to take over 30 hours to get to Lisbon."[63]

Mentally and Physically Challenging Journeys

Whether African players traveled to Portugal by boat or plane, the trip itself often generated challenges for these novice long-distance travelers. For example, the Angolan recruit Carlos Duarte, traveling to Portugal in 1952 to begin playing for FC Porto, endured an extremely difficult voyage at sea. Apparently the food on board didn't agree with Duarte and he consequently lost a great deal of weight, worrying his father, who met him in Funchal on the island of Madeira as the recruit made his way north to Portugal.[64]

Even those players who flew faced challenges while en route. For example, Matateu was set to leave for Portugal from Lourenço Marques via boat in September 1951 when, at the last minute, he received a telegram instructing him to board a plane bound for Lisbon. During this inaugural flight for the player, the plane experienced a great deal of turbulence and Matateu later revealed how frightened he was; "I didn't think I was going to make it. . . . The only thing encouraging me was the fact that my mother would receive the money from my insurance policy if I should die."[65] Thankfully, for Belenenses supporters and for football fans everywhere, Matateu's flight was otherwise uneventful.

In Transit: Staying Engaged to the Sport, and to Society

For those players who traveled to Portugal by ship, the two to four weeks that the journey typically lasted afforded opportunities to engage in a variety of activities, while also helping them transition both socially and culturally to metropolitan life. For many players, the time on board was marked by restlessness, as it was a challenge to practice the very game that enabled the journeys. But the migrant athletes ably improvised, exhibiting the same type of resourcefulness they had displayed as child practitioners of the game. For example, the Angolan players Santana and Daniel Chipenda, who traveled together to the metropole in 1954 after they both had signed for Benfica, practiced while on board the ship using a ball composed of old fabric. Santana explained that they engaged in this activity because "I had heard that Otto Glória [Benfica's manager at the time] was very demanding, as was Sr. Valdivieso [the coach of Benfica's junior squad]. And because we had many days without training and without adequate nourishment for a footballer, we knew that the effects of this [inactivity] would show."[66]

Rui Rodrigues similarly stayed engaged with the game during his multiweek trip from Mozambique to play for Académica in 1962, but more so mentally than physically. The player indicated that while on board, "I imagined myself on the pitch, shooting the ball and scoring goals, while on the radio the reporter cried 'goal!' and the public in the stadium called out my name."[67]

Still other players embraced more conventional entertainment options while at sea, utilizing the journey to embrace metropolitan life, or be reminded of its potential harshness. In 1949, for example, Mário Wilson and Júlio Pereira, or "Juca," traveled from Mozambique on board the ship *Mouzinho de Albuquerque* to join their new club, Sporting. According to Wilson, Juca, who was the son of Portuguese settlers, "was handsome and had fantastic elegance. . . . All the women on the ship fell in love with him. . . . He was one of the playboys on this trip. At the dances, Juca was always there."[68] Yet, while Juca was charming his way into the hearts of the Portuguese travelers, Wilson was reminded of the cruelty of racial discrimination, recalling that during this same journey, "We Africans of color, even though [as a mestiço] I was of an agreeable stature, were segregated, violently pushed to one side."[69] Wilson's experiences reveal that at least in the late 1940s, the metropole and a series of liminal spaces associated with it could be every bit as unforgiving and unpleasant as the colonial contexts from which these players derived.

Arrivals in Portugal: Excitement, Apprehension, and More Challenges

As the long journeys to the metropole concluded, African recruits brimmed with excitement, but also with a degree of apprehension as they arrived on Portuguese soil for the first time. Players were met at the airport or docks by varying numbers of club officials, media personnel, and team supporters. Those prospects whose soccer reputations preceded them were often compelled to engage in press conferences at the points of disembarkation, while less-touted signings arrived virtually anonymously, were received quietly, and subsequently escorted by a club representative to their new accommodations.

Arrivals offered high-profile recruits a chance to publicly proclaim admiration for their new clubs and the supporters of these squads and to humbly declare their gratitude and commitment to improving the fortunes of the teams—much in the same way that new signings conduct themselves on such occasions in contemporary football. For example, upon arriving in Portugal in 1951, Matateu offered exactly these sorts of platitudes: "I want to say with much pleasure that in spite of having come from African lands, I feel very Belenenses and that at the club I will do the best that I can and know how to do. . . . Here, I will have a great opportunity to better myself, and for that I am extremely grateful to Belenenses—my new club."[70]

The media aggrandized these arrivals, not missing an opportunity to mix politics, history, and football and, in the process, place the burden of heightened expectations squarely on the shoulders of the new recruits. Shortly after Matateu's arrival, for example, *A Bola*, the leading metropolitan football newspaper, hyperbolically announced:

His journey took him from Portugal to Portugal [i.e., from Mozambique to the metropole]. . . . And today . . . Matateu has risen peacefully from the streets to his new club, and can consider himself a Julius Caesar arriving in Gaul with all his desire to conquer, to exclaim triumphantly. The overseas provinces—that Portugal there, so far away, grand, and immense, model of the virtues of a race that gave "new worlds to the world"—are now paying us a dividend of four centuries. And it is they who are giving us . . . new worlds to our football world: an Espírito Santo, a Peyroteo, an Águas, and many others. . . . And now, Matateu, who came from far away in order to wear, there in the Restelo [Belenenses' stadium], the same Cruz de Cristo [Cross of Christ] that one day we took to his land. He arrives without ostentation, unknown and simple.[71]

Two years prior to Matateu's arrival, in 1949, Juca and Mário Wilson had arrived to similar fanfare, greeted by both staunch supporters and casual fans of Sporting, journalists, and club officials. Matateu's brother Vicente Lucas also encountered a sizable welcoming party upon his arrival some five years later, in June 1954. After traveling from Mozambique for more than three weeks on board the ship *Patria*, Lucas reached the Conde de Óbidos quay in Lisbon, recalling, "I thought we would never arrive!" When they finally did, however, he was met by a large audience, which included Matateu, eagerly anticipating the arrival of "Matateu II." Offering comments to the assembled crowd, Lucas avowed his commitment to carving out his own success, out from under his brother's (albeit significant) shadow, declaring, "I am not Matateu the Second," while also delivering the ultimatum: "If I win, I stay. If not, I go back."[72] Meanwhile, for Hilário, who arrived in Lisbon to play for Sporting in 1958, the initial excitement was palpable and there would be no going back: "After a twenty-two-day journey, I could hardly believe that I would be on the turf at José Alvalade Stadium, training with the stars whose pictures were on the cards that we used to collect."[73]

If some players were feted and others starstruck, many other African recruits experienced rather unremarkable arrivals. Even Eusébio was met at the airport by only three club officials and two journalists. Yet it was Joaquim Conceição, an Angolan prospect who came to play for Vitória de Setúbal in 1962 at age twenty, who endured what was perhaps the most anticlimactic arrival experience. Upon reaching Lisbon during the fall of that year, no one was present to greet him, or even in Setúbal, some thirty miles southeast of the capital. Only later, in a Setúbal café, did a representative from the club finally meet him and take him to the home where the team's players resided.[74] António Brassard, who came to Portugal to play for Académica de Coimbra in 1964, had a similarly deflating arrival experience:

I came to Portugal by plane. The route was Lourenço Marques-Luanda-Kano [Nigeria]-Lisbon. . . . I came to Portugal without having family here; it was an abrupt change for someone who was used to living with family and friends in Lourenço Marques. Suddenly, I saw myself in a different country, without family; it was a weird feeling. When I arrived in Coimbra, the students were on holidays. The city was deserted and it was quite difficult for me. It was a radical change . . . but I adjusted as time progressed. But in the beginning, it was not easy.[75]

Initial Acclimation Challenges

Newly arriving African players faced an array of challenges, some related to football and others to life beyond the pitch. Some of these issues would persist or periodically resurface, but many of them were most pronounced in the immediate aftermath of the footballers' arrivals and would eventually dissipate. The players struggled with, inter alia, the cooler climate, the absence of close friends and family, the intense training regimen, and the competition they faced for playing time now that they were members of some of the most accomplished clubs in the world. Going forward, they would draw upon their mental fortitude and their commitments to footballing success and social integration to help overcome these challenges. The presence of African players already established in Portugal who had preceded the waves of newly arriving recruits helped, over time, to temper some of the transitional difficulties. In situ veterans offered advice regarding how to navigate the metropolitan environment, as well as how to best showcase one's soccer skills, and, perhaps most importantly, provided much-needed camaraderie.

Saudades *for All That Was Left Behind, and the* Social Challenges That Lay Ahead

Among the most immediate challenges for these newly arrived players was the sense of loss, or *saudades*, for everyone and everything they had left behind. Speaking after he had arrived from Angola and was settling in at Belenenses in the late 1950s, Yaúca's comments reflect these feelings of absence: "There is only one thing that gets in the way of my happiness.

The *saudade* that I have for my family; a person can never forget those to whom he owes his life. Also, I remember the good friends I have in Lobito [Angola], who were a part of my childhood. However, I'll never forget the sacrifices I need to make to assure my future. I work . . . to have a good life after I am done with football. However, I know that I also work for those whom I cherish . . . to make their lives easier."[76] Joaquim João, who arrived from Mozambique in 1973 for a tryout with Benfica, echoed Yaúca's sentiments regarding the newfound voids in the recruits' lives: "I stayed at Benfica for thirty-five days, on a probationary period for a precompetition camp. I was happy, but there was a lot that I missed. In particular, I missed my mother."[77]

Following any media engagements upon arrival, club representatives typically took players to their new accommodations to help them begin the adjustment process in a controlled, supportive environment. As Mike Cronin and David Mayall have contended, "By providing a range of services and opportunities for the newly arrived immigrant, the clubs were assisting in their integration into the receiving society by reducing opportunities for conflict and confrontation."[78] The housing provided differed according to the era and, to a great extent, on the stature of the particular club. Regardless, these accommodations were where players first began not only to reflect on everything that had just transpired and the enormity of what lay ahead of them, but also to interact with the roommates/teammates who would be instrumental in helping them overcome their transitional challenges. The case of the Mozambican player António Brassard, who joined Académica in 1964, illustrates the importance of these teammates and, in particular, those with a shared provenance: "In the beginning, it was not easy. . . . I knew Rui Rodrigues, who had played with me at Primeiro de Maio [in Mozambique]. . . . I went to live with him in a house where there were around twelve other people, all of whom were students. We were football players, but [we] were living in a house that belonged to a lady who accepted all kinds of students. She provided accommodation and food and we paid a monthly amount."[79]

On the other end of the accommodations spectrum, Benfica operated the Casa de Benfica, which had been established during the tenure of Otto Glória, the Brazilian who managed the club from 1954 until 1959. This facility housed single players (and, on Friday evenings prior to games, married players as well), and was where virtually all of the club's African recruits resided. Yet, for Shéu Han, who arrived in Lisbon to play for the Encarnados in 1970, reasonably late on in the colonial period, the accommodations weren't as facilitative to his transition because the club was in the process of discontinuing the use of the Casa. Responding to my question regarding his housing upon arrival, he declared: "That was another challenge. When I arrived on July 16, 1970, I went from the airport to the Benfica house. When I arrived there, the most important players were not living there. There were three or four. Why? Because the club was about to close the house. After two months, they told the players that everyone must find a room to rent, and Benfica would pay the rent."[80]

If Han arrived at a time when the Benfica players' residence was about to cease functioning, Augusto Matine experienced even more acute challenges at the club, but would ultimately rely on his fellow countryman Mário Coluna for the companionship he needed to help him persevere during this difficult transitional period. He shared the following during our interview:

> When I arrived there [at Benfica], I was a slightly built player. . . . I was [physically] weak, but I had the build and the will to improve. Therefore, the coach sent me to stay in a motel for three months without touching the ball, without training, without doing anything. It was painful; my vice was playing football and they put me in a motel. But Coluna, at the end of his training session, used to come pick me up at the motel to walk around. We used to walk around, have lunch, and after that he went home because he was already married. And I was staying there in the motel. After three months, I was not feeling well, I was feeling heavy. I thought that I was no longer myself, that if I kept this up, one day I would not even know how to play football.[81]

Matine continued, indicating his gratitude to Coluna, but also citing his Portuguese coach at Clube Central, back in Mozambique, as someone responsible for helping to prepare him for and ultimately overcome these initial challenges: "It helped having a Portuguese coach at Central because the adjustments and demands in Portugal were tremendously intense. . . .

The language we had in common was extremely important. The Central coach himself had knowledge of what I would encounter in Benfica, and that helped prepare me."[82]

Yet even significant preparation or meaningful camaraderie could be offset by the myriad nonsporting challenges that were beyond players' control. For example, these footballers immediately missed their families, the food they had traditionally consumed, and the warmer weather they had left behind. As Hilário explained during our interview:

> One of the biggest challenges was being away from family, and besides that the food [in Portugal] also presented a problem to adapt to because of all the different ingredients and spices we used. But the biggest challenge we encountered was the weather. Africa has a hot climate year-round, so we weren't used to the cold weather. I even have a good story about that. One day early on in my career in Portugal, I went to play in Belgium, in Brussels, and I went there like I was in Africa, so I was wearing shorts and a T-shirt, but when we got there the temperature was below zero degrees Celsius, so I had to buy a hat and an overcoat because I had no idea about the climate—I thought I was still in Africa! We suffered a lot due to the weather and food.[83]

António Brassard echoed these sentiments, similarly critical of the winter weather in Portugal—in this case in Coimbra, where he played for Académica beginning in 1964: "I joined the first team as a second-option goalkeeper. It was a time of adaptation. In Mozambique, the weather is warm and we were not used to playing in the winter. We did not play with gloves. In Portugal, I had to get used to playing with gloves because of the rain. That was difficult to adapt to—especially in Coimbra, where the winter is rigorous."[84]

Footballing Challenges

Coping with the various voids and attendant social tribulations away from the game undoubtedly constituted formidable personal challenges for the migrant players. But these African footballers also faced major challenges on the pitch, as they adjusted to a much stricter training regimen.

Moreover, unlike in their soccer careers in the colonies, they faced competition for playing time, as the metropole constituted a much higher level within global soccerdom than any they had previously experienced—Portugal was, in many respects, at the very pinnacle of it. Comments made by Mário Coluna, whose arrival at Benfica in 1954 coincided with Otto Glória's, the Lisbon club's new Brazilian manager, highlight some of these footballing challenges: "And pronto! There was no time . . . training began, much harder than what I was accustomed to! Professionalism had its exigencies and everyone had to be available for work—both physical and technical—as Senhor Otto didn't make life easy for anyone."[85] Fellow Mozambican Costa Pereira, who also joined Benfica in 1954, would express similar sentiments to Coluna's, declaring later that same year: "An entire month of training in Lourenço Marques corresponds to a week of training in Lisbon. [José] Naldo [a Benfica squad member, also from Mozambique] has already put on four kilos and even appears taller, because over here 'they mean business.' "[86]

Although Coluna and Pereira were sufficiently talented to make immediate impacts as members of Benfica's first team, other African footballers struggled to secure playing time. Augusto Matine explained this challenge related to his experiences at Benfica in the 1960s, which was a result of the significant divergences between the colonial and the metropolitan football environments: "It was difficult to arrive in Portugal and earn your space in the Benfica squad because Benfica had around eighty players; it had four or five teams. . . . They were the champions of Europe . . . and they molded players, emerging talents from Guiné, Mozambique, et cetera. . . . Therefore, it was difficult for a guy to arrive there and gain a place in the main team."[87] Arriving to play for FC Porto in 1951, the Angolan defender Miguel Arcanjo faced a similar challenge. Despite his significant potential, the eighteen-year-old was considered too light and inexperienced to play first-team football and, thus, had to wait two years before breaking into the club's starting eleven.[88]

The Curious Case of "Ruth Malosso," One of the Greatest to Ever Play the Sport

Finally, it is worth mentioning the extraordinary case of Eusébio's arrival because it underscores the control that Portuguese clubs had over African players and the lengths to which they were willing to go to protect the recruits as they transitioned from the colonies to life in the metropole. This account has been told elsewhere in great detail, and the player himself has shared the events surrounding his arrival in Portugal and the immediate aftermath in countless interviews, but given its relevance to the history that this book reconstructs, I have outlined it below.[89]

After being greeted by Benfica officials at the Lisbon airport on the evening of December 16, 1960, Eusébio was spirited off to the southernmost region of Portugal and placed in a hotel, allegedly to avoid being kidnapped by individuals associated with archrival Sporting, which was actively disputing Benfica's claim to the player. To prevent this possible abduction, the club assigned someone "trustworthy" to him during this period.[90] During the roughly two weeks Eusébio was holed up in the hotel, Benfica officials gave him the code name "Ruth Malosso," so as to avoid drawing any unwanted attention to the player or his whereabouts. Meanwhile, given the clandestine nature of Eusébio's hasty in-country relocation, Sporting officials were busy accusing Benfica of kidnapping the Mozambican recruit, a claim the player would repeatedly refute over the years, including in the following interview from 2004:

> Even today . . . Sporting still says I was "kidnapped"; it's a total lie—lies, lies. Let me explain: how could I like someone who kidnapped me as I love Benfica? Another thing: the contract with Benfica was signed by my mother—I was a minor. I have a photocopy of that contract, Benfica has a photocopy of that contract, the flight to Portugal was paid for by Benfica. There has *never* been *any* document drawn up by Sporting and signed by my mother or me—nothing. I think it was Sporting that wanted to kidnap me! To get me away from this confusion and controversy, Benfica sent me to the Algarve.[91]

What became known as the "Eusébio case" took roughly four months to resolve, with the promising prospect not making his first appearance for Benfica until May 23, 1961. In the meantime, the press filled the void with endless speculation about the disputed recruit. As Ana Santos has written, "The letters exchanged between the institutions [Benfica and

Sporting] became public, but those were only the visible part of a deeper dispute between the clubs. The duration of the contention encouraged the media to generate several stories about the situation, including those about an alleged 'kidnapping' of the player by Benfica."[92] Ultimately, Benfica agreed to send the appropriate fee to Eusébio's former club—a Sporting affiliate—in Lourenço Marques, which, in turn, triggered his formal release, with the Mozambican outfit obligingly sending along his carta de desobrigação. As Eusébio would later recall related to this bizarre, unsettling scenario: "My only fear when I arrived in Portugal was not realizing the extent of the rivalry between Benfica and Sporting—in Mozambique there was a lot of rivalry between the clubs, but here it was even worse, and I felt apprehensive."[93]

By the time African players settled into their new accommodations in the metropole, they had already faced and typically surmounted innumerable challenges. From the pressure they had experienced in the colonies to excel in front of scrutinizing scouts—both formal and informal alike—to receiving their parents' blessings to relocate to Portugal in order to continue playing the game they loved, to the painful good-byes, long journeys, and difficult transitions upon arrival in the metropole, these African footballers had accomplished a great deal before they ever ran out on the pitch for the first time clad in the jerseys of their new clubs.

In the short term, the adoration of the metropolitan fans that the African footballers' on-the-field achievements engendered helped to boost the players' spirits and thereby ease their transitions. An account by Acácio Rosa from 1961 regarding Matateu's early footballing exploits for Belenenses illustrates how powerfully uplifting and transformative initial soccer success could be for the new arrivals and how quickly it could improve their plights in the metropole: "He arrived without ostentation, unknown and simple. . . . The man without pretensions defeats Sporting! Then the public indulged themselves . . . satisfied! It granted him . . . the type of popularity reserved for only a half dozen elected officials, and of those, only Matateu was identified by the People for enthronement."[94]

Yet even early football success couldn't completely eliminate the many challenges migrant footballers faced as they continued their transitions into metropolitan life, both on and off the pitch. In order to confront and attempt to overcome adversity, African players strategically drew upon their past experiences in the colonies and the related knowledge and wisdom they had accumulated. It is to these processes that we turn in the ensuing chapter.

4

Successes, Setbacks, and Strategies

Football and Life in the Metropole

If I knew what Sporting [Clube de Portugal] was all about, I would have packed my bags and come to the metropole a long time ago. At times, of course, I miss my family, my friends, and the memories that I left behind in Lourenço Marques. But a man is a man, and life continues. One has to adapt to the new life that destiny selects for each of us and do what is necessary to honor the family traditions or the bonds of happiness that unite us to our comrades, which time and distance are unable to remove from our thoughts.

—Hilário, in an interview from 1960

The contract was relatively good, but at that time when someone stopped playing football that person couldn't achieve economic independence, so he was lost because he didn't know how to do anything professionally, only football. The money a footballer made at that time was something that one could live well from, but it wasn't anything extraordinary, which is different from today when someone can be a player and not even start for the team, but is still able to achieve financial independence because of the status of the club and the salary paid.

—Mário Wilson, explaining in a 2010 interview why he left
Sporting Clube de Portugal to study and
play for Académica de Coimbra

With the long voyages from Africa behind them, players could begin to settle into their new clubs. Some of the challenges associated with the immediate aftermath of their arrival persisted or even deepened, including the feelings of absence related to their distant friends and families, or even racial discrimination, subtler though it was in the metropole. Many other challenges waned, however, such as those associated with the demanding football training regimens. Yet African players were also confronted with a host of new challenges, including an inability to transfer to clubs beyond Portugal's borders or, at times, even within the country; once-promising careers that began to stagnate; and contract renewal negotiations that left many players feeling powerless toward their employers. In response, the footballers drew upon a set of experiences and related strategies from their upbringings. In particular, the assiduousness they had developed via soccer-facilitated employment opportunities in the colonies would serve them well in the metropole. As Nuno Domingos has argued, "This [work] ethic approximated what would be required of them as professional athletes . . . an ethic that was put to the test in the metropolitan environment."[1] Thus, even as African players negotiated daily life in a foreign environment, they drew upon a labor ethic and a host of associated social strategies that they had learned and cultivated while working as, for example, plumbers, pass-stampers, and railroad employees in the colonies. The constituent tactics—including their solicitation of occupational advice and engagement in secondary migration to improve their short- and long-term prospects—constituted vital methods for footballers who sought to capitalize on these sporting opportunities before their athleticism faded. In the ensuing chapter, these social and occupational processes are examined via a reconstruction of the migrant athletes' lives in the metropole, both on and away from the pitch.

Saudades *and Social Challenges*

Even after settling in to their new environments, players continued to have *saudades* (feelings of loss and remorse), missing the friends and family members they had left behind in Africa, as well as the food, the more forgiving weather, and many other aspects of life in their now-distant home-lands. For some footballers, the feelings of loss grew less acute over time, but for most of the migrants these absences continued to constitute their most significant nonfootballing adversity in the metropole. As Matateu candidly stated to his sibling Vicente Lucas while the two were playing for Belenenses in 1956, "What I would like more than anything is to have Mother here, where we live."[2]

If these brothers lamented their mother's absence in Portugal, they were fortunate to at least have each other to temper this sense of familial privation. Most African players in the metropole were much less fortunate, and perhaps none more so than Augusto Matine, who commented during his first year with Sporting in 1966:

I missed my family. In the first four months alone in a hotel, I was crying every day. I knew that I had improved my living conditions, but I had to pay the high price of separation from my family and friends with whom I had lived for a long time. I started to have hallucinations, accompanied by pain, especially the first Christmas. That first Christmas was painful for me because I was living with Benfica's youth and junior players. At Christmastime they went home. Each one went home: if he was from Porto, he went to Porto; if he was from Guimarães, he went to Guimarães. I stayed alone because I was Mozambican. The other Mozambicans who were there were already married; therefore, I stayed alone in the hotel. That took a lot out of me.[3]

If African players' words powerfully highlight their sense of loss and isolation, their ameliorative actions were often just as revealing. Many of the athletes attempted to stay connected with their friends and families via telephone calls or written correspondence, but physically reconnecting was the ultimate aim. Personal reunions were made during the summer off-seasons as frequently as possible, as many metropolitan clubs sanctioned and even funded annual trips home for African squad members. For those players who weren't able to return home for a series of years following their departure, homecomings were even more emotional. For example, Jorge Calado, a Mozambican who played for Benfica in the 1960s, before moving on to Leixões, Belenenses, and União de Tomar, replied to a question posed to him in 1968 about the happiest moment in his life: "Returning home to Lourenço Marques, after four years away. Four years that seemed like four centuries. The hugs of my parents and friends made me cry."[4] Eusébio echoed the importance of these reunions: "In the first years of my career, I would go to Mozambique during every one of my vacations to spend them with my family. Before the last game each year [in Portugal], I would pack my bags and get my tickets and then I would tell my friends, 'See you in fifteen days.' I would never spend a month, only fifteen days, but it was great because I was with my family and friends and I missed them. I was eighteen, nineteen, twenty, or twenty-one years old, and every vacation I had I would spend with my family because we were very close."[5]

Saudades for friends, family members, and their homelands also manifested themselves in players' postfootball intentions. Although many plans changed with the outbreak of civil conflicts in Mozambique and Angola following, or even preceding, independence, thereby compelling African players to remain in the metropole, during their athletic careers many of them candidly expressed their desire to return home upon retirement. Miguel Arcanjo, the Angolan fullback who starred for FC Porto beginning in the early 1950s, stated during a 1956 interview: "I was hoping to go to Africa last year, but I couldn't because of the FC Porto [summer] tour to Brazil and Venezuela. However, as soon as I can, I will go to see my mother and my siblings, whom I haven't hugged in a long time. . . . I want to play football for as long as I can, then go back to my homeland."[6] Or, as fellow Angolan José Maria declared in the late 1960s: "My dream is simple: I intend to buy a building together with my brother in Luanda, so that, when one day we return, we will be able to live peacefully for the rest of our lives."[7] Unfortunately for José Maria and his brother, Conceição, teammates at Vitória de Setúbal, the civil war that commenced prior to independence in 1975 and raged until 2002 rendered life anything *but* "peaceful" for virtually every Angolan.

Racial Discrimination in the Metropole—
Subtle or Even Imperceptible?

During my interviews with former players, they uniformly indicated that they didn't personally experience racism while in the metropole—in conspicuous contrast to their experiences in the colonies. I contend that their status as athletes, many of whom were propelling Portuguese club teams and the national team to unprecedented levels, coupled with the paucity of Africans in the metropole and their attendant exoticism, largely insulated these athletes from this type of discrimination. But of course racism did exist in Portugal—then, as it does now. For example, interviews of players following independence reveal that some of them felt that their salaries were inferior to the wages paid to their Portuguese teammates, though it remains unclear whether any compensatory discrepancies that may have existed were attributable to racial discrimination or to the clubs' rather cynical calculations that players coming from Africa would be grateful simply for the opportunity and, thus, not as focused on their incomes. Finally, it's important to resist extrapolating the experiences of these African footballers onto members of other racial minority groups in Portugal during this period, including other Africans. Historical reconstructions of the prevailing racial sentiments toward, and experiences of, other, albeit numerically small, segments of the metropolitan population await further research; an account of African soccer players constitutes but one modest contribution to this broader effort.

In Compensation

Examining players' salaries does offer insight into issues of racial inequality, but this endeavor is also fraught with analytical problems, as clubs don't open their files to even the most persistent researchers, and exact income levels from decades past are, in general, extremely difficult to identify. Moreover, what salary discrepancies do exist are attributable to a host of factors, namely, talent. For example, when I asked Nuro Americano, who played for Benfica in the early 1970s, about this issue, he replied, "Yes, there were different salary categories, but not based on race. Eusébio was Eusébio; he was playing on the senior team, he was in the national team, and he had his own status. The rest of us—as we were but 'boys' comparatively—we had our own salary category."[8] Fernando Gomes, who played in both Portugal and Angola, also discounted any suggestions that Portuguese players earned more based on race: "The African players who came here [to Portugal] would receive the same salary [as a Portuguese player]. The first black player who came to Sentrensa to play was from Guiné. . . . They would make the same as me or the other players; it wasn't that they were black, and, therefore, they would make less."[9]

Although my informants may have been dismissive about race generating wage discrepancies, former Sporting forward António Joaquim Dinis, who hailed from Luanda, admonished metropolitan clubs for exploiting African talent, suggesting—though never explicitly invoking—racial discrimination, while also absolving the Portuguese public. Speaking in the late 1970s, he declared:

> The majority of the Angolan players who immigrate to Portugal never experience a sense of satisfaction. Not because they lacked a warm reception by the public, but rather because of the attitudes and behavior of the patrons of Portuguese football. Angolans and Mozambicans have continually suffered shameful exploitation by the big clubs. I signed a very inexpensive contract with Sporting. I won the National Championship and the Taça de Portugal [in the early 1970s]; I am an international [squad member], and, in spite of all this, I used to earn less than the team's reservists.[10]

Unfortunately, it's impossible to substantiate Dinis's claims, though the conviction with which he spoke lends the allegations significant plausibility. Writing decades later, authors João Nuno Coelho and Francisco Pinheiro echoed Dinis's accusations:

> African players, especially in Portugal, where currently they are quite numerous, are not—on the level of salaries—privileged. On that front, much was lacking. . . . Dinis isn't an isolated case. "I say clearly"—affirmed one of his colleagues from Sporting— "the player who came from Angola or from Mozambique is exploited. First, they made him proposals, some promises that are never fulfilled. And once he signed, he became a 'prisoner.' He has to choose between

unemployment or [an ashamed] return home." In the eyes of the patrons of the clubs, the African from overseas has difficulty finding work . . . outside the metropole [this is true because the resources of the clubs from the "colonies" are very modest]. Consequently, he will accept all the conditions that are proposed.[11]

In Society

If certain players and observers of the game accused the clubs of racial exploitation, these same critics failed to level charges of discrimination against the general public in Portugal. In addition to broad tolerance of the players, black African footballers regularly dated and even married Portuguese women, though there were occasional protestations by relatives of some of these girlfriends-cum-wives during the courting process. Moreover, as African footballers began to produce on the field, they quickly became pitchmen for an array of products, suggesting that companies weren't concerned that racist sentiments within the Portuguese citizenry would jeopardize prospective sales.

An exoticization of black Africans in the metropole partially explains this apparent racial tolerance. Indeed, Lilica Boal, a black student from Cape Verde who arrived in Portugal in 1958 to continue her studies, indicated in a recent interview that "there wasn't racism in Portugal, but [Portuguese] mothers with ill children would hand us [Africans] the children because they believed if a black person touched a child, it would cure them."[12] Uninformed sentiments of this type were accentuated by the extremely small number of Africans in Portugal during the colonial period—especially outside urban areas—rendering the migrants a type of human novelty. Indeed, speaking in 2011, Fernando Gomes suggested that the seeming absence of racism toward these players may well have been based on this erstwhile socioracial phenomenon:

> There were no issues with the African players. They were popular players, because, for example, today you see black people everywhere [in Portugal], but at that time blacks were a rare sight so everyone wanted to know if the blacks were nice or not nice, if they were something else or they were not. Therefore, black players were naturally popular, which made it easy for them to integrate into social circles.

Back in those days, there was a huge admiration for soccer—people would go to their jobs, go to church, and go attend soccer matches, and that was it; there were no other forms of entertainment, there was no television or Internet.[13]

Nuro Americano's comments further confirm this type of social curiosity. Responding to my question about racial prejudice in Lisbon, he stated: "I never experienced or felt it. I grew up in Pemba, a small community, but among white people. Blacks and whites, we played without any problem. I went to Portugal and found the same thing. I was even happy when people arrived and found me there and saw my skin color because it was not any black man who managed to go to Portugal at that time. They used to touch my hair and I was happy, far from thinking about racism."[14]

Demographics notwithstanding, Africans during this period confirmed the comparative dearth of racial discrimination in the metropole, vis-à-vis its pervasiveness and intensity in the colonies. Indeed, even as thousands of young Portuguese men began returning home from the colonial wars against guerrillas associated with the various African nationalist organizations in the 1960s and 1970s, wounded physically and often mentally, animosity was never directed at the migrant footballers. As Augusto Matine indicated during our interview, "It was easy to adapt to Portuguese society. . . . Contrary to what was happening in Africa [Mozambique] regarding racism, in Portugal we did not feel racial discrimination because we were a minority and soccer players were respected in all aspects, and so we did not feel that animosity. . . . Even the supporters of other clubs never provoked or denigrated us."[15] Elsewhere, Matine has echoed these comments, citing the contributions African players had made to Portuguese football: "The Portuguese were curious about us; we were treated kindly. After all, it was we who took Portugal out of its marginal position in [global] football. It was we, of Mozambique, who did that."[16]

Given his unparalleled contributions, perhaps it's not surprising that Eusébio, too, failed to experience any sustained racial discrimination while playing in the metropole. Responding to the question "Did you ever find racial prejudice in your footballing career in Portugal?" during a 2004 interview, the Mozambican great replied, "No. I never encountered anything—here we are in the twenty-first century, and you cannot go to a football match without hearing these so-called hooligans shouting racist taunts about black footballers—when I played for Benfica, almost all the clubs had black players and there was never any problem. I could go out, go to the cinema, and no one said anything bad; I never felt that I was different. . . . Benfica's greatest successes were always with Portuguese-speaking players from Angola and Mozambique."[17]

Perhaps the greatest testament to the racial tolerance that players encountered in the metropole is the case of David Júlio, née Julius. A black South African, Júlio first migrated to Mozambique to play in Lourenço Marques before attracting the attention of Sporting Clube de Portugal and making the jump to the metropole in 1957. By 1960, he had obtained his Portuguese citizenship and was a member of the national squad. That year, he commented on these remarkable developments: "I never imagined that by coming to Portugal I was going to stay here. Now, I am naturalized. I won't leave here. I feel great, I and those close to me. Here, I have found friends, colleagues, good managers. . . . I feel like this is my nation and Sporting is a great club. . . . I'm making progress in the eyes of others and speaking Portuguese and I hope that before the end of the year I will be dominating the language, without any difficulties."[18]

On the Pitch: Challenges, Successes, and Setbacks

If players encountered a range of challenges in the metropole away from the game, they also faced myriad trials in their new footballing environments. The migrant athletes newly had to contend with playing on grass (as opposed to dirt) fields; intrasquad competition for playing time; a much more rigorous training regimen; positional assignments based upon race; injuries and other physical setbacks; and, for many, conscription into the military, which often took them away from their respective club teams (even if many of them did experience considerable success on Portugal's military football squad). In spite of these challenges, numerous African players realized success for both club and country, securing trophies and setting records that still stand and, ultimately, achieving legendary sporting status. Yet it would be misleading to suggest that footballers hailing from Africa met with much greater or lesser success than did their Portuguese counterparts. For every successful African player, there were many others from the continent who failed to thrive in the metropole. And, although some of them helped propel their clubs and the national team to unprecedented levels, the majority of their teammates were Portuguese, and many of the latter were just as instrumental to these sporting achievements.

Demanding Regimens: "Professionalism Is No Joke"

Jacinto João made the above statement regarding the seriousness of the football regimen in the metropole during a 1969 interview while playing for Vitória de Setúbal. In fact, numerous African footballers echoed this sentiment upon arriving in the metropole. Professional football in Portugal was, indeed, no laughing matter. Players' preparatory experiences in the top colonial leagues did help temper, at least somewhat, the demands of the game in Portugal. Indeed, Domingos has argued that "the development of the sport in the capital of Mozambique guaranteed for these athletes a technical and tactical apprenticeship and a minimum physical preparation that facilitated their integration into the more professionalized environment of metropolitan football."[19] This preparation notwithstanding, African players endured much more rigorous training sessions in Portugal and newly stringent regulations away from the pitch to ensure that they maintained proper fitness. Moreover, some metropolitan managers were more demanding than others, instituting conditioning regimens that were even more exacting. Overall, although African footballers typically adjusted well to metropolitan football, this transition often included a great deal of physical discomfort.

For most African players, the training regimen was significantly more challenging and relentless than what they had experienced in the colonies, especially when off-the-pitch conditioning and health requirements are considered. For example, during the same interview cited above, Jacinto João remarked that the training demands constituted the major impediment to his footballing success: "Only one obstacle came in my path: I was used to Luanda and only practicing when I could. In Setúbal, we work every day and it is very hard. I soon realized that I needed to take it seriously and honestly and demonstrate an unbreakable will to fight and to surpass all difficulties imposed by the training system established by the club and the coaches."[20]

Training regimens included rigorous daily practice sessions as well as highly demanding weekly routines. Mondays were often the only off-days for players; the other six days of the week belonged to the club. Hilário, who played for Sporting, explained, "Monday was our day off; we could do whatever we want. But Tuesday was a work day, so we would go to bed by 11:00 p.m. [on Monday nights] because we would have practice in the morning, and Thursdays we would go into concentration [at the team facility] for Thursday, Friday, and Saturday if we were to play on Sunday. If we had a game on Wednesday for a European competition, we couldn't go out. . . . If we wanted to go to a club or disco, that had to be done on a Monday."[21]

Although Mário Coluna played for Benfica and Hilário at Sporting, the training schedules for the two clubs appear to have been virtually identical. Yet, in accessing Coluna's comments on the subject, it's also clear that individual managers could render the regimen more or less stern: "Otto Glória [the Brazilian manager of Benfica from 1954 to 1959] changed many things via the discipline he imposed at Benfica, including the [practice] schedule, meals, when you could eat and when you couldn't, the hours of rest, etc. Only on Monday were liberties permitted, but even so, at the Tuesday afternoon sessions, the coaches pushed due to the necessity of disintoxicating the excesses of the previous evening. Béla Guttmann, Glória's successor, was even more of a disciplinarian."[22]

Confirming this restrictive environment in metropolitan soccerdom, a 1954 issue of the sporting journal *Guardian Desportivo* featured the Regulamento Geral da Secção de Futebol, a document that "established a series of norms regulating a player's life, his schedules, his activities, and options."[23] In one passage, the regulation states:

It is expressively forbidden to go to places that intrinsically have a pernicious environment—dance halls, gambling establishments, etc.—that considerably reduce the moral and physical cleanliness so important to sports activity. These establishments generate for the player an inaccurate notion of an easy and comfortable life, and corrupt his sense of duty, prompting him to take part in gambling and to perpetrate . . . excesses, including the abusive use of alcoholic drinks and smoking, which go against the minimum conditions necessary to produce an ideal physical performance.[24]

Although the spirit of these regulations was strong and influenced club policies and, thus, players' behavior, they were ultimately just guidelines or suggestions. African players' selective engagement with these so-called regulations is well illustrated by Matateu, who played at Belenenses from 1951 to 1964 and then with a series of less prominent Portuguese clubs until 1974. Perpetuating a penchant he had developed in Mozambique that he believed enhanced his performance, the striker was extremely fond of beer—before, after, and even during matches! Yet, even at forty-one years of age, Matateu was still contributing, scoring twenty-one goals for Amora FC over the course of the 1968–1969 season, and informing the sporting paper *A Bola*: "I'm forty-one years old, but I look like [I'm] nineteen, because I'm conserved in beer. . . . Believe it or not, when I don't drink beer, I'm not the same. I feel badly and my performance is always inferior. . . . It's true—if I didn't drink beer, I would have hung up my boots long ago."[25] Rumored to have habitually hidden beers in toilet cisterns in the clubhouse, there was also a memorable episode in which these "pernicious" beverages apparently facilitated a key Belenenses victory. According to Vicente Lucas, Matateu's younger brother and teammate:

Once, we went to play at the Stadium of Light [Benfica's stadium], and my brother approached the manager and insisted that he give him two beers before the game. Matateu said—"I drink two beers and I kill Benfica!" [Fernando] Riera [the club's Chilean manager] responded to him: "If I give you the beers, rather I will be killing you," to which Matateu responded that it wouldn't affect him poorly because he was used to it. Riera packed up two bottles of beer and gave them to my brother, but asked him to drink them in a place where no one else could see. I remember that before the game, Costa Pereira, the goalkeeper for Benfica, said that Matateu had never scored a goal against him. Matateu drank the two beers and I saw the confidence that Costa Pereira would come to see and that would bite him, because Matateu was determined to score a goal. And he did score the goal that gave Belenenses the victory, scoring from a very difficult angle.[26]

Competition for a Spot

As outlined in the previous chapter, players often struggled upon arrival in Portugal given the higher levels of ability of their new teammates. Even those African players who would go on to star for club and country often experienced these types of setbacks in the early years of their metropolitan careers. The most successful footballers quickly regained their confidence, though, and given their prodigious talent, surged forward, quickly cementing spots on the first team. Many others, however, were unable to secure consistent playing time. For African players who rarely made the headlines, soccer in the metropole often meant a place on the bench or, worse, on the reserve squads, or even a humiliating trip back to the colonies following an unsuccessful stint in metropolitan football.

Santana, a midfielder from Angola, experienced many of the highs and lows associated with heightened competition for playing time. Arriving in 1954 to play for Benfica, Santana was suffering from rheumatism and kidney issues and was actually cited and fined by the club for failing to "fully contribute in the manner expected." Once his condition was properly diagnosed, club officials forgave him and rescinded the fine, but he still struggled to break into the first team, playing with the reserves his first three years at the club and again following the end of the 1957–1958 campaign, after spending that season with the first team. After this setback, Benfica's manager, Otto Glória, apparently informed Santana, "You are a good player, but you are at a dead end at Benfica. There are men on the team who have paid their dues and are not leaving their spots anytime soon. Your youth is going to fly by, time is ruthless, and it makes you lose your skills. Do you want to try your odds at another club? If you want, Benfica will loan or release you to Tirsense. Think about it and tell me later what you think."[27] Resolute, Santana refused to leave the club and ultimately did earn a spot on the first team, spending a remarkable fourteen seasons in total with the Eagles, including five with the national team, suiting up 162 times for Benfica and netting an impressive 79 times.

Other players never made it at the most competitive clubs such as Benfica, but many did find success with smaller outfits. For example, the Angolan forward Domingos António da Silva, popularly known as Mascarenhas, arrived in 1956 to play for Benfica, but after two unsuccessful seasons during which he made only two appearances for the first team, he was shipped off to FC Barreirense, based in the city of Barreiro south of Lisbon. However, in this new setting, Mascarenhas earned significant playing time, and he took advantage of it. Following three successful years there, the "big clubs" renewed their interest and the Angolan agreed to return to the capital, but this time with Benfica's crosstown rival, Sporting. During his three seasons with the Lions, he flourished, most notably scoring six times in a UEFA Cup Winners' Cup match against the Cypriot side, APOEL FC, which remains a European competition record, and netting again in the final to help secure the trophy for Sporting. Ultimately, the allegedly temperamental Mascarenhas enjoyed a seventeen-year career in Portugal that was marked by inconsistency, though punctuated by significant success.[28]

Many other African players who made the jump to the metropole similarly experienced this type of inconsistency, their careers marked by occasional success, but mostly mediocrity as they moved from club to club, unable to secure regular playing time. José Pérides, a midfielder from Tête, in Mozambique, was one such player. Having arrived in Portugal in 1954 to play for Académica, he spent most of his time on the club's junior squad, appearing only briefly for the first team. Yet, after two seasons in Coimbra, he had still managed to demonstrate enough potential to attract the attention of Sporting, though he would subsequently enjoy little success after joining the Lisbon club. In 1957, Pérides remarked on his limited usage by the Lions, while still remaining dedicated to the cause: "Sporting hasn't used me that much in the current season, in the first team. However, whenever I have been called on to defend the colors of my team I have given all that I had, like the honest professional that I am proud to be."[29]

Many other players had careers in metropolitan football that are impossible to reconstruct due to their brevity and the absence of any noteworthy achievements. These athletes remained in Portugal only briefly before returning, often begrudgingly, to Africa. And still other African footballers, of course, never made it to Portugal, despite their promise. Indeed, even players with connections in metropolitan soccerdom and star status in the colonies often lacked the requisite talent. For example, following the 1959–1960 season, as was his custom each summer, Sporting star Hilário returned to Lourenço Marques. At this time, his younger brother, Orlando, was "one of the stars of Mozambican football, playing for Sporting da Beira. . . . When Hilário arrived, Orlando spoke with him about his chances of also going to Portugal to play. Hilário was clear, and clarified: "'The football profession is extremely difficult, even for those who, like Orlando, display great potential.' Hilário, as an older brother, spoke frankly."[30] Eight years later, when this account of the siblings' interaction was published in an issue of *Ídolos*, Orlando was still at Sporting de Beira, destined never to make the leap to the metropole.

Racialism within the Sport

If African players experienced minimal racial prejudice away from the game while residing in Portugal, the sporting arena was generally free of this type of discrimination as well. For example, as established above, salaries were typically commensurate with players' footballing abilities, even during the early years of their careers. Moreover, the practice of "stacking," in which "players are disproportionately assigned to certain positions based on ascribed racial or ethnic characteristics," doesn't appear to have been nearly as pronounced in Portugal as it was, for example, in France.[31] Nor did African players have to endure the racially motivated taunting or hurled projectiles in Portuguese soccer stadiums that they occasionally experienced elsewhere.[32] Yet to claim that racism, or at least racialism, was absent from the sport would be inaccurate. Even if stacking wasn't widespread in the Portuguese league, close observers of the game, including many in the media, invariably commented on players' physical, or "natural" and "instinctual" traits rather than their understanding of the game, suggesting the former compensated for the latter. This comparatively subtle form of racial prejudice inferred that Africans primarily succeeded at the sport due to innate features that were somehow divinely denied Portuguese-born players, whose success was supposedly predicated solely on hard work.[33]

This type of racialist commentary reflected prevailing, contemporaneous sentiments that race bestowed certain physical and intellectual attributes in abundance while withholding others. The following piece that appeared in the journal *Mundo de Aventuras* in the 1950s is indicative: "Fantastic in the short dribble, possessor of a notable violence on the pitch, and a man who shoots powerfully with either foot, Matateu is a force of nature. There is a radiance of happiness on the pitch with an aura of inno-cence when he plays, deriving from the distant African lands of his birth."[34] Of course, the footballing traits of Matateu that the piece describes were, by all contemporaneous accounts, accurate and, thus, were justly con-veyed. But the insistence on the player's physical abilities, coupled with the ensuing passage that reduces his demeanor to that of an oblivious child, reflects the racialist sentiments of the era. By way of a rebuttal, Domingos has rightfully argued, "The recognition of the [Lusophone] African play-ers' technical and tactical expertise is a crucial element of interpretation that leads to the avoidance of the error of considering their qualities as the result of natural gifts. African players intelligently mastered modern football's dynamic."[35]

Without analyzing an individual footballer's various positional abil-ities, that player's teammates, and the judgment of his manager, it's im-possible to confirm the presence of stacking in the Portuguese league. Conversely, evidence of this racialist phenomenon does appear to exist in the French context. As Alegi has argued regarding the usage of African players in France, "Black footballers were perceived as fast, agile, and reac-tive, but lacking in leadership skills, tactical intelligence, and self-control. . . . Stacking in France led to Africans being regularly played in wide posi-tions, or as strikers."[36] Alegi goes on to explain that, by extension, "stacking harmed generations of black players and European teams . . . thus pre-cluding many talented individuals from advancing into coaching careers and football administration."[37] To evince this practice, Alegi cites the fact that during the 1950s and '60s, 49 of the 75 sub-Saharan players, or 65.3 percent, in the top two divisions in France were strikers.[38] Lanfranchi and Taylor echo Alegi's comments, declaring that "Africans were considered, almost unfailingly, as instinctive players. They played the game but easily gave up. They were nice to watch but not really efficient. . . . Such attitudes were reflected in the positions and responsibilities given to Africans on the field of play. Most were employed as wingers or full-backs, two positions on the margins of the field said to require 'natural' qualities rather than thought, vision and reflection."[39]

Although many African players in Portugal played in wide positions, as strikers, or as fullbacks, seemingly just as many were midfielders, cen-tral defenders, or even goalkeepers. Nor were Africans being placed in these positions only in the waning years of the colonial period. One of the first African players to travel to the metropole, Mário Wilson, was a central defender, while Mário Coluna, who followed Wilson from Mozambique just five years thereafter, in 1954, was a midfielder. In fact, Wilson was moved from attack to central defense only *after* he arrived in the metropole, as was the accomplished Vicente Lucas, who played for Belenenses from 1954 until 1967.

Additionally, many African footballers eventually captained their club teams, as well as the national squad, including both Coluna and Wilson; the latter was so revered that early in his Académica career, he was given, and carried well, the nickname "the Captain." Similarly, Coluna remarkably assumed the captaincy of Benfica even before he was in line to do so: the armband was typically passed to the next-oldest player at the club. However, Otto Glória, the Lisbon club's manager at the time, deemed Coluna a "natural leader"—an example of an African player being commended (and rewarded) for attributes other than his physical gifts.[40]

Moreover, many of these former footballers—including both Wilson and Coluna—joined the coaching ranks following the conclusion of their playing careers, overseeing both club and national squads in Portugal and the former African colonies. Thus, although Alegi's claims that stacking precluded coaching opportunities for African footballers appear to be valid in other contexts, the Portuguese/Lusophone African example problematizes a universal application of this contention.[41] Quite simply, there's no evidence that Portuguese clubs handicapped themselves by stacking, nor were the migrant players—from the earliest arrivals, to those footballers who reached the metropole just prior to the conclusion of the colonial period—impeded as they sought, and secured, prominent coaching positions.

Duty Calls

Although racial discrimination didn't inhibit African players from propelling their metropolitan clubs to significant success, military duty could and often did. During the period under examination, many European militaries fielded soccer teams that were quite competitive, with their squads traveling throughout the continent and, ultimately, across the globe, to battle their martial counterparts on the pitch. Although the military typically excluded *mestiço* (mulatto) and black African footballers from duty due to their potential subversiveness, once the wars for independence began they were required to serve, just like Portuguese players and nonplayers alike. Metropolitan clubs were unable to deny the armed services access to their players—even their most valuable ones. Moreover, as Mário Torres remarked during our interview, "The generals, captains, and commanders of the army . . . would look for a football player who was of age to join the army team. . . . The army would go after the players of Benfica, Porto, and other teams."[42] Even if conscription was unavoidable, the Portuguese military sent very few African-born players to the colonies to fight, as their loyalty was still doubted within certain circles of the regime. Rather, most of these migrant athletes were safely stationed at bases in Portugal and, depending on the magnitude of the individual footballer, clubs could try to arrange with military officials for the draftee to be assigned to a base near the team's headquarters so that his soccer contributions could continue uninterrupted. Most famously, Eusébio served at a base proximate to Lisbon and, thus, he remained with his club, Benfica, while also playing for the military team. However, many other players didn't enjoy this type of preferential arrangement and therefore lost time from their professional careers.

Most African footballers resented military duty not because they disliked the rigor associated with service—in many ways, it resembled their soccer practice regimens—but because it interrupted or otherwise detracted from their footballing careers. For example, after spending time at Benfica under Béla Guttmann in the 1960s as a reserve player, the Mozambican midfielder Jorge Calado finally broke into the first team. Yet, shortly thereafter, he was notified that he was obligated to serve thirty-two months in the military. Although club officials arranged for him to serve at Queluz, a base in the greater Lisbon area, which enabled him to continue on at Benfica, Calado felt that the time in the military "interfered with his rhythm and prevented him from demonstrating his full potential."[43]

In other cases, military duty took players too far away from the headquarters of their club teams, precluding their participation even if, as stated above, most of the conscripts remained within Portugal. The career of Augusto Matine, who played for both Benfica and Setúbal during the colonial era, was disrupted in just this manner. The former midfielder from Mozambique explained to me:

I had military service while in Portugal. . . . In my case, I went from Lisbon to Porto. And I served in Coimbra, where I did four months. From Coimbra, I went to Porto for specialization. . . . So, it was not possible to play [for Lisbon-based Benfica]. It took eight months before Benfica succeeded in having me transferred. . . . Benfica had to find a serviceman interested in serving in Porto so that he could exchange places with me. . . . While in the military, I played for the military selecção, which was the last military team that Portugal fielded.[44]

For some African players, military duty did not meaningfully disrupt their club careers, despite its potential to do so. Although Eusébio's case is perhaps the best-known example of an African footballer/conscript performing "double duty," there were many others. For example, Mário Coluna served in the armed forces while continuing to play for Benfica, explaining: "I served the military in Portugal. I also played for the military team at the international level. And I was also able to continue playing for Benfica. I began serving in 1955 when I was twenty years old. . . . At that time, it was not necessary to go far away to serve in the military. Moreover, we had one administrator [at Benfica] who was a military officer. It was easy; there was no war in that time; it was not necessary to go to Porto or to the other provinces."[45] Mário Wilson similarly indicated that such arrangements were reasonably easy to make prior to the outbreak in the early 1960s of the wars for independence in the African colonies: "Académica would have players in the military, but when the club needed those players in the A or B team, the military would release them because there were no wars at that time. Later, when the independence movements began fighting in the colonies, some African players were selected to go to Africa."[46]

Even after the conflicts commenced, it remained possible for African footballers to continue playing for both the military and their respective club teams. For example, former Académica player Rui Rodrigues suggested that although clubs couldn't refuse to release a player for military service, elements within the clubs' administrations and the military could conspire to facilitate double duty: "I played for the military team at the age of twenty-six [in 1969]. We played there to avoid going to war. It was possible to play for both Académica and the military team. I was assigned to the Oeiras military facility [outside Lisbon]. That unit did not even technically exist anymore, but they put us there to make it seem as if we were doing something in the army! I went to play against Holland; we went to play in Funchal [Madeira]; we played against Spain in the Estádio da Luz [in Lisbon]."[47] Via these types of arrangements, Portuguese clubs retained their best players, while the military team also benefited. Indeed, Mário Torres, an Angolan midfielder who played on the military squad in the 1950s and later served in Mozambique, boasted to me during our interview: "We had a great team, the military team could have gone head-to-head with any European national team at that time."[48] Given the talent on these squads, Torres may well have been right.

Challenges Overcome: Footballing Success

Potentially lost in a discussion of the prodigious challenges African soccer migrants faced is the significant *success* many of them achieved, which, in turn, helped the players to integrate socially. Eusébio is, by far, the most widely known of these African footballers, but many others were remarkable talents who regularly hoisted domestic and international trophies, led the domestic league in various statistical categories, and continue to hold various records long after their retirements. In fact, many of them achieved legendary status while they were still playing, adored by the fans. Consider an account of Matateu that appeared in a 1952 issue of *Ecos de Belém*: "The truth is that on this past Sunday, at the end of the 'Belenenses-Sporting' match, Matateu, after a brilliant exhibition, was carried in triumph from the field to the dressing room, a demonstration of 'Belenenses' congratulating themselves, congratulations well-deserved, especially as the club celebrates yet another anniversary of its glorious existence."[49]

African footballers' celebrity also reached the colonies, where throngs of fans typically greeted them upon their returns to the continent. Although this book isn't intended as yet another encomium to some of the most celebrated of these African footballers, it is important to remember that some of them were among the best in the world, while many others made important domestic and continental sporting contributions that continue to be remembered, and exalted, by fans in Portugal and farther afield.

Just as supporters around the world celebrated the footballers' accomplishments, the players themselves were grateful for this support, and also for the opportunities they had to travel the world and to play the game they loved, while never forgetting their African origins. Speaking in 1956, six years into his thirteen-year Benfica career, the white Angolan striker José Águas emotionally declared:

> I owe to Benfica everything that I am in life. My independence as a man and my means of living . . . I hope will constitute a good base for the future. When I remember what a little insignificant boy that I was, when I came from Lobito, six years ago, and I see myself today in my house, married and almost a father, traveling to various continents and with knowledge, relations, and happiness that are my pride, it is then that I perceive how much I owe to football, and especially, to Benfica, which went to search for me in Africa. I am able to guarantee that Benfica will be my only club. I am twenty-six years old, and I hope to play until my thirties; after, I will return to my homeland, of which I already have many *saudades*. I went there in 1952, for a visit, but I haven't returned since. I will make my life there, but Benfica will continue to live inside of me, with the same intensity and the same passion that I already felt before coming, and which has been reinforced with unforgettable memories. My son will know how much I owe Benfica and I will feel very happy if he, one day, leaves our homeland to come to wear the glorious encarnada jersey, in which I have spent the best moments of my sporting life.[50]

Changes of Scenery: Transfer Challenges and Opportunities

Although metropolitan clubs enjoyed a great deal of control over their players—Portuguese and African alike—footballers could request a loan or transfer to another squad in the hopes of improving their plights. In many cases, a lack of playing time was the impetus for such an entreaty. But there existed a much wider array of motivations. For example, some African players wanted to join a more competitive squad in order to achieve further sporting success and, often, for superior wages. Irrespective of the particular reason, clubs could—and often did—reject the requests, refusing to issue the requisite *carta de desobrigação* (release) to facilitate a player's formal disengagement from the team. In these instances, players often complained that they were "prisoners," especially prior to the 1960s, before the game was finally professionalized in Portugal and the players reactively formed a union, albeit a relatively toothless one. Yet, even into the 1970s, clubs still had ways of pressuring and, thereby, controlling their players. For example, Shéu Han heard stories that in the months leading up to the coup d'état in Portugal in 1974, some clubs were declaring to their players: " 'Here is the contract, and there is a boat [heading to the wars in the colonies]. If you sign the contract, you are fine; if not, you may be on the boat to the army.' If you signed the contract, you were guaranteed to stay in Portugal. If not, you might go to fight in the wars in Africa."[51]

Many African footballers had their transfer requests denied during this period, as their clubs remained eager to continue utilizing their exhibited talent or trying to mine their potential. However, other requests issued by these players were granted, their clubs determining that the players in question were expendable or simply that the cash available by selling them outweighed their value to the squad. Having received the consent of their clubs to transfer, African players were able to engage in this form of secondary migration to reach destinations that they deemed would ultimately constitute better fits for them. But this manner of repositioning oneself did have its limits. Of particular frustration to many African players was their inability to sign for outfits beyond Portugal's borders, primarily due to political reasons. Most sensationally, Salazar declared Eusébio a "national asset" in order to preclude his transfer to one of a number of covetous Italian clubs (addressed in detail in chapter 5).

The case of Bernardo da Velha, who arrived in Portugal from Guiné in 1962 and would go on to play for Sporting, Porto, Guimarães, Boavista, and, following the toppling of the Estado Novo regime in 1974, Sporting Clube de Espinho and Leixões, illustrates some of the challenges players faced in the realm of transfers and loans. After signing what he thought was a one-year contract with Sporting, he was allegedly surprised to learn that at the conclusion of the 1962–1963 campaign, the club considered him still legally committed for two additional years. He consequently appealed to the national football federation for his release, a process that took a full year to resolve. In the meantime, despite his considerable success at Sporting, the other clubs that were originally interested in him apparently no longer desired his signature, suggesting collusion. Ultimately, he was able to transfer to FC Porto in 1964, where he played under Otto Glória. But by then he had also been assigned to military duty. Incorporated into a Lisbon-based unit, he was forced to travel to Porto on the weekends for his matches. Following knee surgery, da Velha made his way back into Porto's starting team, but again found himself engaged in a contractual dispute with his employer. Moreover, he had, meanwhile, been invited to sign with a club in Mexico.[52] However, Porto allegedly requested too much money from the North American outfit to secure da Velha's release, which may have simply constituted a creative way to reject a transfer that the Portuguese government wasn't going to sanction anyway. Ultimately, da Velha re-signed with Porto, unable to secure the coveted carta until 1969, at which point he played for a series of less accomplished Portuguese clubs before finally retiring in 1976.

Da Velha certainly wasn't alone in attracting interest from foreign clubs. Over the years, squads based elsewhere in Europe or even in North or South America expressed their interest in signing some of the most talented African footballers playing in Portugal. For example, Matateu received overtures from Reims and Santos; Hilário from Inter Milan, Real Madrid, Vasco da Gama, and Botafogo; Augusto Matine from Cordova; Iaúca from AC Milan and Feyenoord; and so on.[53] Yet these advances almost always came to nothing; African players primarily moved domestically within Portugal or, in many cases, not at all. According to Hilário, "When I arrived in Portugal in 1958, soccer was still an amateur affair. After that, in the 1960s, we players created a union and soccer became a profession. But before that change, all contracts had a lifetime duration. For example, if I entered into a contract with Sporting, the only way I could leave the club was if Sporting was seeking to trade or loan me out. . . . Later, contracts were limited to three years."[54] Rather conveniently, the Portuguese clubs insisted that the offers arriving from abroad weren't financially sufficient, or that these clubs were simply uninterested in selling; although the main Portuguese teams weren't as deep-pocketed as major clubs elsewhere in Europe, they were on sound financial footing. The wide array of reasons that Portuguese clubs cited as impediments to these transfers suggests that the Estado Novo regime was never going to permit the players to leave anyway.

Only on extremely rare occasions—and, according to Mário Coluna—only after the death of Salazar in 1970—did some African footballers manage to travel beyond Portugal's borders to play their soccer. Perhaps the African player who had the most celebrated career abroad was Jorge Mendonça, the son of Portuguese settlers in Angola, who played as a forward in Spain from 1958 until 1970, scoring ninety-five times for Atlético de Madrid, Barcelona, and Mallorca.[55] Interestingly, Matateu, one of the greatest African footballers in the history of Portuguese soccer, also eventually made this jump. Yet, upon closer inspection, it's entirely understandable why the regime permitted him to leave. By the time Matateu relocated to Canada in the early 1970s, he was already over forty years old, having toiled for quite some time in Portugal's lower divisions for minnows such as Atlético Clube de Portugal, Clube Desportivo de Gouveia, Amora Futebol Clube, and Clube Desportivo de Chaves. Similarly, following a decorated sixteen-year career with Benfica, in 1970 the regime permitted Mário Coluna to sign for French side Olympique Lyonnais, where he played for a single campaign before returning to Portugal for a final season, this time as a player-coach with the amateur club Sport Clube Estrela de Portalegre. Over the course of his career, Coluna had drawn interest and offers from numerous foreign clubs, including Vasco da Gama and Flamengo in Brazil, well before his departure to France, but, like Eusébio and many others, he had been prevented from leaving. Only after Salazar died was Coluna allowed to leave, even as Benfica officials implored him to stay at the club until his retirement from the game. According to Coluna:

> I had reached thirty-five years old and Benfica organized a party to pay homage to me. Benfica officials said, "Mário Coluna, stop playing so that you can exit from the 'big door.' We will organize a big event, revenues from ticket sales will all go to you." I consented, but by then I was enrolled in the course to become a soccer coach. . . . Benfica officials said, "Mário Coluna, stay here and train [to become a coach] at our school of football." But while I was training, one administrator and one agent came to me and said, "We know that Benfica discharged you as [a] player, but we think that you can be useful

for at least one season at Lyon, Olympic de Lyon." I said, "Okay," and it was the best contract that I ever had. I played one season; I knew France from one corner to another. We finished in second place in the French league and were finalists in the French Cup, which we lost 1–0. I was well received there. . . . After that, I came back to Benfica again as an overseer and coach. . . . I was responsible for looking for good players around Portugal.[56]

When I asked Coluna if players were more comfortable playing in Portugal, given the linguistic and other cultural connections, than they might have been playing abroad, he dismissed that speculation, declaring, "We were professionals; all we wanted was money."[57] In both Coluna's and Matateu's cases, they were at the ends of illustrious careers, well past their prime years, and each had made significant contributions to Portuguese football, which the regime seemed to be tacitly acknowledging by sanctioning their moves abroad.

Notwithstanding these few international departures, for most African players, transfers and loans were domestic affairs, entailing moving from one Portuguese club to another. At times the relocations were permanent, but just as with the contemporary soccer transfer system, most loans were short-term, enabling a player to move to another club for a single season, or two, in order to secure much-needed playing time to further his footballing development. The case of Augusto Matine underscores the ways that African players strategically requested this type of move, as well as the dividends these loan spells could generate:

In my first year at Benfica, I was loaned out. I demanded this from Benfica because I had not secured a place in the first team. When I first entered Benfica, I played some twenty matches . . . but I suffered an injury. . . . Because of that injury, I lost my place. Another player, Victor Baptista, entered the squad, as did a new coach . . . Jimmy Hagan, the Englishman, and I realized that the new player was also good. As a team that wins is not changed, Hagan stuck with Baptista, and I had to fight to get my place back. It is normal to fight for playing time in big clubs. As Hagan was preparing for the new season, he chose to stick with Baptista, while I was regarded as a substitute. I decided to talk with Hagan. I said, "Coach, if you do not include me in the first team, then give me a chance to go out to play in [an]other club. If I am not in the first team here in Benfica, I will get lost; I will lose my abilities. I want to play." He understood and asked me where I wanted to go. I said I wanted to play in Setúbal, that their coach had approached me and wanted me to play for them. He said, "Okay . . . I authorize you to play for Setúbal, but you also need to talk with the Benfica president."

Therefore, I spoke with the president, Dr. Borges Coutinho, and he authorized me to leave for one year. When I arrived in Setúbal, Benfica had been champion the prior year. But when I was at Setúbal, we beat Benfica in the Estádio da Luz [the "Stadium of Light," Benfica's home arena]. . . . Therefore, all the Benfica supporters saw what had happened—when I was at Benfica we had beaten Setúbal, 5–1, but now we had beaten Benfica at home. They realized that the only new player at Setúbal was me, Matine. So the Benfica coach himself said that I must not continue at Setúbal, that I must come back. Therefore, at the end of that season, I went back to Benfica. Again, there was a competition between me and Baptista, but he got injured, so I took his place.[58]

Social Realities and Strategies

Regardless of where exactly in Portugal players from Africa landed or for how long, their social lives were key to their overall happiness and success. These footballers' weekly existences were fairly routine—and, for the most part, fairly mundane—revolving around daily practices, weekend games, and, otherwise, large quantities of free time. As part of the migrant athletes' social integration, they embraced a range of different leisure activities that, although not peculiar to the metropole, were much more readily available or accessible in Portugal, including watching television and going to the cinema or to the theater. Such activities were almost always engaged in with teammates, often with those players who similarly hailed from Africa, and therefore helped to foster a sense of unity within the clubs and deepened the fraternity among footballers sharing a similar provenance.

Housing

Since each day began according to where the player had slept the night before, it's instructive to consider the different housing scenarios the footballers experienced. As mentioned in the previous chapter, the large clubs often had "homes" that accommodated single players and, in the buildup to weekend matches, married footballers as well. Eusébio described his experience living at the "Benfica House":

I had my own room there, and there was always someone who took care of the domestic tasks. We had television and other games, and it felt like our home. If we had a game on Sunday, "concentration time" started on Friday, which meant that the married players would come to the "home" and we would all be together. With the exception of the married players, no one had apartments elsewhere. We all lived together . . . and we didn't pay rent or anything. . . . Since we were hired by Benfica, we could stay there; and if we got married, we would leave and go to our own house. . . . While in the home, the single players had a set time to go to bed. The married players didn't have that, but they had a curfew, for example at midnight, while the single players had to be back at the home by 11:00 p.m.[59]

By design, clubs were aiming to cultivate unity among their players through these types of communal accommodations, while still respecting the privacy of their married athletes—at least during the week. African players generally responded well to these housing arrangements, appreciating the camaraderie and the attendant diminished feelings of loneliness. Eusébio added:

The housing arrangement was something that created discipline; it would teach us what discipline really is, and the contact with all your colleagues created a sense of union. Everyone knows each other, talks to each other every day, goes to practice together every day, comes back, and has lunch together. Everyone goes to the movies together, comes back from the movies, and has dinner together, and then watches some television. At 11:00 p.m., someone would turn off the lights and we would all go to bed. . . . I could call my mother. I would tell Sra. Altido [the house mother] that I wanted to call my mom, and she would call and I would talk to her. I didn't have to pay. It was all-inclusive. . . . Torres, Cruz, and I used to sleep in the same bedroom. It was a big bedroom with four beds. Because of this arrangement and the support, the process of adaptation was easier.[60]

Owing to these housing provisions, clubs were able to more closely control the players who lived in them. Curfews were obviously easier to enforce, and, in general, the residents remained under closer scrutiny. According to Augusto Matine, commenting about his time at Benfica in the early 1970s, "The professional team used to train in the morning and afternoon, but there were some days that we only trained in the morning. One could rest until 4:00 p.m. or go to the cinema, but it was like military service— we were highly controlled. Therefore, from 4:00 p.m. to 7:00 p.m. we could go out to the cinema or to a show, but at 7:30 p.m. we had to be back for dinner. Even the married players were controlled. The club could send someone to a player's house to check whether or not he was at home, even when he was married."[61]

Notwithstanding this type of potential surveillance, accommodations for married players afforded them a somewhat divergent, more private living experience, even though they shared a similar daily footballing schedule with their single teammates. Rui Rodrigues, who joined Benfica in 1971 following ten seasons with Académica, described his daily routine as a married player with children in a 1972 interview:

My normal day is as follows: 9:00 a.m., wake up; 10:00 a.m., be at Luz [Benfica's stadium] for daily training; 1:00 p.m., medical treatment and massages; 2:00 p.m., lunch in my family residence, in Linda-Velha. Until dinner, rest time at home, which could be sleeping or listening to music in the company of my wife and two children. Here and there, we would go for a walk with the family by the avenue, to Cascais and Estoríl or the other way, to Sintra; 8:00 p.m., dinner, followed by some more rest and a quick look at the TV. Around 10:00 p.m., lights out to prepare for another day.[62]

Camaraderie and Leisure

Although players spent some of their leisure time in their respective residences, as the various testimony above reveals, they also interacted with teammates and others outside their accommodations. The social bonds that African footballers cultivated and deepened served to mitigate their saudades, while also lifting their spirits and helping them adjust to metropolitan life. African players exhibited the same type of humility, deference, and respect toward their new teammates—and fans—that they had while active in colonial soccerdom and at the jobs their soccer skills had facilitated. In somewhat rare cases, players' wives from Africa joined them in the metropole. Such reunions prompted those footballers to move out of team residences and spend more of their free time with their spouses, even as they continued to fraternize with teammates and to welcome newly arriving African players into these athletic brotherhoods. For example, Vicente Lucas revealed that his older brother Matateu greeted Eusébio, Coluna, Hilário, and others upon their arrival in Portugal with the following succinctly reassuring words: "Your father is here."[63]

One of the ways African footballers ingratiated themselves with their new teammates was to respect the more senior players. As Shéu Han explained, "In Benfica, in those days, it was difficult to make one's mark, so abundant were the great players. In training with the older players, we really couldn't dribble past them. To dribble by players of that magnitude was to disrespect them. We had to find other ways to get past them. This helped us learn that sometimes you need both effort and imagination to overcome problems."[64]

An emphasis and reliance on provenance constituted another social strategy used by African players to aid their ongoing adjustments to metropolitan life. Even when these footballers ended up on rival clubs, their common origins eclipsed any sporting rivalries, regardless of how deeply interclub animosities might have run. During our interview, Hilário stressed the importance of having fellow Mozambicans in Lisbon, even if they played, as did Eusébio, for Sporting's bitter rival, Benfica:

We [Eusébio and I] were really good friends. We each had our own
club, but we always tried to get together to have a couple of beers,

grab some lunch or dinner, or during vacations. Back then, there weren't as many African players in Portugal; now there are almost more blacks than whites, but it wasn't like that when I came. . . . My house was really close to Eusebio's. We were only enemies on the soccer field. And even if we didn't live in the same area, we would get together and eat some chicken or have a couple of beers.[65]

Hilário continued, emphasizing the pride that African players had for their homelands and their ardent support for others who shared their provenance:

Matateu, Opusio, and Costa Pregas always helped a lot because they wanted to see the new African players succeed and triumph. Most of the players from Africa had a deep connection with the continent and they would have rather stayed in Africa than Portugal, but we had to leave to play soccer. Therefore, we would support everyone who came from Africa, giving advice or something else they needed. We liked helping one another. . . . Normally, whoever was from Mozambique was proud of being born in that country. I would say I was from Mozambique and I was proud of that, and that's why we like helping the other players. Wherever we were, if there was someone from Mozambique there, we'd have support. The Mozambique nation will always be there to help.[66]

In my interview with Eusébio, he echoed Hilário's testimony:

Friends, we were friends. We knew each other from Mozambique. . . . In my family, one of my brothers played soccer with Matateu, and the oldest played with Coluna and also worked with him. If a new player came from Angola, the other players who were from Angola would help him. . . . There was a connection that we used to call "a half-walked path," because when you got there [to Portugal], you thought you were not going to know anyone, but it wasn't like that and so you grew more comfortable with the situation. . . . In Lisbon, I had Hilário, Mascarenhas [from Angola], Paredes, Matateu, Vicente. . . . We used to get together in a café, which people called the

"Players' Café." We used to meet there to talk, have a coffee, drink water, and then go see a movie. It was one of our pastimes; if you didn't want to go, you could stay in the "Benfica Home." But the television there was black and white and only had one channel—not a lot of options [Eusébio was laughing loudly at this point]![67]

One of the closest relationships was between Eusébio and Coluna, who had grown up near each other in Lourenço Marques. The latter served as the mentor and guardian to the former while in Portugal. As Eusébio has explained on numerous occasions, Coluna was a father figure to him and, more prosaically, helped him navigate life in the metropolitan capital:

> Everything began between our mothers, who were friends. When I arrived in Portugal, I took a letter to the *mais velho* [elder] indicating that he should support me. It was important to me. He supported me in every way; it was Coluna who opened my first bank account. . . . And, because we had the same origins, Béla Guttmann [Benfica's manager] thought that Coluna should keep track of me. On our trips, we always shared a room. I always asked him questions about professional football and received great advice, which I stored away in my head. . . . What's important in football resides beyond the four lines. You need to be disciplined and to follow a code of conduct. Coluna was intransigent regarding the compliance of those rules. Later, he became the godparent of my wife and of my first daughter. We used to speak in Ronga during games so that our opponents wouldn't understand.[68]

Coluna corroborated Eusébio's account during our interview, explaining:

> I had received a letter from Eusébio's mother asking me to take care of him because I am older than him. I was to take care of him because he was young and he had no one he knew in Portugal to take care of him. Eusébio's mother knew me, and I was older than him. Therefore, he had all his "grand" interviews with me present. . . . I am the one who opened his bank account. I am the one who determined how much he should spend per month—500 escudos. I took him to

my tailor to make his clothes so that he could dress the way others were dressing in Portugal.[69]

Of course, this type of interaction, assistance, and fraternity wasn't peculiar to life in the Portuguese capital, even if there were more African players based in Lisbon than there were elsewhere in the country. For example, Mário Torres, who played for Académica in the university city of Coimbra, in central Portugal, indicated that this form of supportive camaraderie also characterized the community of African players in that setting: "We all helped each other. If I left my place, I knew I could go grab coffee at Café Montanha with the other Africans. . . . There, all of us from Africa would get together to have lunch, or if anyone needed anything or needed to solve any problems. that's where you would go."[70]

Each of the former players I interviewed mentioned this sort of camaraderie and the special connections that existed among the African footballers present in the metropole. Shéu Han's explanation of these profound links, however, also featured an interesting metaphor:

> There was no organized network, but there was a closeness among African players. It was one of those things that happened spontaneously. Many of us came from the same place; we shared a language, a similar appearance; there were unspoken signals and body language. . . . And the distance from home . . . Then you might wonder: Why did I spend much more time with Matine, with Antoninho? Well, perhaps because we knew what the player who came from Africa needs. . . . It reminds me of animals' instincts, the way they help each other. For example, a duck has ducklings. When the duckling is about to fall down, the mother will stretch her wings to help, but it is not preplanned. Therefore, these signals, these gestures just happened, and often . . . I have to tell you that there was a kind of African comfort.[71]

Interracial Realities and Strategies

Beyond bonding with other African players, in order to truly feel comfortable in their new settings, migrant athletes also needed to have positive interactions with Portuguese fans, club officials, and other members of metropolitan society. Indeed, when the first African footballers arrived, there were very few other Africans in Portugal. Hilário even remarked that in those early days, when a white person encountered a black person/player, because the latter was so rare, whites took it as a sign of good luck![72] In order to negotiate this society, African players drew upon the intercultural skills they had begun honing in the colonies—in their "downtown" soccer clubs, in their jobs outside of football, and in a host of other contexts. As Coluna explained to me, "I adapted easily in Portugal because in Desportivo [his Mozambican club] there were white players as well: Fernando Lage, João Ribeiro, and Oliveira Dias, for example. . . . Therefore, it was nothing new going to Portugal, interacting with the Portuguese."[73]

Over time, many African players even began dating and, ultimately, marrying Portuguese women, which fully integrated them into metropolitan society. But even short of this amorous, more extreme step, African players typically embraced Portuguese cuisine, music, and other cultural dimensions and features of metropolitan life, which helped them to integrate socially. These footballers encountered few difficulties when engaging in these endeavors, only occasionally experiencing racist, or racialist, challenges, most frequently emanating from family members of the Portuguese women with whom they were romantically involved. However, this type of pushback was rare, and even when it did occur, it wasn't particularly forceful or durable.

The easiest—and, in practice, most expedient—way for African players to build bridges across racial divides was to befriend their Portuguese teammates. Migrant athletes aggressively engaged in this form of interracial camaraderie, and their Portuguese teammates seemingly invariably welcomed and cocultivated these friendships. As Hilário explained to me, "I think I spent the same amount of time with my Portuguese and African teammates. Most of the times I would get together with Malta [a Portuguese player] or Eusébio."[74]

In practice, the personal connections that African footballers developed within the game were not limited to teammates. Given the nurturing and protective approach that clubs adopted toward the athletes, relationships with team officials were almost inevitable. Many times, administrators served as surrogate parents to African players. In these interactions, the footballers again drew upon their experiences in the colonies, namely the trusting relationships that they had developed with officials of the downtown clubs. Many of the club representatives in the colonies had arranged extrafootball employment for African players and had helped to negotiate their initial contracts with metropolitan clubs. For example, as Matine declared during our interview regarding the key role that team administrators for Clube Central, his Mozambican outfit, played during the process of signing his first contract with Benfica, "There were no player agents like there are today. In my case, the people who helped and protected me were the white administrators of Clube Central because I belonged to their club. The Central men protected me during the process of negotiating and signing my first professional contract with Benfica, in 1969."[75] For Abel Miglietti, a Mozambican forward who signed with Benfica in 1968 before realizing greater success at FC Porto (from 1970 to 1976), the ties ran much deeper: The godparents of his first child were Dr. Antero de Carvalho, the director of FC Porto, and the executive's wife. Further, the associated celebration took place in Porto's stadium, the Estádio das Antas, with the club's directors and players all in attendance.[76] Finally, and perhaps most famously, in a letter Eusébio wrote home while at Benfica, he attempted to reassure his family that he was doing well by indicating that he was calling Domingos Claudinho, Benfica's director, and the administrator's wife "my white parents," because they "treat me like their son."[77]

Even more dramatic examples of African players reaching across the racial divide were those—including Coluna, Jorge Calado, Ferreira Pinto, Jacinto João, and Hilário, just to name a few—who married Portuguese women. Although footballers who had achieved celebrity status, including Eusébio and Matateu, often attracted hordes of interested women as they navigated daily life in the public sphere in Portugal, most players met their eventual spouses in much more subdued fashions. For example, while at Académica, António Brassard met his future wife through a friend. As he explained to me, "I had friends from the soccer team and other people with whom I had relationships. Actually, I met my wife through a colleague of mine who was from near Coimbra. . . . He invited me to spend the holidays in his hometown. His grandparents lived there. It was there where I met my wife, whom I married in 1968. After we were married, I socialized with other people and other families."[78] Even Matateu, who rapidly became a celebrity in 1950s Portugal while starring for Belenenses, met his future spouse rather humbly. His wife of five years, Matilda, recalled that "it was a very modern story for the time in which we lived. I met him when I was eighteen years old through my cousin Carlos, who was a huge supporter and assiduous attendee of Belenenses' matches. We used to go to a café on Avenida da Liberdade that was just below Belenenses' headquarters. It was there, at that place, that I met Matateu. He was my brother's idol."[79] Matilda indicated that some family members initially objected to the marriage, both because she was already pregnant and because Matateu was black, but that the family ultimately supported the union.[80] Matilda and Matateu had a daughter, Argentina, though, over time, the footballer was unable to resist the advances of other women, thereby dooming the marriage after only five years.

Although many African players connected to and embraced metropolitan culture through interactions with teammates, club officials, and, for some, Portuguese women, others engaged via local cuisine, music, film, and so on. Players also gravitated toward popular culture trends in Portugal, even when the constituent stars or performers weren't Portuguese: for example, footballers' fondness for American movie stars. In reconstructing African players' preferences, the series of *Ídolos* pamphlets are of particular value, as each featured a section in which athletes articulated their "likes" (i.e., what they enjoyed about life in Portugal). In these issues, players readily shared their penchants for various aspects of Portuguese culture; interviews with these footballers some forty years later suggest that their earlier declarations were, indeed, veracious.

A list of "likes" generated by the Benfica player Santana, an Angolan who arrived in Portugal in 1954, is exemplary of African footballers' embrace of Portuguese culture. In an *Ídolos* issue from 1960, Santana declared that he was "fond of: Lisbon; when his fans telephoned him; Brazilian music; Ava Gardner; blondes and brunettes; playing football; and dressing well."[81] Bernardo da Velha, from Guiné, similarly mentioned his "like" for Western movie stars, including John Wayne, Eddie Constantine, Claudia Cardinale, and Sophia Loren, in his list from 1968.[82] Jorge Calado also cited Sophia Loren, as well as Elizabeth Taylor and Gina Lollobrigida, and indicated that he owned hundreds of records from American musical artists.[83] Many African players also developed a fondness for *fado*, a somber, wistful, distinctly Portuguese musical genre, and for the most famous *fadista* (fado singer), Amália Rodrigues.

If some African footballers embraced film and music, others cited the food on offer in the metropole as a newfound object of their adoration. For example, in 1972, the Mozambican player Abel Miglietti declared his love for the classic Portuguese dish *bacalhau à brás* (salted cod with onions, potatoes, and eggs); while Zeca, a fellow Mozambican, that same year indicated that he fancied *bacalhau cozido* (a simpler version of salted cod, baked and garnished with potatoes and chickpeas).[84] Many players also articulated an admiration for their new land, including Mascarenhas, an Angolan who played for Sporting, who in 1964 declared that his favorite place in the world was Lisbon, as did, four years later, Bernardo da Velha, "due to the city's movement and colorfulness."[85]

Money and Lifestyle

The regular wages that African players earned in the metropole afforded them more financial responsibility and freedom than they had ever previously experienced. In fact, many of these footballers were the highest-paid players on their respective clubs.[86] Although today's athletes can earn significantly more money, the original African migrant players were still well compensated vis-à-vis the average Portuguese worker. A handful of the footballers spent lavishly, living as bons vivants, but most remained grounded, maintaining the humility and restraint they had exhibited in the colonies. In practice, many players were limited regarding what they could spend anyway, due to financial commitments to their families back in Africa. Even after they had satisfied these types of financial commitments, though, they typically were left with adequate disposable income and purchasing power, while the highest earners among them bought houses and cars, and also engaged in discretionary travel.

In order to avoid their football being compromised by the trappings of their newly facilitated wages, it was essential for players to maintain self-control and focus. As Hilário remarked in a recent interview regarding African footballers of his generation, "We were individuals who . . . arrived in Portugal and had a good home, a good car, good food, a good salary, traveled a lot, and played in a stadium with fifty thousand fans, forty thousand fans, but weren't prepared to handle this situation. There were many players who couldn't endure it. Discipline is required after a guy begins to be chased or harassed for this and that. . . . A guy [needed to] arrive in Portugal and be humble and [not] let things go to his head; if [he didn't], then it was bad."[87] During our interview, Mário Wilson offered similar sentiments: "When I came to Portugal at nineteen years old, one of the biggest challenges I had was receiving 40 contos, which at that time was a lot of money. I could have gone all over Lourenço Marques with that money, going out and picking up girls—everything, but I didn't. I knew that I was very privileged. . . . My dad just wanted to free us from depending on others so that we could achieve on our own."[88]

Sending money to families back in Africa helped players stay grounded, laden with the responsibilities they had to relatives who had helped to raise them and to facilitate their financial success. These remittances afforded improved living conditions for players' families, though footballers' salaries weren't so prodigious that they could purchase sprawling homes for their parents (and themselves) the way many contemporary athletes often do. As Hilário indicated, "Of course, it was like an obligation. I would send a lot of money to my mother because I was making good money in Portugal. After I started working, my mother didn't have any problems or difficulty because I would send 300 to 500 escudos to my mother and I was making 2,500 escudos and that was really good money at that time. I was able to have a car, a good vacation, buy an apartment. I was the best-paid player at Sporting back then."[89]

Celebrity Status: Footballing Fame

Although many African players were the subjects of fans' adulation, most footballers' notoriety didn't extend beyond the world of football. Indeed, even though Hilário indicated to me that many players were treated as "big people" during their metropolitan careers, this treatment delivered few material benefits.[90] A handful of players were exceptions to this general rule, however, including Matateu, Eusébio, and, to a much lesser extent, Coluna. These players regularly received preferential treatment in Portuguese society and, as true celebrities, collected endorsement deals and enjoyed both domestic and international fame.

Matateu was one of the first soccer luminaries in Portugal, and the very first from Africa. As his former wife, Matilda, recalled, "People very much liked to see us together and invited us to various parties. In that era, he was the only football idol in Portugal."[91] An anecdote shared by his brother Vicente Lucas confirms this status: "He would drive to the Pasteis de Belém [pastry shop], just to gaze at women and drink something. The staff knew him already, so as he walked through the door they would put two beers on the table for him. The police didn't say anything, because at that point he was already an idol" (56). And the women at whom Matateu was gazing often reciprocated. According to Matilda, "The women always went after him. Even when I went to fetch him at the Lisbon airport, there were many other women waiting for him and I knew that. But I was always in front, with Argentina [their daughter] in my arms. . . . He was never bad to me, but the worst and most definitive element of his character was his attraction to other women" (50). According to Humberto Azevedo, a lifelong fan of Belenenses, and at one point its oldest affiliate member, "Matateu was a 'conquistador.' He always had ladies around him. At that point, the secretary at the Belenenses head office said that there were constant calls from women who wanted to speak with him. . . . Matateu, when he was around us, never paid for anything, because the members and fans of Belenenses didn't permit him to. He was our symbol" (68). Moreover, although undeniably hyperbolic, an article written by Homero Serpa in the Belenenses journal at the height of Matateu's fame further illustrates his status: "Even a child knows who Matateu is; elderly people, who never concerned themselves with football, now go to see Matateu. Residents from the provinces leave, perhaps for the first time . . . to go to Lisbon to admire Matateu. The newspapers, when they want [to] engage in humor, represent Belenenses by a single player of color: Matateu" (81). And, finally, in perhaps the ultimate confirmation of his celebrity transcending the realm of football, the former director of Belenenses, Morais Cascalho, who entered the club in 1954, recalled some fifty years later that "Matateu quickly imposed himself upon Portugal and that meant, for example, that there began to be an increase in black automobiles, which used to be called 'matateus,' and even black cats began to be given that name" (85). In fact, Matateu was apparently the first Belenenses player to own a car, instantiating his fame.[92]

If Matateu was football royalty, Eusébio enjoyed a celebrity standing that outpaced even his countryman's fame. Eusébio's performance in the

1966 World Cup, in which Portugal finished third, rendered him an international star, having already achieved domestic celebrity status shortly after his debut, and again in 1965, when he was named World Footballer of the Year. By the mid-1960s, Eusébio was an idol, a true superstar, securing endorsement deals for shirts, vitamins, coffee, balls, cars, and just about every other product imaginable. He was subsequently featured in the film *Eusébio, a pantera negra* (Eusébio, the black panther), along with his wife, Flora, from which he earned a percentage of the revenues. Yet, for all his fame, Eusébio remained unassuming, regularly recalling his humble roots and drawing upon his experiences in Mozambique to help him negotiate his newfound celebrity status. In a 1965 interview, the Black Panther explained: "I am a simple man. Simple, like the simple things. Since I was very young, I've learned that life is an intense struggle. Although I didn't have a childhood that I would say was tormented, I still struggled. Just as [I do] today on the football pitches. I feel rewarded for this persistence. . . . I had very little from infancy to adolescence. Coming from a poor family, ambitions were limited. But my mom cared for me and I owed her better possibilities now that I belonged to the footballing elite. I don't say this out of conceit. I have never been conceited. My mother counseled me."[93] Some twenty years after uttering these unpretentious words, Eusébio remained grounded—proud of his accomplishments, but still a remarkably humble man. Responding to the question "Did you ever see yourself as a role model for other African players?," Eusébio replied:

> There are always young players who have their idols and want to be like Eusébio. It is good for them that a captain of Benfica was born in Africa. When I came to Benfica, my captains were Coluna and José Águas, both born in Africa. We were proud of the fact that we were captains of our team, and up to 1973–74 [from 1966] I was captain of the Portuguese national team. I am proud of the fact that I tried to teach new, younger players how to behave both on and off the pitch. For example: don't argue with the referee, it's not worth it, just get on with the game. There are thousands of people watching the matches, seeing how we behave and judging us. I tried to be a role model for them. I was the youngest-ever national team captain when I took over from Coluna after the 1966 World Cup.[94]

Migration and Secondary Migration Strategies

African players seeking higher wages, more playing time, or simply new opportunities and challenges often engaged in secondary migration within the metropole. After making the long jump from the colonies, the domestic leaps were significantly shorter, but were often vital to recharge stalled careers or to capitalize financially before a player's productive years in the sport came to a natural conclusion. In practice, these relocations mirror migrant labor flows spanning a wide range of sectors, transcending sports, with destination cities and target employers luring them from one site to another. Indeed, although the following passage by Peter Alegi relates to intercontinental footballing migration, in this case it applies equally as well to intracountry relocations: "The athletes were not passive victims. Migration also represented their efforts to find opportunities, economic, educational and professional, a motivation 'common to both colonial and post-colonial African dispersions' in and out of sport."[95]

Players were motivated to switch teams for a number of reasons, but financial considerations were primary among this array of impetuses. As such, Alegi has perceptively suggested that African footballers in Europe be included in the collection of "white-collar workers in the African diaspora of the last half century . . . mainly economic migrants."[96] The case of the Angolan forward Iaúca is illustrative. After making his mark at Belenenses, he sought to transfer to a more prestigious club in order to increase his earnings. In a heated battle for his signature, which even, if only briefly, featured Italian suitors, Iaúca ultimately opted for Benfica (though it was rumored that he had signed a secret deal with Sporting). Following the finalization of the lucrative agreement, Iaúca was asked if he was "content," to which he replied: "Do I look like it? I just got married and I needed money! It was like I just hit the Lotto! I am not able, however, to forget Belenenses, where I was always well-treated, cherished, and helped. I am, however, a professional and life dictates this move."[97]

The Angolan player António Joaquim Dinis offered further insight into the economic motivation to move between clubs, especially to the "big clubs": "Football as a profession is only financially impressive for some players—those who play for Sporting, Benfica, Porto, Belenenses, and Vitória de Setúbal. Only playing football, players at other clubs are rarely able to save up a large amount of money for the future. It is a known fact that the career of a player is, as a general rule, very short and so it is necessary that the benefits reflect that, so that when the time comes to abandon this career, one has been justly compensated."[98] In this vein, Rui Rodrigues, who played the majority of his career with Académica, was ultimately attracted to Benfica with a three-year contract so as to cash in before his career concluded, his long-term objectives clearly in the forefront of his mind. Indeed, at Coimbra, where he played and studied to become a pharmacist, student-athletes earned only "subsidies" for their efforts. According to a 1972 issue of *Ídolos,* in which Rodrigues was featured:

> The invite from Benfica, the delay in his studies provoked by his military service, and his belief that this was his last opportunity prompted him to relocate to the capital. One year earlier, a similar decision had been canceled due to a family matter, and for that reason Rui Rodrigues, at only twenty-eight years old, became a fulltime professsional player. . . . The money earned as a professional footballer comes in handy for an investor in the sector in which he intends to specialize [pharmacy]. Rui Rodrigues could buy a pharmacy and through that purchase become motivated to complete his bachelor's degree and become fully independent, without having any great [financial] concerns about his future.[99]

During our interview, Rodrigues confirmed that he had, indeed, been motivated by the money that Benfica offered, but also by the opportunity to play for a prestigious club against other major clubs. According to the player:

> I went to Benfica just to make some money. After that, I came back to Académica. . . . I also wanted to play for Benfica because they had 100,000 people watching their games. It also gave you a chance to play big teams, like Arsenal. I liked to play big teams. That was a key factor in my decision to move. I spent nine years receiving invitations to play for Benfica. My friends were calling me.

I was already an international [squad member] when I moved to Benfica. It was not a radical change because I was used to playing on that squad. On the national team, there were eight of us from Benfica.[100]

Forgoing Sporting Glory: Education and Employment

Although many African players attempted to secure their postsoccer futures by earning as much as possible with their Portuguese clubs, this strategy was risky owing to the relatively small salaries on offer during the colonial period. Many of these migrant athletes identified this sobering economic reality, and consequently sought postfootball security in classrooms and corporate offices. In order to achieve their financial objectives, as outlined above, many African players engaged in secondary migration, swapping one metropolitan team for another to improve their long-term prospects. Yet some of the most far-reaching transfers that the footballers made required that they sacrifice potential short-term sporting glory in order to secure longer-term livelihoods. These calculated migrations primarily brought players to Académica de Coimbra and to CUF (Companhia União Fabril), either directly from the colonies or after arriving in Portugal. In Coimbra, players whose families valued education and who could afford to forgo potential earnings elsewhere continued their studies, living with and studying alongside nonfootballing students in pursuit of an education that would serve them well long after their soccer skills receded.

Other African players pursued postsoccer security by securing long-term employment rather than degrees in higher education. As outlined in earlier chapters, this strategy had a long history in the colonies, as local soccer clubs often attracted talented players by offering them salaried jobs or helping to arrange employment elsewhere.[101] In the metropole, this remunerated route took players to Grupo Desportivo da CUF, a conglomerate located in the Barreiro industrial area on the southern shore of the Tejo River. All members of the soccer team affiliated with the enterprise were also employed in capacities unrelated to football and, most importantly, CUF pledged employment to each of the athletes following the conclusion of their footballing careers.

Académica: Soccer and Studies

Some African players came from the colonies straight to Académica. Mário Torres, for example, had attended a high school in Angola at which Coimbra graduates predominated among the faculty. Lacking the type of scouting networks that the "big" clubs enjoyed, Académica was forced to rely on alumni in the colonies to promote their squad, namely, to footballers (and their families) who were equally as concerned with their studies. According to Torres:

> I was playing for the Student Youth team of Villa [high school], which had ties with Académica. It was practically . . . "Académica in Africa." The club had the support of the teachers . . . and they prioritized the academic side. . . . They all used to talk about how great Académica was, and Académica "this and that." So we, at Villa, used to hear about Académica as much as people who lived in Coimbra. The dean kept telling me that I was going to play for Académica. . . . There was no formal affiliation between this school in Angola and Académica; the only connection between the two institutions was the teachers, because most of them had graduated from Académica and they used to tell all of the kids who had talent on the soccer field that they should play for Académica.[102]

By heeding this advice and opting to play for and study at Coimbra, Torres, and other African players who similarly made their way to Académica, strategically strove to safeguard their futures well beyond the end of their playing days (see fig. 4.1). In Torres's case, he enjoyed both a brilliant career on the pitch and, afterward, a long and successful career as a medical doctor in Coimbra, where he was still living when I interviewed him in 2011.

In general, formal recruitment of African players was a gambit of the major Portuguese clubs—Benfica, Sporting, Porto, and Belenenses—as this undertaking was often reasonably expensive. However, even if Académica was unable to attract many players directly from the colonies, the club did become a target for many African migrant athletes after they arrived in the metropole. In order to reach Coimbra, the footballers re-

Figure 4.1. Académica's starting eleven, prior to a March 5, 1961, match versus FC Porto, which featured four African players: Augusto Araújo (standing, far left); Mário Torres (standing, third from right); Mário Wilson (standing, second from right); and Daniel Chipenda (kneeling, second from left).

quested transfers or loans to Académica, away from their existing squads. Although the clubs who lost players to Coimbra in this manner understandably disdained this practice, the Portuguese regime saw the enrollment of Africans at its best university as valuable propaganda material and therefore sanctioned the players' strategic requests. In fact, it was the Estado Novo regime's minister of education, Pires Lima, a former Académica student-athlete, who first created this dispensation for footballers wishing to transfer to Coimbra to pursue a degree. The Portuguese regime's advocation of this measure meant that clubs were no longer able to deny players' loan or transfer requests to move to Coimbra to suit up for the Equipa dos Estudantes, or "Students' Team."[103]

One of the first African players to benefit from this measure was Mário Wilson, who initially signed with Sporting in 1949, but who, by 1951, had transferred to Académica. According to Wilson, "Sporting didn't want me leaving the club, so only after the secretary of education created the law was I able to leave Sporting to go to Coimbra. . . . With just soccer, you could live well for five or six years and then fall off the map. . . . It was a huge risk. Therefore, many players would choose Académica so that they could achieve more in their lives."[104] Indeed, even while Wilson was toiling with Sporting, he continued to study. During an interview from 2009, on the occasion of his eightieth birthday, he attributed this commitment to his father's influence: "My father, because of his education, knew that football was something that was fleeting."[105] Wilson also astutely remarked, "Sporting exposed me to a school of learning about football in all of its different aspects, but Académica and Coimbra showed me an authentic 'school of life,' which went far beyond football."[106]

Augusto Araújo, an Angolan who first arrived in Portugal in 1956 to play for Benfica, exhibited similar priorities. Just two seasons after his arrival, Araújo made his way to Académica, loaned out by the Lisbon club. In a 1960 interview, he explained his motivations: "Benfica is a great club. And I am its player . . . but Académica offers me more possibilities to rise socially, and by studying, a secure future. My ambition has always been to become an engineer. I came to Lisbon with this intention, ready to fight for it, and I haven't relented. I know that through this achievement I will give my parents and brother great happiness."[107]

Although metropolitan clubs were legally required to release their players to Académica, the squads that were poised to lose footballers in this manner were typically resistant and occasionally succeeded in sabotaging the transfers. In one such case, Ferreira Pinto, an Angolan midfielder who played for Sporting from 1958 until 1962, requested a move to Coimbra that the Lisbon club rejected. Pinto was always interested in pursuing his studies, knowing that the life of a footballer was "ephemeral and that the future was not something with which you can fool around."[108] As such, he had continued to study while in Portugal, with Sporting paying his schooling expenses. At the end of the 1958 season his first with the club, his lack of playing time prompted him to approach the club's directors regarding the possibility of a transfer to Coimbra. Sporting declined, however, following which the player spent three more seasons in Lisbon before the expiration of his contract finally enabled him to transfer away from the club.[109]

In order to pursue their sporting and educational dreams in Coimbra, players sacrificed some short-term income, receiving "subsidies," rather than salaries, from Académica, which covered their basic expenses but not much more. As Mário Wilson declared, "At Coimbra, no one was getting rich and buying cars from the subsidies, but . . . we could live well."[110] António Brassard, who played in Coimbra from 1964 to 1970, offered similar testimony regarding the subsidies: "My subsidy was 1,500 escudos at that time. I spent 800 to pay for housing and food, so I was left with 700 to handle other expenses, such as coffee, clothing, and smoking. We did not receive bonuses for winning a game because we were not professionals. The only bonus we had after the match was a sandwich and a juice. We received these items even when we lost the game [laughs]. There were no negotiated salaries. They paid 1,500 to single players and 3,000 to married players."[111] These limited incomes also precluded most travel back to the colonies during the off-seasons, as did the long, round-trip boat rides—the only transportation that would have been affordable. Consequently, unless African players' clubs were touring the colonies (or elsewhere) over the summer, they typically remained in Portugal during the off-season. For example, Mário Torres reported, "Consequently, we would spend our vacations here [in Coimbra]. We were residents of Coimbra. We weren't only here temporarily, and we were treated as residents because we would stay here year in, year out. We only went home when Académica went to Angola or Mozambique to play. . . . We went about three or four times during the fifteen years I played here."[112]

In some cases, African footballers began at Coimbra, transferred elsewhere, and eventually found their way back to Académica to complete their degrees. Perhaps the best example of this scenario was Rui Rodrigues, who, like Mário Torres, went straight from the colonies—in his case, Mozambique—to Coimbra. Arriving when he was only nineteen years old, Rodrigues stayed at Académica for nine years (1962–1971) before transferring to Benfica. In fact, in order to keep his dream of becoming a pharmacist alive, three times he rebuffed extremely lucrative offers from Benfica (and another from Sporting) before finally relenting and agreeing to join the Lisbon outfit. Although he had a reputation as a "slacker" student during his early years in Coimbra, following his military service in the mid-1960s, he committed himself to his studies and had completed a significant portion of his pharmacy degree by the time he left for Lisbon in 1971.[113] In an interview the following year, Rodrigues noted that the money he earned as a professional footballer would help facilitate his pharmaceutical career, as he planned to purchase a pharmacy and, using his degree in the field, "become fully independent."[114] Rodrigues eventually returned to Académica from 1976 to 1979, following a brief stint at Vitória de Guimarães (1974–1976), to complete his studies and, thereby, fulfill his professional dreams.

Finally, the experiences of Cape Verdean central defender Carlos Alhinho illustrate both the appeal of Académica and the importance of provenance, especially at clubs in which African players lacked teammates with similar origins. Alhinho made the jump from Cape Verde to Coimbra in 1968, enrolled in agricultural engineering at the university, and played four years for Académica. Lured by the possibility of playing for one of the "big clubs," in 1972 he transferred to Sporting and stayed on at the club through the Portuguese revolution, leaving for Spain in 1975. He returned to Portugal in 1976 to play for Porto, and then for Benfica the following year, before relocating to Belgium to play for the Brussels-based club Molenbeek. Once in Belgium, however, he longed to return to Portugal, lamenting during a 1979 interview, "Everything was different in Belgium and the relations between people were extraordinarily cold. It was a difficult time in my life. I didn't integrate in the team or make friends in the squad. I preferred to spend my time with students from Leuven University, who were originally from Cape Verde. Fortunately, I also had relatives living in Rotterdam, 140 kilometers away from Brussels. I could not possibly have stayed there for more than a season."[115] Despite this setback, Alhinho would go on to play another eight years in Portugal and, eventually, in the United States. Following the end of his playing career, he managed various teams for roughly another twenty-five years, including the national teams of both Cape Verde and Angola, before his untimely death in 2008.

CUF: Soccer and Employment

Other African players sought postsoccer security by securing long-term employment rather than by pursuing an academic degree. But as former player Fernando Gomes explained, these dual strategic paths, in practice, constituted two sides of the same coin: "At the time, CUF worked almost like Académica. The difference is that a player would go to Coimbra to seek a degree, while at CUF a player would have a guaranteed job for life. Both prepared them for life after football."[116] Unlike Académica, however, CUF paid salaries that were comparable to the sums on offer from other teams in Portugal's top league, and on the pitch was slightly more competitive than the "Students' Team."

Testimony from Manuel de Oliveira, a Portuguese who both played for and subsequently managed CUF during the height of the club's success in the mid-1960s—a time when the starting eleven regularly featured up to four African footballers—explains the appeal of the club/company:

> In 1957, I had to find a job [new team] because at that time [football] salaries were small. So I ended up . . . at CUF, and to my understanding it was the fourth-strongest club in the country and they employed around ten thousand people. I played until 1962 . . . and I was the captain. . . . As coach of CUF, sometimes players would come and stay for a month and "try out," and if I gave the okay, they would stay and play, and also work for CUF. If not, CUF would give them a job or send them to other teams in, for example, the second division; and to the players that was already a significant improvement because they could "play their way" on to other big teams. Players liked coming to CUF because of the jobs they were also offered. The job and the opportunity to play soccer was a good combination.[117]

Given this dual appeal, CUF consequently attracted a number of African players, including Angolan midfielder Ferreira Pinto. After joining Sporting in 1957, he took classes in his spare time, still aspiring to become an engineer following his retirement from football. Although in 1960, he proudly declared, "I belong to the group of men who knows how to wait and I will wait for my turn, and I am sure it will come at

Sporting," it never did.[118] Conscious of his postfootball future, at one point he considered Académica and also lodged a formal request with the "Lions" for an improved salary. However, although Sporting was willing to part ways with the discontented player, the club steered him instead to CUF. With his new squad, Pinto excelled, propelling the team to a third-place finish in the league in 1964–1965, and concomitantly earning a place for himself on the Portuguese national team. While playing for CUF, he also completed his military duty, worked as an office employee, and was even offered a contract to assume a management position with the soccer club following his playing days, though he ultimately declined, confident that he now possessed the necessary skills to succeed in the private sector.[119]

Similarly, an Angolan teammate of Pinto's, João Monteiro, who had traveled from Luanda to join Sporting in 1958, eventually joined his fellow countryman and former squad mate. After three years in Lisbon, marked by scant success, the striker declared, "I've only played two games: one against Braga and one against Benfica. . . . It isn't easy to succeed in a big club like Sporting."[120] Monteiro would go on to toil for two more years at the Lisbon club, doing enough to subsequently earn a one-year deal with Benfica before gravitating to CUF. Attracted to the outfit due to the long-term financial security it offered, Monteiro played there for nine years, from 1965 to 1974.

African footballers encountered and overcame numerous challenges during their spells at clubs throughout Portugal during the colonial period. Drawing upon their experiences in the colonies, most of these athletes ably, and resourcefully, negotiated the various social, sporting, and professional impediments that life in the metropole daily presented. Meanwhile, following the commencements in the early 1960s of the colonial wars, players were also forced to navigate an increasingly charged political climate in the metropole. Even before the outbreaks of these conflicts, nationalist rumblings in Africa and the nascent political consciousness of certain players granted their relocation to the metropole a political dimension. While the vast majority of migrant footballers assumed an apolitical posture as they attempted to negotiate this increasingly taut environment, a handful abandoned their sporting careers and fled to the colonies to take up arms against the Portuguese. In the ensuing chapter, I examine the shifting political atmosphere in the metropole and the ways that African players creatively, and cautiously, negotiated it.

5

Calculated Conciliation

Apoliticism in a Politically Charged Context

The only time I had any trouble with the PIDE [the Portuguese secret police] was after I visited the poet [José] Craveirinha in jail in
Mozambique. I had a friend who was in the PIDE, and he called me
and told me that my phone was now being tapped. I told him that
they could put ten thousand taps on my phone: I wasn't political and
was not politicized, so I had nothing to worry about.

— Hilário da Conceição, former Sporting and
Portuguese national team player, 2010

We remember that one afternoon, in a European Cup match in
March 1963 in Prague, we participated in a passionate political discussion with the African players from Benfica: Coluna, Santana, and
Eusébio, the youngest of the three. And we concluded that it was
wrong to consider these athletes as agents of Portuguese colonialism,
as some "revolutionaries" insinuated.

— João Nuno Coelho and Francisco Pinheiro, 2002

Nineteen sixty-one was a tumultuous year for Portugal. In January, members of Iberian leftist movements hijacked the *Santa Maria*, a Portuguese luxury liner.[1] In February, the war for independence in Angola broke out. And in December, India forcefully annexed Portugal's territories on the subcontinent. In the wake of this upheaval, an attendant tide of nationalism washed over the country, exacerbated by Portugal's growing international isolation. Nationalist sentiment was encouraged by the regime but was also fomented by the clubs—namely, Benfica—and especially the media, though in many respects this "pride in country" was purely organic, genuinely driven by a population that felt increasingly defensive owing to the multiple pressures heaped upon it.

In response to this domestic turbulence, most African players in the metropole eschewed politics, at least overtly, remaining socially conciliatory and professionally focused. This apoliticism was, at times, difficult to maintain, especially during ensuing moments of unrest. The subsequent disquiet was almost always prompted by the University of Coimbra's increasingly restive student body, with Académica, the squad that represented the institution, repeatedly thrust into the center of developments. During turbulent episodes, football was intertwined with both oppositional and regime politics, and correspondingly exploited for popular protest and statutory repression, respectively.

Notwithstanding these periodic flashpoints, the Portuguese government consistently attempted to co-opt African players in the metropole for propagandistic ends, though most of the footballers discreetly avoided deliberate efforts to engage them. Regardless of the state's limited success on this front, it did actively attempt to suppress any potential political dissidence within the community of athletes through its secret police force, the PIDE. This undertaking was highly efficacious as, unlike their Francophone African counterparts, most of the Lusophone athletes abstained from revolutionary politics; nor did the nationalist movements operating in Portugal's colonies actively seek their assistance. Yet a small number of African players—four, to be exact—did flee the country to take up arms in the colonies against the Portuguese. And many more of the footballers cultivated an increasingly deepened political consciousness while in the metropole, often through interactions with African students who had been invited to Portugal by the regime to further their studies. Unlike the migrant athletes, these students typically held revolutionary political views, actively honing them through regular engagements with elements associated with the banned Portuguese Communist Party.

In the ensuing chapter, I consider the array of political and politicized entities with which African footballers in the metropole interacted, ranging from radical students to menacing PIDE agents. I also examine the ways migrant athletes navigated the shifting political landscape in the metropole, arguing that their outward apoliticism—whether genuinely expressed or calculatedly adopted to provide effective cover—was at the core of their negotiatory strategies.

Inextricabilities: Politics, Nationalism, and Football

As the Cold War progressed, the Socialist bloc of nations increasingly criticized the Estado Novo's colonial project and pressured the regime to abandon it. Owing to Portugal's imperial obstinacy and racially exploitative policies, following the independence of Ghana in 1957 the rapidly growing number of decolonized, left-leaning African states newly joined this chorus and engaged in a range of associated efforts. Even staunch allies, such as the United States, were privately beseeching Lisbon to relax statutory controls in the empire.[2] Rather than entertain these appeals, however, the regime grew ever more intransigent. The New State demanded loyalty from its citizenry, brooked no dissent, insisted upon the dissolubility of the metropole and colonies, and aggressively fostered nationalism, while Salazar famously claimed that even if Portugal were to lose its traditional allies, it would "go proudly alone."[3] It was into this increasingly politically charged environment that footballers from Africa continued to arrive.

State Politics

In 1951, in a stratagem intended to fend off mounting criticism of the perpetuation of empire by stressing the unity of the metropole and its imperial possessions, Portugal refashioned its colonies as "overseas provinces." Shortly thereafter, the regime formally embraced "Lusotropicalism," the theory proffered by Brazilian sociologist Gilberto Freyre suggesting that the Portuguese were uniquely disposed to pursue empire and that their allegedly more empathetic and tolerant brand of imperialism was manifested in its colonial governance. Rejecting these political maneuvers, African nationalist movements had begun to form in the colonies and, as mentioned above, in February 1961 committed the first acts of violence against their European overlords. With Lisbon's imperial authority now formally challenged, Salazar emphatically and unyieldingly maintained that the colonies were "vital parts of Portugal's national community, multiracial and multicontinental."[4]

Following the commencement of the wars for independence in Angola (1961), Guiné (1963), and Mozambique (1964), the regime mobilized Portugal's young men to wage counterinsurgencies in these three theaters. Until the conclusion of the conflicts in 1974–1975, roughly "800,000 Portuguese fought in Africa, almost 8,300 died in combat, 40,000 returned home gravely wounded, and some 150,000 permanently suffer[ed] from post-traumatic stress syndrome."[5] Naturally, the distress that the nation endured at the hands of African guerrillas caused certain elements within Portuguese society to critically eye the most accessible approximation of the black nationalists: African students and athletes in the metropole. Yet this form of potentially retributive racial animosity never resulted in any physical violence toward these Africans. Although the students were, on the whole, much more overtly political than the generally reserved, compliant footballers, neither group became a retaliatory target. Indeed, the Portuguese masses continued to exalt these athletes owing to the myriad sporting successes they were helping to deliver. This adulation notwithstanding, any African residing in Portugal during this tumultuous period had to be careful, perceptive, and deferential, lest they elicit political or social hostility.

Media-Generated Nationalism Related to Sporting Success

While the regime was busy promoting its domestic and imperial policies and rejecting any suggestions that it change tack, the domestic sports media did what it could to bolster these statutory efforts. Writers for football newspapers, such as *A Bola*, relentlessly framed African players' sporting successes as national accomplishments, casting the athletes as embodiments of Lusotropicalism and symbols of the greatness of the pluricontinental Portuguese nation. The media also echoed the government's calls for national unity and pride, and unapologetically embraced the regime's siege mentality, which posited that the diminutive country was the victim of aggressive action by a growing number of antagonistic states and unpatriotic citizens. As João Nuno Coelho has argued, following the 1961 outbreak of hostilities in Angola, the dominant thrust of the sports journalism featured in *A Bola* was both "laudatory, evincing a preoccupation with the international prestige of Portuguese football, as well as accusatory, directed at those who demonstrated their lack of patriotism by failing to fully support the national team."[6] Correspondingly, victories by the Portuguese *selecção* (national team) and domestic clubs in international competitions prompted an outpouring of hyperbolic, nationalist prose in various media outlets. And although the African footballers themselves weren't the target audience for these paeans, the athletes certainly felt the pressure that this epistolary praise generated.

When the sporting press wasn't preoccupied with intensifying Portuguese nationalism, it was enthusiastically defending the regime-spun notion of "one nation"—the assertion that the colonies constituted integral parts of Portugal—and highlighting the footballing implications that this alleged unity had. In 1962, for example, following Benfica's second straight European Cup title, *A Bola*'s director, Silva Resende, who was close to the regime, proclaimed that African players on Portugal's teams had introduced to the game "a new element . . . to a public that perhaps hadn't understood that Portugal, without losing its intrinsic nature, was a multiracial nation."[7]

Members of the sporting media also aggressively rebutted charges that African footballers should not be permitted to play for the Portuguese national team or even for club teams in the country. In 1958, for example, ahead of a match in Milan between Italy and Portugal, *A Bola* writers responded to Italian media contentions that Portugal's African players were not, in fact, Portuguese, waxing poetically that "the Portuguese take to Milan eleven athletes born and raised in Portuguese lands, sons of Portuguese fathers, servants, and if it was necessary, members of the Portuguese Army, speaking Portuguese, feeling Portuguese."[8] The paper further suggested that Portugal was set *not* to "play against Italy, but rather 'Italy + Argentina + Uruguay,' as there were various key players from the latter two countries who had been naturalized as Italian citizens."[9]

Going forward, the 1966 World Cup saw these types of accusations resurface. In this episode, Eusébio and Coluna were the clear targets of the foreign (primarily English) media, which asserted that these players should not be allowed to represent Portugal in the tournament. Again, the Portuguese media responded both defensively and affectively. In one compelling retort, following the conclusion of the event, Silva Resende linked Eusébio's famous "Portuguese tears," shed in the wake of Portugal's 2–1 semifinal loss to England, to the "euphoria in Mozambique that Portugal's string of preceding victories had provoked."[10]

Football-Generated Nationalism

Although both the Estado Novo regime and the domestic media encouraged nationalism, territorial unity, and imperial integration, success on the pitch also organically generated these emotional sentiments among the Portuguese populace. As a small nation, the country has historically exhibited a defensive posture toward its only, often invasive neighbor, Spain. But, as Portugal's perpetuation of empire increasingly provoked international condemnation, the self-protective sentiments were newly directed at any state that criticized its policies or practices. As Benfica, and subsequently the national team, began to succeed at the highest levels of international soccerdom, however, Portugal's acute sense of victimization steadily morphed into national pride. The importance of the African players in these achievements was not ignored; indeed, their contributions seemed only to reinforce the regime's integrationist propaganda, such that, ultimately, the state, the media, and the footballing squads themselves were collectively generating nationalism among the citizenry.

The victories that helped usher in this swell of national esteem began to arrive shortly after African players started relocating to Portugal. In 1962, for example, Benfica won its second consecutive European championship—with the Africans: Coluna, Eusébio, Águas, and Costa Pereira all in the starting eleven—defeating the mighty Spanish side, Real Madrid. Given the historic rivalry between the two countries, the game took on a "we versus them" dimension and, owing to the power asymmetries, also predictively featured a "David versus Goliath" story line, though Benfica was, in fact, an extremely strong side by this point.[11] Ana Santos has even suggested that Real Madrid was further aggrandized in the Portuguese popular imagination to lend additional satisfaction to Benfica's supposedly unlikely victory.[12] Santos further contends that this Benfica squad perfectly served the regime's political aims:

The team provided the symbolic elements that illustrated an ideal: young men from the "big city" and young men from the "Overseas provinces" collaborating for the team, disciplined in the conquest of a common goal. The team symbolized the ideal colonialism. The celebration of a victory in the sport worked as an instrument of national cohesion. . . . In the context of the colonial war . . . the champions of the sport [Benfica] exalted important values linked to the construction of manhood: virility and courage, both of which were essential to the defense of the nation and were necessary to mobilize [the country] for the colonial wars. . . . Benfica's victories also emphasized territorial and political unity in the midst of a community marked by tension, owing to the political conflict and the wars.[13]

So intent was the state to manipulate and rechannel Benfica's success that government censors apparently suggested that the club change the color of its famous jersey from *vermelho* (red) to *encarnado*, a slightly darker, carnation red, because of the former's widely recognized communist/anticapitalist connotations.[14]

While the club ultimately rebuffed these sartorial petitions from the right-wing government, Benfica officials were highly aware of the pride they were generating for the beleaguered nation. In 1965, for example, the club appealed to the regime to sanction a proposed match in Lisbon against the Russian club Dynamo Moscow, explaining:

A victory, absolutely within our reach, would bring, without a shadow of a doubt, even greater reverberations, for the honor and prestige of Sport for our Country. This initiative involves the following benefits: from the sporting point of view, it would show to the World and therefore also to the Soviet athletes, that we are a people with a defined position, standing out and duly integrated in Sport at the global level; from the social point of view, because the Management of Benfica would propose to make all the arrangements for Dynamo and a reception appropriate to the circumstances, as is our honorable practice for all the foreign teams that have visited us, we would take advantage of the opportunity to show them who we are, how we are, and that our people know how to welcome guests. . . .

We are once again certain that S.L. Benfica will be a fundamental element of propaganda for Portugal through Sport.[15]

Cynical Applause: The Regime's Attempts to Exploit Africans' Footballing Success

Dovetailing with the Estado Novo regime's efforts to generate nationalism in the increasingly isolated and fraught country were its attempts to exploit the footballing success African players had helped deliver, which included co-opting the athletes themselves for political ends. Indeed, because the state had sanctioned the relocation of these players, it was naturally keen to reap the political dividends that their sporting achievements were sowing. The regime had long cast football as one of the three pillars of the Portuguese nation, alongside the musical genre fado; and Fátima (famed location of a shrine to Christianity).[16] However, by the mid-1960s, these alleged foundations of Portuguese society newly featured a political dimension in the wake of the tumultuous events of the first half of the decade, and the hemorrhaging of citizens due to both the lack of domestic employment opportunities and the prospect of conscription for young men.

In this increasingly tenuous domestic environment, the state moved aggressively to twin football and politics. As journalist João Malheiro has averred, "The narrow link between football and politics cannot be dismissed. In colonial-era Portugal, to make Eusébio—a black African—the grandest symbol of the country served perfectly the perverse intentions of the government officials. The fondness dispensed to our athlete of the century . . . had the intention of protecting the regime, of softening its racial intolerance, and of exhibiting to the world an artificial generosity. Eusébio was hypocritically exploited."[17]

State propaganda also linked Amália Rodrigues with Eusébio: the greatest Portuguese singer with the country's greatest footballer. Perhaps most famously, prior to the 1966 World Cup semifinal match against England, the vocalist sent a telegram to the squad that read "We conquered the world by sailing the seas from one end to the other, and the conquest continues, this time by kicking [the football]. Proudly grateful. Small kisses from my heart."[18] Over time, the two cultural icons would get to know each other on a personal level. The "king of football" and the "queen of fado" first met in October 1968 and eventually became good friends.[19] In the ensuing years, the celebrities—both of extremely humble origins—appeared together periodically in Portugal, and also abroad, perhaps most notably at "Portugal Day" as part of the International Fair in Osaka, Japan, in August 1970. Coelho and Pinheiro have argued that "they represented the possibility of transcending the, at times, apparently impassable borders of ethnic and social difference via their professional excellence. Of course, the regime profited from their humility and its distorted vision of magnificent social ascension, the defender of the simplicity and sincerity of the 'poor.' But that didn't impede what was almost inevitable: the identification of each Portuguese with them, their 'idols.' "[20]

The regime also regularly invited the most accomplished African players, including Eusébio, to state ceremonies, adorned them with medals for their "contributions to the nation," and rendered them "ambassadors" of the country—official representatives of Portugal both domestically and, perhaps more importantly, internationally.[21] These athletes were not completely unaware of the ways the regime was attempting to exploit them, but their focus on football often served to blinker their general perceptiveness. As Eusébio would exemplarily later remark: "I never was political and much less in that period. I was used by the regime, but only later did I realize that."[22]

Benfica's second consecutive European club championship in 1962 provided the regime with an ideal opportunity to exploit politically the achievements of the African players. At an ensuing ceremony in Lisbon to celebrate the victory, Portugal's president, Américo Tomás, presented the squad with state medals, publicly declared Eusébio and Mário Coluna to be "advertisements for the country," and suggested that the former's "actions and achievements dignified the club, the sport, and the country, itself."[23] Santos has argued that this type of overt acknowledgment of the players' successes, coupled with the associated media coverage that chronicled their accomplishments, reinforced the "imagined community" that the regime was attempting to cultivate so as to bridge the metropole and the colonies.[24]

If Benfica's accomplishments on the European stage in 1961 and 1962 had provided the regime with an opening to interlace football success, national pride, and imperial righteousness, the national team's third-place finish at the 1966 World Cup was even more pregnant with these sorts of propagandistic opportunities. Upon returning home, the government organized a parade through Lisbon's main arteries to celebrate the achievements of the accomplished squad, which included four African players in the starting eleven. In appreciation of their efforts, high-ranking state officials formally honored the players and coaches with silver medals of the Ordem do Infante Dom Henrique, which essentially bestowed upon them Portuguese knighthood, for their efforts to promote "Portugal's good name and prestige."[25] On the occasion, the president of the Portuguese Football Federation declared that "the World Championship has passed, but your effort and sportsmanship endure, making men speak of Portugal in the highest terms during those days when you were able to honor the country."[26] As Santos has contended, "Sport was, in this sense, used by the state in order to maintain national cohesion around the ideals of the maintenance of the colonial empire. At the international level, the victories of Benfica, and of the national team, were used as instruments of pressure, and helped reinforce an image of stature, vigor, and efficacy, flowing legitimately from the Salazar regime."[27]

Later on during the electric World Cup summer of 1966, the Portuguese prime minister, Salazar, invited Benfica's Mário Coluna and other African footballers to the inauguration of the recently completed Salazar Bridge (now the 25th of April Bridge), which connects Lisbon to the southern shore of the Tejo River. The event constituted yet another high-profile opportunity for the political co-option of the African footballers. As Coluna explained during our interview, "Salazar gave the highest consecration of the country to me and my colleagues. After the 1966 World Cup in England, he honored me at the inauguration of Salazar Bridge. I sat with him, side by side, and I went with him to cut the ribbon and to cross the bridge by foot."[28]

The attention lavished on the World Cup team was arguably even more prodigious due to Portugal's 2–1 victory in the otherwise meaningless third-place game against an archenemy of the regime: the USSR. According to Hilário, a Mozambican defender and member of the 1966 squad: "In that World Cup, we did something that no one in the world was expecting, and the Portuguese people and government presented us with medals and awards for what we had done. We were very well received. . . . In fact, the best gift we gave Salazar was beating Russia, because at that time we weren't allowed to play against Russia—only in the World Cup."[29]

Only two years after receiving this sporting/political "gift," Salazar would fall in a bathtub, incurring brain hemorrhaging that led to his death in 1970. In recounting these events, the Mozambican footballer António Brassard recalled returning to Portugal from an overseas tour with Académica in 1968 and being greeted by government officials at the airport, who mandated that the squad pass by the hospital to salute the newly incapacitated dictator and to sign a book wishing him a quick recovery.[30] Clearly, the "gift-giving" season that opened with the victory over the Soviet Union two years prior had been forcefully extended.

The conscription of African players, including Eusébio, into the Portuguese armed forces also constituted an attempt by the regime to exploit footballing success for political ends. These players' participation on the military soccer squad propelled the team to unprecedented levels, which, in turn, generated national pride. The sporting newspapers were quick to chronicle the squad's many successes, including following one victory in which A Bola triumphantly declared, "Eusébio the soldier, promoted to General."[31] Notwithstanding their football achievements, the mere act of having the African players in uniform was a calculatedly exploitative act by the regime. As Cardão has argued:

> The organisms of official propaganda took advantage of the public notoriety of Eusébio in order to consolidate the ideological positions of the authoritarian regime and to trivialize the colonial wars. In one of these campaigns, an aspect of the extrasporting life of Eusebio was exploited: his incorporation into the Portuguese army, in order to propagandize the multiracial composition of the armed forces. During the colonial war, images in the press of young black men dressed in Portuguese army uniforms proliferated, in an attempt to Africanize the army.[32]

Again, the regime deftly—if overtly—attempted to exploit accomplishments on the pitch and the attendant notoriety that they generated to galvanize support for its political agenda.

Political Pressure and "National Assets"

Although African players could and did proceed to the highest levels of the Portuguese football firmament, this universe was, in practice, highly circumscribed. Indeed, as outlined in the previous chapter, the migrant athletes were almost always prohibited from accepting offers that originated beyond Portugal's borders. Having secured the services of African players who were taking their respective Portuguese squads and the national team to new heights, both the regime and the beneficiary clubs were determined to keep the athletes in the country. Moreover, as explained above, for the government, sporting achievements had unequivocally assumed political importance. Perhaps no case illustrates this politico-sporting resolve better than Eusébio's.

Having already attracted interest from clubs across Europe in the wake of Benfica's success in the early 1960s, Eusébio's accomplishments at the 1966 World Cup generated a new wave of suitors. However, the Mozambican star would soon discover that Salazar's ostensibly complimentary classification of him as a "national asset" in 1962 also precluded employment abroad.[33] This decision cost both Benfica and the player dearly: the club had signed Eusébio for 700 contos, while the Italian giant Juventus was reportedly offering more than 20,000 contos for his signature.[34] Naturally, Eusébio was bitter about this politically motivated ruling. For example, in an interview from 2004, the former striker declared, "After the '66 World Cup, Italy made a big offer, one that would have made me the highest-paid player in the world. And yet I was not allowed to move. Why? Salazar was not my father and he certainly was not my mother. What gave him the right? The truth was that he was my slave master, just as he was the slave master of the entire country."[35] During this contractual controversy, Eusébio had actually traveled to Italy with his wife, Flora, to scout out possible accommodations, thereby missing the aforementioned August 6, 1966, consecration of the Salazar Bridge.[36] Ultimately prevented from realizing his Italian dreams, Eusébio resignedly explained in another interview from 2004: "What could I do? Although I was not paid by the government, in those days we could not argue, and if I tried to leave the country I could be arrested and imprisoned."[37]

During my interview with Eusébio in 2010, he was in a decidedly lighter mood, but he still harbored some of the resentment he had displayed in the aforementioned interviews from six years earlier, while also underscoring the steadying influence and importance of his fellow Mozambican teammate Coluna: "Salazar told me not to think about leaving the country, because I was 'patrimony of the state.' Coluna and I would speak in dialect when we met with Salazar so that he wouldn't understand us. . . . Coluna would tell me not to say anything, to shut up, and he would explain everything to me later. . . . Afterwards, Coluna told me that Salazar was the boss of everything in the current political regime."[38]

Although Salazar's power was unrivaled within the country, Portuguese football clubs almost certainly played a supporting role in preventing the players from moving beyond the diminutive nation's borders. Although evidence to substantiate this hypothesis is still wanting, it's possible to infer from the acutely asymmetrical power relationships that Portuguese clubs enjoyed with their players—perhaps most patently manifested in the very late initiation (1960) of formal professionalism in Portuguese soccerdom—that the former played an influential role in ensuring that they retained these prized footballers, and at wage levels far below what the players could have fetched elsewhere.

Negotiating a Politically Charged Environment

The deference that Eusébio displayed to his senior countryman Coluna in the audience of Salazar and, ultimately, to the head of state himself, is emblematic of African players' strategic approach to negotiating Portugal's fraught political environment. And the caution these footballers exhibited only grew following the outbreak of the wars for independence in the colonies. In response, African players comported themselves apolitically, which facilitated their successful navigation of the increasingly charged political atmosphere. Players were even able to maintain an air of impartiality, despite the fact that many of them donned both Portuguese national team jerseys and, as conscripts, military uniforms. Yet there were some exceptions: four African athletes returned to the continent to fight for independence from colonial overrule.[39] For the remainder of the migrant athletes in Portugal, though, even if many of them harbored sympathies for the African liberation movements, they remained outwardly detached. As Eusébio once famously declared, "I don't get involved in politics. I don't like politics. My only politics is football."[40]

As outlined in chapter 3, immediately upon arrival in the metropole, the migrant athletes made public declarations that highlighted their political disengagement and their associated commitment to football, family, and seemingly little else. Their comments disarmed potentially suspicious Portuguese, while endearing the players to the supporters of their new clubs, as well as to the regime. Even after they settled in to their new squads, the players continued to deliver acclamatory statements. For example, three years after arriving from Angola to play for Académica, located in the city of Coimbra in central Portugal, Mário Torres effusively declared in an interview, "I was blessed at that time [1956] when destiny wrote in my life's book the beautiful chapter that I have been living in the beautiful city [Coimbra] of the Mondego River. Here, I have lived the most beautiful moments of my existence. Here, I encountered a future, glory, and happiness!"[41] Apparent sincerity aside, the Portuguese regime could hardly have crafted a more rapturous declaration for Torres to make.

Throughout their careers, players continued to make positive, politically disarming statements resembling Torres's declaration. For example, in 1968, as the wars in the colonies were raging, Ferreira Pinto, an Angolan midfielder who suited up for Sporting, CUF, Benfica, União de Tomar, and, briefly, the Portuguese national team during his twelve-year career in the metropole, was asked, "If you were given a small space of time to guide the destiny of the world, what would you do?" Ferreira responded, "I would call for the immediate cessation of the hostilities that divide people."[42] Echoing Pinto's efforts to distance himself from any type of bellicosity, Eusébio initially decried the nickname "Black Panther" given to him by journalists, as he was alarmed that there was no way to differentiate between this allegedly complimentary moniker and the African American militant organization in the United States.[43] In an interview from the early 2000s, the former Benfica player explained, "It was the English press that first called me the 'Black Panther.' At the time, I had misgivings because in the U.S.A. there was a sect called the Black Panthers. . . . I was worried about the connection, but then I thought: they are in the U.S.A., I live in Europe. I have nothing to do with politics, I am football."[44] African footballers also articulated a flurry of apolitical sentiments in conjunction with the 1966 World Cup matches in England, objecting to the practice of being presented to the fans in attendance over the public address systems as: "born in Mozambique." Eusébio explained, "We didn't like it because it was perceived to be political. They wanted, by force, to link us to the colonies, to everything that was happening. I was born in Mozambique, it's true, but I was Portuguese. And I didn't like it because I never liked it when politics was mixed with football."[45]

When African players weren't expressly dissociating themselves from radical movements or, in practice, violence or controversial ideologies of any sort, many of them apparently weren't talking about politics at all, even with one another. As Hilário explained in a recent interview, "Académica, for example, had [Daniel] Chipenda and [Augusto Germano] Araújo, who were Angolans and activists for the MPLA [Movimento Popular de Libertação de Angola—one of three liberation movements active in the colony]. But there I was with Eusébio . . . in that clique, and we never had any conversations about FRELIMO [the Mozambican nationalist organization fighting for independence]. I don't remember any, ever."[46] Augusto Matine echoed these sentiments: "By nature, us football players, we rarely talked about politics, even about what was happening in the overseas wars, though we were feeling the pain of being colonized."[47] Matine's testimony captures perfectly the internal conflict that African players were experiencing as well as their strategic decision to embrace apoliticism. As Coelho and Pinheiro have contended, "In Portugal, it wasn't advisable that a 'man of the colonies' should demand or challenge [anything]. . . . Everything that was contested took on a political tinge. Beyond their situation as exploited employees, the athletes from Angola and Mozambique were colonized, a thing that they never forgot, though they didn't openly shout out their displeasure."[48]

Honing More Than Football Skills: Developing Political Consciousness

Even as these footballers demonstrated prudence and caution in the metropole, it was in the same setting that they meaningfully developed their political consciousness. Indeed, for all the approbatory declarations the players made following their arrivals, while in Portugal they began to become more broadly aware, and consequently critical, of Lisbon's imperial politics, often owing to interactions with left-leaning African students. Perhaps most acutely, those footballers who studied at the University of Coimbra and, thus, played for the university-sponsored club, Académica, found themselves operating in a milieu in which revolutionary ideas progressively circulated. Very few of the footballers, however, acted decisively upon their newfound, or merely heightened, political consciousness. Instead, virtually all these athletes opted to remain in the metropole rather than surreptitiously returning to the colonies to assist with the various struggles for political independence. Yet simply by congregating with subversive elements in Portugal and engaging in discussions about dissident politics, or even the mere possibility of decolonization, the African footballers were rejecting, even if only discretely and somewhat selectively, the political roles the regime had assigned them.

One of the African players who regularly walked the fine line between sedition and cooperation was the Mozambican defender Mário Wilson. The Académica legend indicated that he regularly discussed African independence with teammates, classmates, and others, including Agostinho Neto, who had been invited to Portugal to continue his studies. Neto, who would eventually assume the leadership of the socialist MPLA liberation movement–cum–political party and go on to become Angola's first president, was highly critical of Portuguese colonialism during his time in the metropole. According to Wilson, "Neto and I used to meet in Lisbon [where Neto was studying]. . . . We came many times . . . to send correspondence to Angola and Mozambique. I began to perceive things that I previously had not, coming to see Mozambique with a new set of eyes."[49] These regular gatherings also included Guineans and Cape Verdeans, who met to discuss politics and life in general. In Portugal, Wilson indicated that over time, African footballers exchanged ideas even when not in the presence of a political revolutionary such as Neto, while the sport afforded them the requisite cover: "After more African players started to arrive, we got together because we wanted the independence of the colonies. We enjoyed a lot of protection because of football; therefore, we were important elements for the decolonization of Africa. I played with guys from Angola ... who did the same thing."[50]

Wilson also revealed that he had first been exposed to this type of radical thinking in the colonies, which was somewhat rare for these primarily "football-first" African athletes. The former Sporting and Académica player confirmed, "It is true that in Lourenço Marques [and again in Portugal] I was a close colleague of Marcelino dos Santos [a fellow Mozambican], who would come to be, many years later, one of the leading figures in FRELIMO. But, in that era, independence was still far away."[51] Tomás Medeiros, a São Toméan who was in Lisbon to continue his studies, verified that the type of political exposure and inclinations that Wilson had were reasonably unique among the African footballing community in the metropole. During our interview, Medeiros characterized the political consciousness of the athletes in the following manner: "The players who came from Africa did not have political consciousness. . . . They received it here from other students and, for some, from the Portuguese Communist Party. You know what? Many footballers who came from Africa were from poor social strata. Some were almost illiterate. But they were good athletes."[52]

Another African who arrived in the metropole to play football shortly after this sporting opportunity materialized, and who similarly harbored nationalist sympathies, was the Benfica midfielder Mário Coluna. In Portugal contemporaneously with fellow Mozambicans Marcelino dos Santos and Pascoal Mocumbi, the latter of whom would eventually flee the metropole to help form FRELIMO and would go on to serve as Mozambique's prime minister (1994–2004), Coluna frequently interacted with individuals deemed "dangerous" by the state. Moreover, Coluna's Angolan wife, Maria Fernanda, actively supported the MPLA and regularly congregated with like-minded individuals in Portugal. Mindful of his football career, though, and not wanting to "transform his house into a liberation movement cell," Coluna strategically assumed an external, apolitical posture.[53] Yet the Benfica star also repeatedly problematized this guise by meeting with individuals that the PIDE had labeled "subversive types," especially when he traveled abroad for matches. Regarding one of these instances, Coluna explained:

Once, I had contact with Marcelino dos Santos and Pascoal Mocumbi, in Paris, in the presence of the Angolan, Mario Pinto de Andrade [founder and first president of the MPLA]. I brought with me Costa Pereira and Santana [Benfica teammates, the former a white Mozambican and the latter a black Angolan]. They spoke to us about the liberation struggle and suggested small ways that we could help. Contrary to my compatriots, Mario Pinto de Andrade was brusque. He even said to Santana: "It is your obligation to support us, or else when we win the war, we are going to take everything."[54]

Although Santana may have initially been unreceptive to the message, following an illustrious career with Benfica and the Portuguese national team that ran from 1954 until 1968, he would eventually embrace the cause, ultimately serving five years for subversion in the regime's political prisons for his espousal.

African players also interacted with elements in Portugal who held critical views of the Estado Novo and, increasingly, toward the regime's unwillingness to abandon the colonial project. Many migrant footballers played for Académica in Coimbra, where they daily conversed with left-leaning university students. Testimony from António Brassard, who began his Académica career in 1964, highlights the politicization process that some athletes experienced in this setting:

In Mozambique, we had little notion of politics. I started gaining political consciousness after my contact with the Republic of Milenares [his accommodations in Coimbra, which he shared with other students from the colonies]. . . . Later on, some of these students became members of FRELIMO, PAIGC, or MPLA. . . . many of them were connected to the political parties that struggled for independence. I started to understand the problems of the overseas territories here in Portugal. I started to understand what Mozambique had as an option, which was to fight for independence. That opened my mind in terms of political knowledge. It opened my eyes about the problems of the overseas colonies. I also started reading books and articles from our friends about politics. They had to hide the books, but they provided them to us. We had a chance to know other realities and ideas of what Portugal's policy was in the colonies. I was tempted to go back to Mozambique to join the struggle, but after my marriage I had to adjust to a new reality and I decided not to go back. I eventually returned to Mozambique in 1970.[55]

Other footballers who played in Coimbra had similar experiences, but only a handful of the athletes did anything more extreme than discussing revolutionary politics. Nuro Americano was one of them. Having arrived in Portugal from Mozambique in 1970 to play goalkeeper for Benfica, he was largely a squad player, seeing very little first-team action. Even if he wasn't flourishing on the pitch, though, he was developing in other ways. During our interview, he acknowledged: "It was in Portugal that I gained my political consciousness. . . . One could not speak openly, but people talked in other ways. It was from there that I started to have an understanding of some of the things that were occurring in my country. . . . I borrowed books about Marxism and Leninism from a fellow Mozambican. I was very innocent at the time; I only perceived the danger [of this endeavor] later on."[56] For all this political exposure, however, Americano admitted that although he and his Mozambican colleagues and teammates in Lisbon occasionally spoke about politics, independence, and "returning to Mozambique to transform the nation into a soccer power, these were just 'conversations over coffee.' "[57] Yet, following his selection for the Portuguese armed services, Americano decided that he would return to the island of Pemba, off Mozambique's northern coast, where he had been raised. Promising to return to Portugal, he secured permission to travel home on holiday prior to reporting for military duty, never intending to fulfill this commitment. The motivation was simple. As Nuro expressed during our interview, "I was receiving information from my friends about the death of this person and that person because of the wars [in the colonies]. I was afraid of being sent to Angola where I did not know anyone, or to Guiné, where I did not know anyone either. I preferred to come back to Mozambique, to my country, and I knew I would not return to Portugal. But as the 'Pemba world' was so small and my father was socially well-connected, someone warned me that the military had issued an arrest warrant for me."[58] Americano consequently fled to Lourenço Marques, and by the time the military police tracked him down at the Marisqueira Café, in the capital city, it was the eve of the April 25, 1974, coup d'état in Portugal, and, according to the player, "They were very preoccupied and forgot about me. Freitas Branco, who was a referee, also bumped into me, and similarly let me go."[59] Although Americano was certainly not a revolutionary, it's also clear that he was unable to reconcile his political views and personal safety concerns with the regime's designs for him or, more broadly, with Portugal's imperial objectives.

Although Americano didn't return to the continent to fight for independence, there were four African migrant footballers—all of them Académica players—who did flee Portugal to join the liberation movements in the colonies. Beyond developing a political consciousness in the metropole, these players strove to participate in the unfolding revolutions, leaving behind the game in the name of a higher, more pressing cause. Three of the dissident athletes were Angolan: Daniel Chipenda, Augusto Araújo, and António "Ndalu" França; while José Julio was a white Mozambican (see fig. 5.1). These players had already been identified by the regime as "dangerous elements," and immediately following their return from a summer 1962 football tour to Africa with the club, they slipped out of the country just before training resumed. After exiting Portugal through the country's southernmost Algarve province, they reached the safety of Morocco, where they were greeted by the media. A former teammate of the fugitive players, Mário Torres, himself from Angola, would later remark that "for some, their flight might have been a surprise, but not to others. To me, it wasn't; I was informed of what was going on. It wasn't a surprise that when we came back from Angola, they weren't at training. I recall perfectly, Wilson, our captain, saying that the boys saved themselves. We knew that it was going to happen."[60] As testament to their efforts and commitment, Chipenda and Ndalu would go on to play pivotal roles as military commanders for the MPLA during the movement's struggle for independence in Angola, and then, subsequently, during the ensuing civil war in the country.[61]

Figure 5.1. Street scene in Coimbra, 1958, with Araújo in front, Mário Wilson on the right, and Chipenda next to him, in the middle.

Coimbra: The Epicenter of Political Radicalism

It's no coincidence that these "fugitive" footballers played for Académica, which necessitated that they reside in the "city of students." Coimbra students were unquestionably more radical than their counterparts elsewhere in Portugal, and, as full members of the student body, Académica's African footballers were daily exposed to the leftist political sentiments that circulated around campus and, more broadly, throughout the municipality. Ricardo Martins has described Coimbra in this period as "an academic pole. . . . The university had students from all over Portugal and its colonies who, in the city's streets and cafés, exchanged ideas and shared impressions as part of a unique process of cultural enlightenment, in sharp contrast to the dictatorial reality of the country."[62] Mário Torres, who played for

Académica during this lively period, confirmed the atmosphere and the constituent activity: "In Coimbra, there was a bigger political opening. I'm from the time that you had to watch what you said. But in Coimbra, you could say things without getting into serious trouble."[63] It was in this milieu that many players from Africa arrived and would ultimately flourish.

The politics that pervaded the city naturally affected the footballers at Académica. João Santana and João Mesquita have contended that the political tone within the squad was also influenced, arguably irreversibly, by its manager, Cândido de Oliveira, who oversaw the team from 1956 until his death in 1958: "Académica was a place where the [political] opposition planted seeds, at least after Cândido de Oliveira arrived."[64] As an opponent of the regime, the player, manager, and football journalist was incarcerated a number of times, including at the infamous Tarrafal political prison in the Cape Verde Islands. Uncurbed, de Oliveira's politics colored his political and social interactions with the players at Académica.

If exposure to dissent of this nature prompted the gradual development of political consciousness among the African footballers at the club, two flashpoints in the 1960s at the University of Coimbra sparked by student opposition to the colonial wars and resultant crackdowns by the regime thrust the players directly into the cross fire. The first incident occurred in 1962 during a period of general unrest prompted by the education minister's decision to prohibit the student union at Coimbra from organizing the first "national students' summit." In protest, students declared a day of mourning and boycotted classes. With the turmoil persisting and threatening to spread, the government postponed all soccer matches for one week (including Académica's scheduled affair versus SC Beira-Mar). Due to face Sporting following the prospective resumption of the football season, the Académica squad gathered to vote whether to play or to refuse to suit up as an expression of their unity with the politically discontent student body. At the time, the Coimbra students had adopted an ardent leftist stance, accusing football players—among others—of being capitalists, "professionals in the service of Salazar," and, thus, insisted that Académica decline to play.[65]

To address the disquiet, the government dispatched troops to the city, and, for a brief moment, it wasn't clear whether or not the regime would disband the club. As captain of Académica, Mário Wilson was now in a patently unenviable position. The Mozambican defender recalled, "There was a serious student protest against colonialism, which led to the stoppage of the league for a week. Soldiers appeared and we were called in . . . to define our position. I was the first to be heard because I was the captain. 'Are you playing or not,' they asked me. 'Sorry, but I need to speak with the players,' I replied. We all met in a room and I spoke: 'We will have time for our struggles; let's not commit collective suicide now. I think we should indicate that we will play.'"[66] Convinced by Wilson's sobering analysis of the situation, and wanting to retain their athletic stipends, irrespective of how small this income stream was, the squad members voted in favor of playing, thereby generating tension between themselves and the students, who had been boisterously advocating for a boycott.

Following this decision, the match versus Sporting did, indeed, take place, with the National Guard surrounding Coimbra's municipal stadium to prevent any potential student interference. Many observers of that game still feel that the general crisis, coupled with the players' lack of training during the imposed break, led to Académica's 3–0 home loss at the hands of the Lisbon outfit. According to Crispim, an Académica player at the time, "We felt great pressure. I played ten years for Académica, and that was the only match in which the Académica supporters were supporting Sporting and howling at the Académica players. The pressure was enormous . . . but, I'm certain that later on the students understood our decision."[67] Irrespective of the result, the decision by Wilson and his teammates to play was, ultimately, prescient: it would take a further twelve years before the nation, led by mid-level military officers weary of participating in the colonial conflicts, was ready for revolution.

In the summer of 1969, roughly five years before the revolutionary events of April 1974, Coimbra was again the center of political upheaval. Once more, leftist university students opposed to Portugal's ongoing imperial resolve instigated the tumult. Protests again boiled over, and, reactively, the government cracked down, transforming the campus into a police state. With the Portuguese military also occupying the city, the entire municipality resembled a war zone. According to the radical former head of the student union, Alberto Martins, who was eventually arrested during the calamity, "Coimbra had become the guiding light of freedom and hope for the entire country."[68] Amid all this chaos, which coincided with the university's exam period (though only 15 percent of the students ultimately opted to sit for the tests), Académica somewhat improbably advanced through the successive rounds of the annual Taça de Portugal (Portuguese Cup) tournament. A 1–0 semifinal victory over Sporting meant the squad would face mighty Benfica in the cup final, which was held annually in Portugal's national stadium in Jamor, just outside Lisbon, following the conclusion of the domestic season. In their defeat of Sporting, Académica players had expressed solidarity with the student protesters by wearing black armbands, and after the Portuguese Football Federation banned this sartorial maneuver, the team's jerseys newly featured a white stripe above the "AAC" (Associação Académica de Coimbra) emblem so as to signal the squad's continued support. Unlike during the 1962 unrest, this time around the Académica players were firmly and overtly supporting their costudents, and vice versa.

Ahead of the June 22 cup final clash, members of banned leftist political parties courageously circulated thousands of antigovernment flyers. And despite a heavy police presence on match day, opponents of the regime smuggled banners with politically subversive messages into the grounds. Once inside, these homemade signs were unfurled to reveal popular battle cries, such as "Better education, less police," and "More freedom," before they were passed back through the crowd to sympathizers, largely evading the clutches of the many undercover PIDE agents posing as fans in the stands. Even the Académica squad openly participated in the dissent: the team's players entered the stadium at a deliberately slow pace and wore the university's traditional black capes draped loosely and untidily in a manner that suggested political lamentation. According to Mozambican player Rui Rodrigues, who started for Académica in the match, "We entered slowly and with the cape on our shoulders, in . . . mourning, to express our solidarity with the students."[69]

Fearful of exactly these types of overt displays of dissidence, the regime prohibited the national television station, RTP, from broadcasting the game and censured coverage by the popular sports newspaper *A Bola*. Further, Américo Tomás, the Portuguese president, opted not to attend the match in order to avoid embarrassment—the first time in tournament history that a president had been absent from the cup final. The regime also made contingency plans to substitute Sporting Lisboa for Académica

should the latter's players refuse to participate.[70] Clearly, the whole country was on edge and, consequently, the contest constituted much more
than just a football match. Ultimately, Benfica won 2-1, in part because
Académica's best player, Artur Jorge, was confined to military barracks in
nearby Mafra, which prevented him from playing, though he did manage
to reach teammate Vítor Campos via telephone to indicate that if the team
won, the cup should be symbolically delivered to Coimbra's student union
leader, Alberto Martins.[71]

The victorious Benfica players were also well aware of the political significance of the match, and many of them were sympathetic to the protesters' cause. In fact, following their victory, some members of the Benfica
squad donned the black jerseys of their opponents as they rounded the
track that encircled the pitch to thank their fans. Indeed, many former
Benfica players regretted that Académica had been the challenger for the
cup, while many of the team's supporters opted "not to celebrate, as they
knew how socially important a victory by Académica would have been."[72]
As João Nuno Coelho and Francisco Pinheiro have argued, Benfica's win
may well have "saved the regime," as, had Coimbra won, the victory likely
would have grown into something larger and broader.[73] Perhaps most importantly, the students had succeeded in widely publicizing their political
and social discontent and in giving voice to the dissatisfaction toward the
regime that so many Portuguese citizens harbored privately.

Reaffirming the importance of the developments surrounding the cup
final and, more broadly, the political turmoil of the 1960s, Mário Wilson
continues to insist upon Académica's centrality to the independence of the
colonies: "We lived in a time and atmosphere that we took advantage of
to . . . help the colonies achieve their independence through our studies,
because we, the ones who came here [Coimbra] to study and play, were
the ones who had to help the cause."[74] Indeed, former player Zeca Afonso
rightfully declared: "Académica wasn't [just] a club, it was a cause."[75]

Subversive Spaces: The Casas dos Estudantes do Império

Individual elements hostile to the Estado Novo were not only prevalent
within Coimbra's student body, but also at the Casas dos Estudantes do

Império (CEI), or "Houses of the Students from the Empire." These centers, including the landmark entity in Lisbon and smaller versions in Porto and Coimbra, accommodated and served as gathering sites for students of all races deriving from Portugal's colonies (see fig. 5.2). The state invited these promising young men and women to the metropole to continue their studies in the hopes of generating a loyal coterie of Africans who would return to the continent amenable to the Portuguese colonial project.[76] The Lisbon CEI opened in 1944, and eventually featuring more than six hundred members, functioned until 1965, at which point the regime shuttered each of the houses, declaring them loci of anticolonialism and anti-Salazarism.[77]

Regarding this assertion, the government was entirely accurate. Diametrically *opposite* to the original purpose of the CEIs, Africans instead honed their political consciousness and outlook in these settings: clandestinely consuming Marxist and Harlem Renaissance literature; interacting with members of the Portuguese Communist Party; embracing their constitutive cultures; and eventually generating their own condemnatory cultural-political output (namely, the magazine *Mensagem*, or Message), much to the consternation of an increasingly intolerant and attentive state.[78] Jorge Querido, a Cape Verdean engineer, activist, and member of the Lisbon CEI who was later imprisoned for his political activity, recalled: "The CEI was one of the few oases of democracy and liberty that survived in the vast colonial-fascist desert; it was a body alive, an authentic institution of informal education. . . . And, above all, for us Africans, it awoke in us our own identity and taught us how to combat the mental and cultural alienation provoked by centuries of colonial domination."[79]

Given that the CEIs functioned as a type of incubator of what John Marcum has called "intellectual radicalism," it should come as no surprise that many of the African liberation movements' leaders, including Amílcar Cabral (Guiné); Agostinho Neto (Angola); Mário Pinto de Andrade (Angola); Pedro Pires (Cape Verde); and Marcelino dos Santos (Mozambique), as well as a number of other future African heads of state, transitioned through these houses.[80] Moreover, following the outbreak of war in Angola in 1961, a total of sixty CEI members, representing each of the African colonies, daringly fled Portugal. These activists made their way to France via Spain before dispersing worldwide to aid the fledgling

Figure 5.2. The former site of the Lisbon CEI.

nationalist parties.[81] Their audacious flight, and the political dissatisfaction it signaled, stood in sharp contrast to the conciliatory approach that the collection of African footballers in the metropole adopted. Smarting from the significant embarrassment this international episode had generated, however, the regime was hardly disposed to reward these players for their compliance. Instead, the state heaped even greater pressure on these athletes, subjecting them to even greater scrutiny and surveillance in order to ensure that they remained model "citizens of the empire."

Because the African footballers in the metropole were keenly aware of the revolutionary political bents of many of the members of the CEI, many of them gave both the "intellectually radical" students and the centers a wide berth.[82] Yet, as the CEI students were among the only other Africans present in Portugal during the colonial period—and were also active football fans and practitioners themselves—other African players openly engaged. Augusto Matine, a Mozambican midfielder who arrived in Portugal just as the Lisbon CEI was being closed, confirmed the relations between African footballers and students from the empire, but also the precautions that the former took regarding these interactions: "Yes, we interacted with students from the CEI, but we avoided being seen with them, so it was only on a few occasions. The most convenient place to meet was at the cinema. . . . We chatted a lot. In fact, we used native languages—Angolans or Mozambicans, this was the way we chatted. We also were careful, as if more than five of us were together, someone would be watching."[83]

Domestic Surveillance and Suppression: The PIDE

The "someone" to which Matine was referring would have been an agent of the PIDE, Portugal's secret police force. Members of this agency closely surveilled African footballers in the metropole, and even more pronouncedly so when Portuguese squads traveled behind the "Iron Curtain." Yet, even within Portugal, this form of monitoring was a regular feature as African athletes gathered with friends at cafés, attended movies, and engaged in other activities. In particular, the state was keen to avoid the humiliation that any subversive activity—up to and including formal defection or flight—could have generated, as many of the African players had become the global faces of Portuguese football. Consequently, these migrant athletes were forced to exhibit judiciousness regarding when and with whom they congregated, both domestically and, especially, while abroad.

Although there was nothing comical about this surveillance or the potential consequences for any perceived or actual indiscretions, during my interviews with former footballers they often chuckled as they recounted the PIDE's oft-unsophisticated methods. For example, the police service often dispatched agents to accompany Portuguese clubs and the national team when the squads traveled abroad, posing as journalists or even unoriginally pretending to read newspapers in foreign hotel lobbies while observing their targets' every move. Due to his interactions with other African students at Coimbra, Mozambican player António Brassard even discovered, some years after he had retired, that the PIDE had sent an undercover photographer to his wedding ceremony and that the pictures taken by the agent were on file at the bureau's headquarters![84]

Although African players were cognizant of, or at least suspected, this level of surveillance, they still occasionally drew unwanted attention. For example, on more than one occasion, Mário Coluna was accused of exhibiting socialist sympathies owing to his interactions with African students and nationalists while traveling for matches elsewhere in Europe.[85] Upon his returns to Portugal, the player would be called in to the PIDE offices and aggressively interrogated. Yet, in each instance, his celebrity status endowed his explanations—namely, that the Mozambicans or Angolans with whom he had interacted were simply requesting tickets so that they could watch him play—with sufficient plausibility, or simply adequate heft. Regarding an incident of this nature that occurred in Bratislava in 1965, Coluna explained:

> Some Mozambicans called me and came to the hotel and we talked. Meanwhile, some journalists who were traveling with the team were police informants. They saw me having a conversion with Marcelino dos Santos [a Mozambican nationalist] and others and then informed the PIDE in Lisbon. Upon returning to Portugal, I was called in by the PIDE, and they said, "We know that you had contacts with FRELIMO guys, and the MPLA." I replied, "They [the Mozambicans] came to meet me at the hotel to ask for tickets to watch the match and to support Benfica. Our contact was about football, not politics, because I am not a politician." It was in this way that I saved myself.[86]

A similar incident occurred following a 1966 trip to Prague, though this time involving Angolan rather than Mozambican students. Again Coluna was called into the PIDE office in Lisbon. Although he did receive a "final warning" following this interrogation, he again escaped punishment, in great part due to the fact that the inspector was an ardent Benfica supporter! But as Coluna biographer Renato Caldeira explained, "From that day forward, without ever approaching him directly, the PIDE fixed their eyes on him. Black cars for some time went around his house on interminable nighttime patrols in order to register who entered and who departed."[87] The agency even suggested to officials at both Benfica and the Portuguese Football Federation that Coluna forfeit his captain's armband. However, Caldeira indicated, "the prestige that Coluna had already earned prevailed. . . . To have a captain 'of color' at the head of the Portuguese national team was already a testament to the [alleged] multiracialism trumpeted by the regime, which paid more dividends than all of the speeches by the Minister of the Colonies combined ever could."[88]

If Coluna periodically drew attention from the PIDE, the agency was continuously suspicious of Daniel Chipenda, an Académica player from Angola who, along with three of his Coimbra teammates, fled the country in 1962 to assist in the nationalist struggles in the colonies. A series of PIDE reports from 1961 link certain "radical" CEI Coimbra students to Chipenda, accusing him of leading an "anti-Portuguese group" in the city that often frequented the café Montanha—a popular hangout for African footballers and students.[89] The PIDE reports explicitly refer to this cohort as a *pretalhada*, a pejorative term for an assembly of black individuals. In fact, as early as 1955, the head of the PIDE in Coimbra, José Barreto Sacchetti, had rancorously declared that "all of the members of the Coimbra CEI are politically evil. . . . Only the dissolution [of the chapter] would be appropriate to extinguish the evil that from there spreads itself through academic means."[90] Ironically, Sacchetti had actually apprehended Chipenda and his fellow absconders prior to their flight from Portugal, convinced that this seizure had foiled whatever scheme in which these subversive athletes might be involved. According to Mário Wilson, who played a central role in their subsequent release:

> Before the players eventually escaped to Africa, they had been caught near Figueira da Foz [in northern Portugal], from where they most certainly would have left. But Sacchetti, who ruled the PIDE in Coimbra, caught them and took them back to the PIDE headquarters and then came to me and said, "Captain, you and I have a wonderful relationship. We caught them escaping. I'd like you to speak to them." And I said, "Okay." I spoke and joked with them, but always fearing that the walls had ears. And Chipenda said, "But I must take the mathematics oral exam." And I said "Okay, I'll tell Sacchetti you have to go to the math exam." In Sacchetti's Mercedes . . . I just chatted with the math teacher, and automatically Chipenda completed the class. . . . All these things were simply delaying the process until the last hour, at which time, after our return from Angola [on a tour with Académica] they [the four players] completely disappeared.[91]

Although the files that the PIDE kept on Chipenda and Coluna were rather robust, most African players had much more prosaic, less noteworthy inter-actions with the agency. For example, the Mozambican player Hilário indi-cated that oftentimes, prior to departing Portugal for matches abroad, African footballers were brought into the organization's offices and intimidatingly "re-minded" of their focus: "The only thing that the PIDE did to me was when the teams traveled to the communist countries, the African players who were on the club or in the national team were called in to the PIDE, and asked: 'Do you know to where it is you're going? Do you know what you're going to do?' And, we would respond: 'Yes. I know. To play football.' For all of these trips, the Africans were contacted."[92] Given their broader commitment to apoliti-cism, the vast majority of players complied with the directives. But even when the traveling footballers did engage in conversations with fellow Africans that could be construed by the agency as subversive, Hilário and others indicated that they spoke in dialect, rendering their articulations beyond the compre-hension of any PIDE agent who might be attempting to eavesdrop.

Finally, it is worth noting that in addition to aggressively monitoring African players, the PIDE also attempted to safeguard these "national as-sets." And, naturally, foremost among these athletic and propagandistic resources was Eusébio. Consequently, after the PIDE received news from "absolutely trustworthy sources" in the early 1960s that the Benfica star was to be abducted—variously by Spaniards, Venezuelans, Algerians, and others—while abroad with the club, they actively investigated the possi-bilities related to each of his travel destinations and took whatever preven-tive measures they could. In this precautionary manner, the agency strove to thwart a potential attack against Eusébio—and, by extension, the re-gime.[93] These supposed threats recurred throughout the 1960s, including prior to the 1966 World Cup, with the PIDE working closely with police forces in other countries to ensure the safety of the player, as well as other African footballers who might be seized for "propaganda purposes"—the agency apparently unaware of, or simply indifferent to, the irony.

Following the loss of Goa and the outbreak of the wars for independence in Portugal's African territories in the early 1960s, the political climate in both the metropole and the colonies darkened. From the late 1940s until 1975, the stream of migrant African footballers from the colonies were, thus, thrust into an increasingly charged metropolitan environment. Yet, rather than being drawn into engaging in dissident dialogue or even insurrectional activities, the overwhelming majority of the migrant athletes eschewed the political currents that daily circulated around them. Instead, they largely remained focused on football, even if some of them privately discussed politics and harbored empathy for their countrymen who were fighting for independence.

As African footballers navigated this political minefield, their outward apoliticism served them well. Indeed, even as Portugal underwent a democratic transition in the aftermath of the events of 1974, many of the players continued to shun politics. Although both Portugal and the colonies-cum-independent African nations attempted to claim these athlete-heroes as their own, even today most of the retired footballers consider themselves as dual nationals, resisting exclusive association with Portugal or their respective African lands of provenance. Despite their obvious political utility—then and now—Eusébio's self-protective declaration that "I don't like politics. Football is my politics," continues to characterize the position of most of these former sporting luminaries.[94]

Epilogue

It was out of the question that any of us accept [Portuguese] natu-
ralization. Our interest and our duty, which we imposed upon ourselves, was to remain Angolan, even if it was necessary to continue
to pursue our profession in Portugal.

—António Joaquim Dinis, an Angolan forward who signed with
Sporting Lisbon in 1969, speaking shortly after the 1974 coup d'état
in Portugal that toppled the Estado Novo regime and led to the
independence of the African colonies

I met Rui Rodrigues in Parreira, a small town in central Portugal featuring
a population of less than a thousand, on a hot and hazy day in mid-June
2014. Upon finally finding the place, and the former player, Rodrigues
turned out to be just as welcoming and unassuming as the town itself. As
we began to converse, he repeatedly remarked how amazed he was that an
American professor had tracked him down in this little corner of the world
and, even more remarkably, that I wanted to interview him. Rodrigues's
incredulity aside, he was in many ways the ideal informant to illustrate
the focus of this section: African migrant footballers' lives following their
playing days and, in particular, after the conclusion of the colonial period.

Having arrived in Portugal from Mozambique in 1962, Rodrigues
played for nine years with Académica before moving on to Benfica for
three seasons. Following the coup d'état in Portugal on April 25, 1974, Rodrigues transferred to Vitória de Guimarães, in northern Portugal, for two
years before concluding his footballing career back at Académica, finally

retiring in 1979. Although Rodrigues enjoyed a successful initial stint at Académica and a similarly productive ensuing spell at Benfica, for the purposes of this epilogue, I am primarily interested in his decisions and actions following the transformative events of 1974.

Upon transferring to Guimarães, he made arrangements to travel to Coimbra, roughly one hundred miles to the south, on Mondays, Tuesdays, and Wednesdays of each week in order to resume his pharmaceutical studies. This concord with the club was realizable only because Rodrigues's fellow Mozambican, former teammate, good friend, and eventual best man at his wedding, Mário Wilson, was managing Guimarães at the time. Rodrigues ultimately earned his degree during his second stint at Académica and would go on to open and oversee a pharmacy quite close to where we sat for our interview.

Following our conversation, Rodrigues and I had a beer, took some photographs, articulated our mutual gratitude, and exchanged good-byes. My departure entailed a drive back to Lisbon, while Rodrigues casually walked back toward his nearby home, steadily fading in my rearview mirror as the haze of the mid-afternoon sun gradually engulfed him, the town reclaiming him.

For all of the seeming prosaicness of Rodrigues's post-1974 experiences, they offer significant insight not only into the lives of these players after their athletic careers concluded, but also into the ways they had foresightedly prepared for this eventuality. In particular, his experiences underscore the industry and endeavor that African footballers continued to exhibit following their playing days, their strategic resolve to consolidate their postfootball lives, and the coaching paths down which many former players traveled. In this section, I examine the life decisions and divergent plights of these migrant athletes, who eventually composed a far-flung diaspora, spanning multiple continents.

~⌐‿◠

On April 25, 1974, a group of mid-level Portuguese army officers, disaffected after waging counterinsurgency campaigns in the African colonies for over a decade, turned against their superiors and, by extension, the Estado Novo, prompting a popular uprising that swept the durable regime from power.[1] The so-called Carnation Revolution radically altered the political landscape in Portugal and would shortly deliver independence to the colonies. What the revolt would deliver to the African footballers playing in the metropole at the time, however, was much less clear.

Predictably, the players at Académica were the most profoundly affected by these political developments. With a wave of left-wing radicalism sweeping the country, the footballers again found themselves targets of attacks by riotous Coimbra students. Jorge Campos, an Académica player at the time, explained, "After the revolution, Communist students were running the club and they held a referendum to close football operations. We [the players] were labeled 'professionals,' which was a tremendous affront at that moment."[2] In fact, this contentiousness and the uncertainty surrounding the club were what prompted Rodrigues to choose Guimarães over Coimbra. In the ensuing disorder, Académica was, indeed, eventually dissolved, and, in its stead, an amateur football squad, the Clube Académico de Coimbra, would newly represent the university in the various national competitions. Roughly a decade would pass, during which time the squad experienced a series of relegations to the lower division, before the team was reprofessionalized and returned to play as Académica de Coimbra, its historic moniker. Meanwhile, for the CUF football squad, the revolution was even more traumatic and enduring. In the aftermath of the revolt, the conglomerate was nationalized, the name of the club changed to Grupo Desportivo Quimigal, and the following year (1975–1976), the squad finished in last place and, thus, was relegated following twenty-two straight years in the first division. It was never to return.

Although these two mainstays in Portugal's top football league suffered in the wake of the revolution, the remaining clubs persisted intact.[3] African players, such as Shéu Han, who were affiliated with one of the more stable squads continued on with their careers—in his case, remarkably, all the way until 1989, exclusively with Benfica—while other footballers, such as Eusébio, took the opportunity to finally move abroad, signing with Monterrey (Mexico), and then taking his regrettably age- and injury-diminished skills to, in quick succession: the Toronto Metros-Croatia (Canada); Beira-Mar (Portugal); the Las Vegas Quicksilvers (USA); União de Tomar (Portugal); the New Jersey Americans (USA); and the Buffalo Stallions (USA), before finally retiring in 1979.

Once their playing days finally concluded, many of these ex-footballers turned to coaching. Although Peter Alegi has demonstrated that racism prevented many African players from joining the coaching ranks in other contexts, these retired Lusophone players enjoyed, and continue to receive, ample opportunities.[4] Among the first African players to arrive in Portugal, eventually retire, and subsequently coach was the Mozambican Mário Wilson. Regarded as a masterful tactician and widely respected in Portuguese soccerdom for his managerial acumen, his first job arrived in 1964 at his former club, Académica. Wilson's extraordinary coaching tenure would extend another thirty-five years, and included multiple stints at Benfica, a spell at the helm of the Portuguese national team, and even two seasons in Morocco as the manager of Forces Armées Royales de Rabat. During his lengthy managerial career, Wilson became known as a "firefighter" due to his ability to remedy "crises" at clubs, quickly right the ship, and often secure trophies in the process, before moving on to another outfit. At Benfica, he won the league in 1976 and two Portuguese Cups, in 1980 and 1996, in this "firefighting" fashion; interestingly, after the 1976 title, the Mozambican was considered the first "Portuguese" manager at Benfica to win the Premiere League since its inception in 1938.

Mário Coluna was another African migrant footballer who would go on to extend his professional engagement with the game following the end of his playing days. Unlike many African footballers who remained in Portugal following the revolution, Coluna answered the call to return to Mozambique to help the fledgling nation develop.[5] Responding to the summons of the country's first president, Samora Machel, Coluna would go on to oversee the country's national team and, eventually, assume the presidency of the Mozambican Football Federation.[6] Prior to these major appointments, he also managed club teams Textáfrica da Cidade de Vila Pery and Maputo-based Ferroviário.[7] In fact, reminiscent of a labor strategy that African players of his generation regularly employed, before agreeing to manage Ferroviário, Coluna insisted on also being given a formal, nonfootballing job with the railroad company that sponsored the team. Following the club's acquiescence, Coluna reported for work each morning in the company's offices in Maputo and coached the football squad in the afternoons. In fact, during our interview, Coluna boasted to me that he was an official retiree of the Caminhos de Ferro de Moçambique, the local name of the railroad entity. Writing years later, Mozambique's second president, Joaquim Chissano, lauded the former Benfica star's commitment to the nation, declaring, "Mário Coluna is a true patriot who never forgot his country. Because of that, his footballing career has brought him back to his country where, whether serving as a [club] manager, national coach, or director, he transmits his deep knowledge of football matters."[8]

Augusto Matine similarly returned to Africa following the coup in order to coach, though not until his playing days concluded, some eight years after the tumultuous developments of 1974. Playing for Vitória de Setúbal at the time of the Carnation Revolution, he extended his career until 1982, finishing as a player-coach at the now-defunct Clube de Futebol Estrela da Amadora, formerly located in greater Lisbon. When I asked Matine about the events of 1974 and their aftermath, he offered a common refrain: "Everything changed, things changed totally. . . . I saw everything in Portugal, everything changed. Even the Portuguese did not know what was coming. . . . Therefore, the revolution was undefined, as we did not know what it would lead us to."[9] Having successfully navigated the volatile postrevolution environment, the Mozambican midfielder eventually returned home and joined the coaching ranks, first at the helm of the national team and then with two Maputo-based clubs: Ferroviário and Grupo Desportivo. Explaining his decision to repatriate, he remarked:

There was something inside me. I always liked my home country. Each year that I was in professional football [in Portugal], I came back to Mozambique . . . which contributed to keeping me updated about my home country, my origins . . . which have never disappeared. I always missed my youth, my friends, et cetera. . . . And those guys, this generation of mine is here [in Mozambique]. . . . I always missed coming home to relax with friends who grew up with me, the ones who played with me; even today I do that.[10]

Although space limitations preclude the inclusion of the postfootballing trajectories of each of these former players, there is a verifiable diaspora of these ex-footballers that extends from Europe, to North America, to Africa, and most likely beyond. Their assorted geographical termini were typically associated with post-career remunerative endeavors, which range(d) widely. Many of these retired players found work within the game as coaches, including Vicente Lucas, Carlos Alhinho, Shéu Han, Abel Miglietti, and Belmiro Manaca, while many others, including António Brassard, Nuro Americano (who also served as a member of the Mozambican Parliament), Mário Torres, and the aforementioned Rui Rodrigues, would go on to have successful careers as professionals of various types in Portugal, North America, or back in Africa.[11] In short, there was, and is, no single career path down which the majority of these former athletes traveled. They were, of course, never a homogeneous collection of individuals anyway.

The Former Colonies and the Persistence of Neocolonial Football Networks

Although the vast majority of African players in Portugal ably navigated the political and social uncertainty following the 1974 revolution, the football landscape in the former colonies changed dramatically, temporarily precluding exactly the types of migratory opportunities these athletes had enjoyed. With Socialist-Marxist regimes of various levels of dogmatic commitment assuming power in the former Portuguese territories, the governments officially disparaged athletic professionalism due to its intrinsic capitalist relations and dimensions. Moreover, the new regimes were keen to use sport—and, in particular, football—to cultivate national unity. In Mozambique, this thrust prompted the FRELIMO government, from its 1975 inception, to ban the migration of domestic players abroad. FRELIMO also adopted measures to "de-Europeanize" the sport, "decreeing that Mozambican teams drop their Portuguese appellations and replace them with local, indigenous names, while Portuguese touring teams were no longer welcomed in the country."[12]

Ultimately, the ban on athletic out-migration proved to be untenable and was, therefore, abandoned in 1987.[13] With FRELIMO engaged in civil war with its adversary, RENAMO, and Mozambican players eager to increase their earning potential and escape the conflict, beginning in the 1980s neighboring South Africa became a target destination for many of these footballers.[14] Following the rescindment of the ban, however, the soccer flows to Portugal recommenced, though the interdiction had never completely stemmed them.[15] Indeed, as Lanfranchi and Taylor have contended, following independence, "the migration of African footballers became more complicated legally, but continued at a similar pace and rhythm."[16] Indeed, by the mid-1980s, "the top three Portuguese leagues featured 340 foreigners, many of them Lusophone Africans."[17] Moreover, by 2000, "Portugal was the third largest importer of African football labor, with 65 percent of all African players in Portugal hailing from the former colonies of Angola, Mozambique, and Guinea-Bissau."[18] In fact, at that time, every Mozambican footballer playing abroad was based in Portugal.[19]

That these former colonial networks persist should not be surprising. Lusophone African players can dramatically increase their wages by relocating to Portugal, while also experiencing reduced linguistic and cultural impediments as they engage in the integrative process—just as the initial generations of migrant footballers from the colonies did. Meanwhile, for the Portuguese clubs, these talented African players are typically inexpensive to sign and, as just mentioned, bringing them into their squads is less risky, as they already speak Portuguese and most have more than a passing familiarity with Portuguese culture.

It is due to the generally depressed prices paid for African footballing prospects that observers such as Amady Camara and, more recently, Paul Darby, have decried this practice as exploitative and the overall nature of these club-player relationships as neocolonial.[20] And, in many respects, their accusations are accurate, especially if one considers these players as "raw materials," being "mined" in Africa and brought to Europe for "consumption."[21] Yet, if we adopt a player-centric perspective and consider them as laborers, strategically offering their services to employers that provide the most favorable working conditions, the decisions and corresponding actions of these athletes can instead be interpreted as both highly pragmatic and calculated, which problematizes a narrative of victimization. Indeed, I would argue that studies that sound the alarm regarding the exodus of African soccer players risk ignoring the migrants' aspirations to compete against and play with the best and, more importantly, to improve their lives and, by extension, the lives of family members, just as millions of Africans do in an expansive array of other professions.

Sports and Beyond: African Footballers'
Durable Impacts and Legacies

In considering contemporary African football migration, it would be difficult to overemphasize the durable impact and legacies of the players on which this book has focused. Their significant sporting contributions ushered in a "golden age" of Portuguese football that, although approximated in the mid-2000s, during which time the national team reached the finals of the Euro 2004 tournament and finished fourth at the 2006 World Cup, has yet to be repeated. Moreover, the athletic and social success of many of these players has prompted countless African footballers over the past decades to make the transition to Europe, or elsewhere abroad, seeking both soccer glory and financial stability. Although only a fraction of the aspirant athletes ultimately realize their objectives, the initial flows of African players continue to serve as models for current, and presumably future generations of, footballing migrants.

The original Lusophone African players also indelibly placed Portugal on global footballing maps. For example, although Benfica rarely makes waves at the highest levels of European football any longer, the club remains a familiar name to even moderately serious soccer fans, while Portugal's national team—often utilizing players born either in the former colonies or to parents hailing from these stops—regularly qualifies for both continental and global tournaments. Most recently, the national squad won the Euro 2016 championship in spectacular fashion, with Eder, who was born in Guinea-Bissau, netting the winning goal. The high-level footballing profiles these teams contemporarily enjoy are unquestionably rooted in the sporting success they enjoyed beginning in the 1960s, which was facilitated by the prodigious contributions of their African squad members.

Beyond the realm of sports, these African players also arguably helped raise the stature of Portugal as a nation. Hoisting on their backs a country that was losing roughly one hundred thousand citizens annually during the 1960s, the footballers generated pride in Portugal and in its capacities. And, in many ways, this elevated sense of national accomplishment and status endures. An anecdote related to Eusébio and the 1966 World Cup semifinal loss helps highlight the durability of this esteem. In recounting the late change of venue from Liverpool (where the Portuguese team was based following its sensational, 5–3 comeback quarter-final victory over upstart North Korea) to Wembley Stadium in London for the match against host nation England, the former star has, in multiple interviews, voiced his lingering bitterness.[22] For example, in an interview from 2004, he declared:

> It was terrible. We had prepared to play in Liverpool, but the sudden change forced us to scrap all of our training plans. I looked up to God in heaven and screamed at the top of my lungs: "What have we done to deserve this?" There was no reply. I knew the answer. We were poor and small. England was rich and powerful and they were the host nation. And then I cried. I cried for a long time. Had we played in Liverpool, like we were supposed to, we would have won that game and reached the final. There is no question about it.[23]

Eusébio's regrets notwithstanding, it's his next sentiment that perhaps best underscores the far-reaching significance of the African footballers of his generation. Imagining a rematch between the two nations later during the same interview, the Mozambican legend proclaimed, "And if we play them again, it will be different. We are still small, but we are no longer poor."[24] The myriad contributions made by these African players have, indeed, rendered Portugal a very *rich* nation.

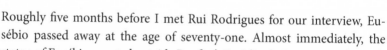

Roughly five months before I met Rui Rodrigues for our interview, Eusébio passed away at the age of seventy-one. Almost immediately, the statue of Eusébio, erected outside Benfica's Estádio da Luz in 1992, became an impromptu shrine to the fallen player and a powerful testament to his enduring impact and legacy (see fig. E.1). Following national periods of mourning in both Portugal and his native Mozambique, Eusébio was laid to rest in Portugal's Panteão Nacional, or National Pantheon, where only the most significant Portuguese, including past presidents and writers, are buried, though there are also cenotaphs for famous historical figures from the country's past, such as Henry the Navigator and Vasco da Gama. Also interred in the converted seventeenth-century cathedral is Amália, the inimitable fado singer and former friend of the footballing legend. Highlighting the unifying contributions that Eusébio made to both nations, former Mozambican president Joaquim Chissano eulogized, "Portuguese football has lost one of its greatest idols. Football brought Mozambique and Portugal together, and everyone in Mozambique is proud of Eusébio."[25] Everyone in Mozambique, indeed. And Portugal. And beyond.

Figure E.1. Eusébio monument/shrine, January 2014.

Notes

Introduction

1. In the book, I use the terms "soccer," as the sport is known in the United States, and "football," as it's known virtually everywhere else in the world, interchangeably.

2. Footballers from Angola and Mozambique, Portugal's largest and most important colonies in Africa, made the greatest impact in the metropole and were also significantly more numerous than were players from Guiné, Cape Verde, and São Tomé; thus the text primarily focuses on athletes deriving from these two countries.

3. Fátima is the site in central Portugal where, in 1917, apparitions allegedly sent from the heavens appeared, and it remains an extremely popular pilgrimage destination, as well as an enduring symbol of the country's religious devotion.

4. "José Maria: O 'pulmão' do Vitória," *Ídolos do desporto* 6, no. 13 (December 6, 1969).

5. Gerald J. Bender, *Angola under the Portuguese: The Myth and the Reality* (Berkeley: University of California Press, 1978), 151.

6. Mário Wilson, interview by author, October 29, 2010.

7. Two scholars who have spearheaded this effort are Peter Alegi and Paul Darby. See, for example, Darby, *Africa, Football and FIFA: Politics, Colonialism and Resistance* (London: Cass, 2002); and Alegi, *African Soccerscapes: How a Continent Changed the World's Game* (Athens: Ohio University Press, 2010).

8. Nuno Domingos has written extensively about soccer in colonial Lourenço Marques (Maputo), but generally focuses on the introduction and development of formal leagues and the African appropriation of the European-introduced game, while Paul Darby is more concerned with the underdevelopment of African soccer. See Darby, "African Football Labour Migration to Portugal: Colonial and Neo-Colonial Resource," *Soccer and Society* 8, no. 4

(October 2007): 495–509; Domingos, "Football and Colonialism, Domination and Appropriation: The Mozambican Case," *Soccer and Society* 8, no. 4 (October 2007): 478–94; Domingos, "Urban Football Narratives and the Colonial Process in Lourenço Marques," *International Journal of the History of Sport* 28, no. 15 (October 2011): 2159–75; Domingos, "O desporte e o Império Português," in *Uma história do desporto em Portugal*, vol. 2, *Nação, império e globalização*, ed. José Neves and Nuno Domingos (Lisbon: QuidNovi, 2011), 51–107; Domingos, *Futebol e colonialismo: Corpo e cultura popular em Moçambique* (Lisbon: Imprensa de Ciências Sociais, 2012).

9. For complementary accounts of these players' sporting accomplishments, see, for example, Mário de Aguiar, *Coluna: O grande capitão* (Lisbon: Filtro Estúdios Gráficos, 1968); Eugénio Silva, *Eusébio: Pantera negra* (Lisbon: Meribérica, 1992); Fernando Correia, *Matateu: O oitava maravilha* (Lisbon: Sete Caminhos, 2006); and João Malheiro, *Eusébio: A biografia autorizado* (Vila do Conde: QuidNovi, 2012).

10. Scholars have previously examined the historical and contemporary arrival of African soccer players in other European settings, including England and France, which this book complements. See, for example, Phil Vasili, *The First Black Footballer—Arthur Wharton, 1865–1930: An Absence of Memory* (London: Cass, 1998); Vasili, *Colouring over the White Line: The History of Black Footballers in Britain* (Edinburgh: Mainstream, 2000); and Rodney Hinds, *Black Lions: A History of Black Players in English Football* (London: Sportsbooks, 2006).

11. See, for example, Pierre Lanfranchi and Alfred Wahl, "The Immigrant as Hero: Kopa, Mekloufi and French Football," in *European Heroes: Myth, Identity, Sport*, ed. Richard Holt, James A. Mangan, and Pierre Lanfranchi (London: Cass, 1996), 114–27; and Pierre Lanfranchi and Matthew Taylor, *Moving with the Ball: The Migration of Professional Footballers* (Oxford: Berg, 2001), 170–76.

12. Phyllis M. Martin, *Leisure and Society in Colonial Brazzaville* (Cambridge: Cambridge University Press, 1995).

13. Phyllis M. Martin, "Colonialism, Youth and Football in French Equatorial Africa," *International Journal of the History of Sport* 8, no. 1 (1991): 56–71; Martin, *Leisure and Society*; Laura Fair, "Kickin' It: Leisure, Politics and Football in Colonial Zanzibar, 1900s–1950s," *Africa* 67, no. 2 (1997): 224; Fair, *Pastimes and Politics: Culture, Community, and Identity in Post-Abolition Urban Zanzibar, 1890–1945* (Athens: Ohio University Press, 2001); Marcelo Bittencourt, "Jogando no campo do inimigo: Futebol e luta política em Angola" (Lisbon: Seventh Congress on African Studies, 2010), 1–21; and Peter Alegi, *Laduma! Soccer, Politics and Society in South Africa, from Its Origins to 2010* (Scottsville, South Africa: University of KwaZulu-Natal Press, 2010).

14. David Goldblatt, *The Ball Is Round: A Global History of Soccer* (New York: Penguin, 2006), 91, 492.

15. Pierre Lanfranchi, "Mekloufi, un footballeur français dans la guerre d'Algérie," *Actes de la recherche en sciences sociales* 103, no. 1 (1994): 70–74; Lanfranchi and Wahl, "Immigrant as Hero"; Lanfranchi and Taylor, *Moving with the Ball*, 170–78.

16. See, for example, Fair, "Kickin' It"; Domingos, "Football and Colonialism," 478–82; and Alegi, *African Soccerscapes*. In practice, this vernacularization phenomenon occurred the world over, as local adoptees infused cultural values and styles into the sport to create something different from what had been originally introduced.

17. Fair, "Kickin' It," 244; Marissa J. Moorman, *Intonations: A Social History of Music and Nation in Luanda, Angola, from 1945 to Recent Times* (Athens: Ohio University Press, 2008); Alegi, *Laduma!*; Alegi, *African Soccerscapes*.

18. This statement alludes to Frantz Fanon's insightful and durable 1952 study, *Black Skin, White Masks*, in which he argues that colonial hegemonies prompted a pathological sense of admiration among Africans for European culture. Fanon, *Black Skin, White Masks* (New York: Grove Press, 1967).

19. Hilário da Conceição, interview by author, October 19, 2010.

20. See, for example, Michael A. Gomez, *Exchanging Our Country Marks: The Transformation of African Identities in the Colonial and Antebellum South* (Chapel Hill: University of North Carolina Press, 1998).

21. See, for example, Heidi Gengenbach, " 'What My Heart Wanted': Gendered Stories of Early Colonial Encounters in Southern Mozambique," in *Women in African Colonial Histories*, ed. Jean Allman, Susan Geiger, and Nakanyike Musisi (Bloomington: Indiana University Press, 2002), 19–47.

22. The theory was coined by Brazilian sociologist Gilberto Freyre in the 1930s and subsequently adopted and promoted by Salazar, the Portuguese dictator throughout most of the period that this study examines. Although the critics of Lusotropicalism are legion, Gerald Bender's critique of Freyre's theory is perhaps the most powerful. See Freyre, *Casa-Grande e Senzala* (Rio de Janeiro: Global Editora, 1933); and Bender, *Angola under the Portuguese*.

23. See, for example, Timothy H. Parsons, *The African Rank-and-File: Social Implications of Colonial Service in the King's African Rifles, 1902–1964* (Portsmouth, NH: Heinemann, 1999); Benjamin N. Lawrence, Emily Lynn Osborn, and Richard L. Roberts, eds., *Intermediaries, Interpreters, and Clerks: African Employees in the Making of Colonial Africa* (Madison: University of Wisconsin Press, 2006); Michelle R. Moyd, *Violent Intermediaries: African Soldiers, Conquest, and Everyday Colonialism in German East Africa* (Athens: Ohio University Press, 2014).

24. For a detailed examination of the "propagandistic" tours that the metropolitan teams made to the colonies, see Marcos Cardão, "Peregrinações exemplars: As embaixadas patrióticas dos clubes metropolitanos ao 'ultramar português,'" in *Esporte e lazer na África: Novos olhares*, ed. Augusto Nascimento, Marcelo Bittencourt, Nuno Domingos, and Victor Andrade de Melo (Rio de Janeiro: 7Letras, 2013), 109–28.

25. Lawrence, Osborn, and Roberts, *Intermediaries, Interpreters, and Clerks*, 9.

26. Judith A. Carney, *Black Rice: The African Origins of Rice Cultivation in the Americas* (Cambridge, MA: Harvard University Press, 2001); Frederick C. Knight, *Working the Diaspora: The Impact of African Labor on the Anglo-American World, 1650–1850* (New York: New York University Press, 2010).

27. Although I previously employed "professionalism" in a study on Angolan diamond miners, albeit to explicate a reasonably different set of occupational approaches, elsewhere scholars of Africa have rarely invoked this term, instead reserving it for studies of indigenous soldiers or simply to describe remunerative activity, rather than a collection of occupational behaviors. See, for example, Joseph B. Rukanshagiza, "African Armies: Understanding the Origin and Continuation of Their Non-Professionalism" (PhD diss., State University of New York, Albany, 1995); Boubacar N'Diaye, "Ivory Coast's Civilian Control Strategies 1961–1998: A Critical Assessment," *Journal of Political and Military Sociology* 28, no. 2 (2000): 246–70; and Todd Cleveland, *Diamonds in the Rough: Corporate Paternalism and African Professionalism on the Mines of Colonial Angola, 1917–1975* (Athens: Ohio University Press, 2015).

28. Lanfranchi and Taylor, *Moving with the Ball*, 167.

29. Hilário da Conceição, interview by author, October 19, 2010.

30. See, for example, Paul Darby, "The New Scramble for Africa: The African Football Labour Migration to Europe," in *Europe, Sport, World: Shaping Global Societies*, ed. James A. Mangan (London: Cass, 2001), 224; Darby, "African Football Labour Migration to Portugal," 501, 503.

31. This general rule notwithstanding, for an examination of the relationship between the regime and Eusébio, see Marcos Cardão, "Um significante instrumental, Eusébio e a banalização lusotropicalismo na década de 1960," in *Esporte, cultura, nação, estado: Brasil e Portugal*, ed. Victor Andrade de Melo, Fabio de Faria Peres, and Maurício Drumond (Rio de Janeiro: 7Letras, 2014), 172–88.

32. Lanfranchi and Taylor, *Moving with the* Ball, 168.

33. Paola Rolletta, *Finta finta* (Maputo, Mozambique: Texto Editores, 2011).

34. Indeed, many of these former athletes and, in particular the more famous among them, are accustomed to discussing their sporting exploits but are rarely asked to retrieve memories of their daily lives away from the pitch.

In perhaps the most extreme example, I would argue that Eusébio even had a type of mental script from which he repeatedly read, given how many times he had answered similar questions about his remarkable sporting career.

35. While a handful of African players had relocated to Europe to play at the end of the nineteenth century and earlier in the twentieth century, these migratory trickles paled in comparison to the post–World War II flows to France and Portugal and, moreover, were extremely brief in their duration and also failed to prompt subsequent, sustained flows. In Portugal, the sole case was of Espírito Santo, who arrived from Angola in 1936 and subsequently starred for Benfica and, eventually, the Portuguese national team. However, even the "Pérola Negra" (Black Pearl), as he was known, had been born in Lisbon, and, regardless, it would take over a decade from his initial arrival for other black or mestiço players to follow in his migratory footsteps.

Chapter 1: Foundations

1. Isabel Castro Henriques, "Africans in Portuguese Society: Classification Ambiguities and Colonial Realities," in *Imperial Migrations: Colonial Communities and Diaspora in the Portuguese World*, ed. Eric Morier-Genoud and Micel Cahen (New York: Palgrave Macmillan, 2012), 79.

2. Ibid.

3. Gerald J. Bender, *Angola under the Portuguese: The Myth and the Reality* (Berkeley: University of California Press, 1978), 20.

4. Nuno Domingos, "Dos subúrbios da Lourenço Marques, colonial aos campos de futebol da metrópole,' uma entrevista com Hilário Rosário da Conceição," *Cadernos de Estudos Africanos* 26 (2013): 227.

5. Bender, *Angola under the Portuguese*, 20; Nuno Domingos, "Urban Football Narratives and the Colonial Process in Lourenço Marques," *International Journal of the History of Sport* 28, no. 15 (October 2011): 2163.

6. Domingos, "Dos subúrbios da Lourenço Marques," 227.

7. Bender, *Angola under the Portuguese*, 151.

8. Nuno Domingos, "Football in Colonial Lourenço Marques: Bodily Practices and Social Rituals" (PhD diss., University of London, 2008), 235.

9. Marcelo Bittencourt, "Jogando no campo do inimigo: Futebol e luta política em Angola" (Lisbon: Seventh Congress on African Studies, 2010), 17.

10. "Miguel Arcanjo: O homem duas vezes quase perdido para a futbol," *Ídolos do desporto*, no. 42 (1956).

11. "Armando: O '115' do Sporting," *Ídolos do desporto* 5, no. 1 (December 30, 1967).

12. Paola Rolletta, *Finta finta* (Maputo, Mozambique: Texto Editores, 2011), 165.

13. "Conceição: O 'Grande Capitão' Sadino," *Ídolos do desporto* 6, no. 17 (March 14, 1970).

14. Fernando Correia, *Matateu: O oitava maravilha* (Lisbon: Sete Caminhos, 2006), 41.

15. Domingos, "Football in Colonial Lourenço Marques," 237.

16. Rolletta, *Finta finta*, 21.

17. Ibid.

18. Nuno Domingos, "Football and Colonialism, Domination and Appropriation: The Mozambican Case," *Soccer and Society* 8, no. 4 (October 2007): 480.

19. Nuno Domingos, "O campo de desportivização imperial português," in *Esporte e lazer na África: Novos olhares*, ed. Augusto Nascimento, Marcelo Bittencourt, Nuno Domingos, and Victor Andrade de Melo (Rio de Janeiro: 7Letras, 2013), 87.

20. Patrick Harries, *Work, Culture and Identity: Migrant Laborers in Mozambique and South Africa, c. 1860–1910* (Portsmouth, NH: Heinemann, 1994).

21. "Águas: 'Esse desconhecido' que veio do Lobito," *Ídolos do desporto*, no. 5 (1956). The Taça Latina was an annual (summer) tournament for club sides from the "Latin European" nations of France, Italy, Spain, and Portugal that ran from 1949 until 1957, featuring the champions from each country's domestic league.

22. Domingos, "Football in Colonial Lourenço Marques," 240.

23. Domingos, "Urban Football Narratives," 2171.

24. Domingos, "Football in Colonial Lourenço Marques," 240.

25. The first broadcast of Portuguese football in Lourenço Marques occurred in March 1934, with the game resulting in the defeat of Portugal's national football team by its Spanish counterpart in Madrid. The broadcast allegedly took place "before a huge crowd." Domingos indicates that "the match report reached Lourenço Marques with a two-minute delay, a minimal distance to people who were used to reading the news several days later in the newspapers." Ibid., 49.

26. Domingos, "Football in Colonial Lourenço Marques," 222.

27. Rolletta, *Finta finta*, 86.

28. Paul Darby, "African Football Labour Migration to Portugal: Colonial and Neo-Colonial Resource," *Soccer and Society* 8, no. 4 (October 2007): 502.

29. Domingos, "Urban Football Narratives," 2164.

30. Domingos, "Football in Colonial Lourenço Marques," 232.

31. Allen Guttmann, *Games and Empires: Modern Sports and Cultural Imperialism* (New York: Columbia University Press, 1996), 179.

32. Gary Armstrong, "The Migration of the Black Panther: An Interview with Eusebio of Mozambique and Portugal," in *Football in Africa: Conflict, Conciliation and Community* (New York: Palgrave Macmillan, 2004), 249.

33. Domingos, "Football in Colonial Lourenço Marques," 222.

34. Correia, *Matateu*, 41.

35. Augusto Matine, interview by author, November 20, 2012.

36. António Lobo Antunes, introduction to *Monstros sagrados: Benfica anos 6os*, by Pedro Vasco and Ricardo Galvão (Lisbon: Primebooks, 2011), 10.

37. Bittencourt, "Jogando no campo do inimigo," 6.

38. Ibid.

39. Due to the racist acuteness that the apartheid system featured, black and mestiço players were often left off Portuguese colonial squads that either traveled to or hosted South African teams, though local fans often criticized these omissions.

40. Domingos, "Football in Colonial Lourenço Marques," 48.

41. Ana Santos, *Herois desportivos: Estudo de caso sobre Eusébio, de corpo a ícone da nação* (Lisbon: Instituto do Desporto de Portugal, 2004), 92.

42. See Michael Billig, *Banal Nationalism* (London: Sage, 1995).

43. Pierre Lanfranchi and Matthew Taylor, *Moving with the Ball: The Migration of Professional Footballers* (Oxford: Berg, 2001); Darby, "African Football Labour Migration," 502; Marcos Cardão, "Peregrinações exemplars: As embaixadas patrióticas dos clubes metropolitanos ao 'ultramar português,'" in *Esporte e lazer na África: Novos olhares*, ed. Augusto Nascimento, Marcelo Bittencourt, Nuno Domingos, and Victor Andrade de Melo (Rio de Janeiro: 7Letras, 2013), 109–28.

44. Cardão, "Peregrinações exemplars," 121.

45. Ibid., 122.

46. Ibid.

47. This list would include the following teams, with the years they toured in parentheses: Aberdeen (1937); Newcastle (1952); Dundee United (1953); Djurgardens (1955); Dinamo de Praga (1956); Ajax (1958); Portuguesa de Santos (1959); and Ferroviário de Araraquara (1960).

48. Augusto Matine, interview by author, November 20, 2012.

49. "Miguel Arcanjo: O homem duas vezes quase perdido para a futbol," *Ídolos do desporto*, no. 42 (1956).

Chapter 2: Engaging with the Game

1. Nuno Domingos, "Football in Colonial Lourenço Marques: Bodily Practices and Social Rituals" (PhD diss., University of London, 2008), 41.

2. See, for example, Laura Fair, *Pastimes and Politics: Culture, Community, and Identity in Post-Abolition Urban Zanzibar, 1890–1945* (Athens: Ohio University Press, 2001); Peter Alegi, *African Soccerscapes: How a Continent Changed the World's Game* (Athens: Ohio University Press, 2010), 15.

3. John Bale and Joe Sang, *Kenyan Running: Movement Culture, Geography and Global Change* (London: Cass, 1996), 49–50.

4. *Pelada* in Portuguese literally means "naked."

5. Paola Rolletta, *Finta finta* (Maputo, Mozambique: Texto Editores, 2011), 179.

6. Gary Armstrong, "The Migration of the Black Panther: An Interview with Eusebio of Mozambique and Portugal," in *Football in Africa: Conflict, Conciliation and Community*, ed. Gary Armstrong and Richard Giulianotti (New York: Palgrave Macmillan, 2004), 256.

7. Ernesto Baltazar, interview by author, June 24, 2014.

8. Rolletta, *Finta finta*, 179.

9. "Dinis: O ídolo do asa que triunfa no Sporting," *Ídolos do desporto* 7, no. 5 (January 1, 1972).

10. Rolletta, *Finta finta*, 165.

11. Hilário da Conceição, interview by author, October 19, 2010.

12. Augusto Matine, interview by author, November 20, 2012.

13. Domingos, "Football in Colonial Lourenço Marques," 142.

14. For a more detailed account of the development of Armando's relationship with soccer, see "Armando : O '115' do Sporting," *Ídolos do desporto* 5, no. 1 (December 30, 1967).

15. Domingos, "Football in Colonial Lourenço Marques," 68.

16. Rolletta, *Finta finta*, 51.

17. Fernando Correia, *Matateu: O oitava maravilha* (Lisbon: Sete Caminhos, 2006), 54.

18. "Abel: Chave mestra para abrir defesas," *Ídolos do desporto* 7, no. 6 (January 7, 1972).

19. "Hilário: O 'rapazinho' do Alto Mahé," *Ídolos do desporto* 2, no. 2 (October 24, 1959).

20. See Nuno Domingos, "Football in Colonial Lourenço Marques: Bodily Practices and Social Rituals" (PhD diss., University of London, 2008); and Domingos, "Urban Football Narratives and the Colonial Process in Lourenço Marques," *International Journal of the History of Sport* 28, no. 15 (October 2011): 2159–75.

21. Nuno Domingos, "'Dos subúrbios da Lourenço Marques colonial aos campos de futebol da metrópole,' uma entrevista com Hilário Rosário da Conceição," *Cadernos de Estudos Africanos* 26 (2013): 228.

22. Ernesto Baltazar, interview by author, June 24, 2014.

23. Nuro Americano, interview by author, November 27, 2012.

24. Domingos, "Football in Colonial Lourenço Marques," 52.

25. Rolletta, *Finta finta*, 160.

26. Victor Andrade de Melo, "(Des)mobilização para a luta: O esporte como estratégia nos conflitos de Guiné Portuguesa (décadas de 1950 e 1960)," in *Esporte, cultura, nação, estado: Brasil e Portugal*, ed. Victor Andrade de Melo, Fabio de Faria Peres, and Maurício Drumond (Rio de Janeiro: 7 Letras, 2014), 68–82.

27. Richard Cashman, "Cricket and Colonialism: Colonial Hegemony and Indigenous Subversion?" in *Pleasure, Profit, Proselytism: British Culture and Sport at Home and Abroad, 1700–1914*, ed. James A. Mangan (London: Cass, 1988), 261.

28. See Allen Guttmann, *Games and Empires: Modern Sports and Cultural Imperialism* (New York: Columbia University Press, 1996), 69; C. L. R. James, *Beyond a Boundary* (London: Yellow Jersey Press, 2005); David Goldblatt, *The Ball Is Round: A Global History of Soccer* (New York: Penguin, 2006), 489; Nuno Domingos, "Football and Colonialism, Domination and Appropriation: The Mozambican Case," *Soccer and Society* 8, no. 4 (October 2007): 482; and Fahad Mustafa, "Cricket and Globalization: Global Processes and the Imperial Game," *Journal of Global History* 8, no. 2 (2013): 330.

29. Melo, "(Des)mobilização para a luta," 74–75. The squad was the Clube Desportivo a Recreativo de Bissau.

30. Although they are beyond the scope of this study, Domingos has contended that these "notables" had "mastered bureaucratic instruments and official procedure" essential to oversee the associations, which became sites in which "education, command of the Portuguese language, integration into the labour market, the adoption of a European lifestyle and participation in associations recognised by the colonial power, were valued qualities." Domingos, "Urban Football Narratives," 2166.

31. Alegi, *African Soccerscapes*, 15. Alegi's example is seemingly drawn from Anglophone Africa, in which the British had more closely shared their sporting traditions with indigenous elites in an attempt to co-opt them. This phenomenon is largely absent in the Lusophone context. See, for example, James A. Mangan, ed., *The Cultural Bond: Sport, Empire, Society* (London: Cass, 1992).

32. Domingos, "Football in Colonial Lourenço Marques," 66.

33. Domingos, "Urban Football Narratives," 2167.

34. Club owners did, however, occasionally sponsor poor but highly talented players.

35. Goldblatt, *Ball Is Round*, 491. As Goldblatt explains further, "In Brazzaville they refused. The native sports federation was abandoned and organized African football was set back a generation." See also Phyllis M. Martin, *Leisure and Society in Colonial Brazzaville* (Cambridge: Cambridge University Press, 1995).

36. Domingos, "Urban Football Narratives," 2167.

37. Ibid., 2168.

38. Alegi, *African Soccerscapes*, 32.

39. Domingos, "Football in Colonial Lourenço Marques," 137.

40. Ibid., 208.

41. "Yaúca: 'A pérola negra,'" *Ídolos do desporto* 2, no. 3 (October 31, 1959).

42. Alegi, *African Soccercapes*, 34.

43. Domingos, "Football in Colonial Lourenço Marques," 139.

44. The newspaper, which appeared in various forms until 1974, was created by the Grémio Africano, a proto-nationalist organization based in Lourenço Marques composed primarily of educated, urban black and mestiço Mozambicans, which advocated for greater indigenous rights as part of the "nativist" movement. In 1928, the paper announced that it had the widest circulation in the colony. See Aurélio Rocha, "Associativismo e nativismo em Moçambique: O grémio Africano de Lourenço Marques, 1908–1938" (PhD diss., Universidade Nova de Lisboa, 1991).

45. José Craveirinha, *O Brado Africano* (January 22, 1955), 8.

46. Domingos, "Football in Colonial Lourenço Marques," 12.

47. Rolletta, *Finta finta*, 205.

48. In Portuguese, *baixa* means "low" or "under," an allusion to the lower-elevation areas of the original city centers that the Portuguese constructed, in contrast to the higher elevations on the peripheries where Africans resided.

49. José Magode, *Pouvoir et reseaux sociaux au Mozambique: Appartenances, interactivité du social et du politique, 1933–1994* (Paris: Connaissances et Savoirs, 2005), 119.

50. Brian Stoddart, "Sport, Cultural Imperialism, and Colonial Response in the British Empire," *Comparative Studies in Society and History* 30, no. 4 (1988): 649–73.

51. Mangan, *Cultural Bond*.

52. "Ferreira Pinto: Um médio que dá sempre tudo por tudo," *Ídolos do desporto* 5, no. 13 (March 23, 1968).

53. "Bernardo da Velha: O 'Tapa Buracos' do F. Clube do Porto," *Ídolos do desporto* 5, no. 19 (March 23, 1968). In an analogous case from Mozambique, Augusto Matine explained that when he joined Clube Central in Mozambique for the 1963–1964 season, the team requested formal permission from

the Ministry of Education for him to also be able to play on the senior team. Eventually, a compromise was reached that allowed him to play up to half a match for the juniors, who played on Saturdays, and a full match for the senior team on Sunday afternoons. Naturally, he claimed that this helped his football development and continued with this arrangement before playing exclusively for the senior team. Augusto Matine, interview by author, November 20, 2012.

54. It wasn't until the 1950s that these teams began accepting black players, a full decade after their metropolitan-based parent clubs began employing the athletes. See Marcelo Bittencourt, "Jogando no campo do inimigo do inimigo: Futebol e luta política em Angola" (Lisbon: Seventh Congress on African Studies, 2010), 4.

55. Domingos, "Football in Colonial Lourenço Marques," 220. Domingos indicates that this inclusion shifted most mestiço fans' focus from the suburbs to downtown.

56. António Brassard, interview by author, June 19, 2014.

57. Most African players who eventually joined the top leagues already resided in the colonial capitals, but many others were identified by scouts in secondary cities or in even farther-flung areas, but whose considerable talents attracted the attention of the right people.

58. Peter Alegi, "Football and Apartheid Society: The South African Soccer League, 1960–1966," in Armstrong and Giulianotti, Football in Africa, 122.

59. Fair, Pastimes and Politics, 247.

60. For example, Augusto Matine, interview by author, November 20, 2012.

61. Fernando Gomes, interview by author, June 26, 2011.

62. António Brassard, interview by author, June 19, 2014.

63. Nuro Americano, interview by author, November 27, 2012.

64. Ibid.

65. Augusto Matine, interview by author, November 20, 2012.

66. For a fascinating, comprehensive discussion of the evolution of soccer tactics and their global circulation, see Jonathan Wilson, Inverting the Pyramid: The History of Soccer Tactics (New York: Nation Books, 2013).

67. Hilário da Conceição, interview by author, October 19, 2010.

68. "Yaúca: 'A pérola negra,'" Ídolos do desporto 2, no. 3 (October 31, 1959).

69. This system was devised in response to a change in 1925 of the offside rule, which newly reduced the number of opposing players required between attackers and the goal line from three to two.

70. Nuno Domingos, "A circulação de um esquema táctico: O exemplo do WM em Inglaterra, Portugal e Moçambique," Esporte e Sociedade 5, no. 14 (March–June 2010): 22. This article provides an extensive discussion of the

progression of the "WM" from its origin in England, to Portugal, and eventually to the overseas empire.

71. *Notícias da Tarde*, April 11, 1959, p. 6.

72. Domingos, "A circulação de um esquema táctico," 29.

73. Domingos, "Football in Colonial Lourenço Marques," 208.

74. This term is used throughout the Lusophone world. For example, the Portuguese national team is simply called the *Selecção*, as it is composed of the best Portuguese players. Similarly, in the Spanish-speaking soccer world, *Selección* is regularly used for national squads.

75. Eventually, "junior" squads were also assembled to give rising but still young players opportunities such as this. For example, Vicente Lucas, who would go on to play in the Mozambican *Selecção* and Portugal's *Selecção*, much earlier on played against, and defeated, a South African all-star squad as a member of the Mozambican junior squad. See "Vicente Lucas: O homem que não quis ser 'Matateu II,'" *Ídolos do desporto*, no. 34 (1956).

76. Eusébio, interview by author, October 28, 2010.

77. Melo, "(Des)mobilização para a luta," 69, 72.

78. Augusto Matine, interview by author, November 20, 2012.

79. Rolletta, *Finta finta*, 155.

80. Jacinto Veloso, *Memories at Low Altitude: The Autobiography of a Mozambican Security Chief* (Cape Town: Zebra Press, 2012), 14.

81. Rolletta, *Finta finta*, 46.

82. Mário Coluna, interview by author, November 21, 2012.

83. Correia, *Matateu*, 54.

84. Rolletta, *Finta finta*, 155.

85. Fernando Gomes, interview by author, June 26, 2011.

86. Guttmann, *Games and Empires*, 69.

87. Domingos, "Football in Colonial Lourenço Marques," 146; Domingos, "Dos subúrbios da Lourenço Marques colonial," 233. "Jackals" (*chacais*) was also a derogatory Portuguese term used locally to describe South African whites.

88. Armstrong, "Migration of the Black Panther," 257.

89. Apparently, Sporting was reluctant to release him, but in order to gain employment at Ferroviário he had to join the football club, so he sat out a year until he achieved the result he had been seeking. "Costa Pereira: O 'goleiro' do Maracanã," *Ídolos do desporto*, no. 5 (1956).

90. Correia, *Matateu*, 21, 54.

91. Domingos, "Dos subúrbios da Lourenço Marques," 233.

92. Alegi, *African Soccerscapes*, 37. This practice began in Lagos before spreading to other areas of the colony. In fact, the oldest organized football

club in Nigeria is believed to be the Public Works Department, which was formed in 1929. See Wiebe Boer, "A Story of Heroes, of Epics: The Rise of Football in Nigeria," in Armstrong and Giulianotti, *Football in Africa*, 66.

93. Fair, *Pastimes and Politics*, 246.

94. Alegi, *African Soccerscapes*, 37.

95. *O Brado Africano* (August 9, 1941): 3.

96. José Craveirinha, "Clubes Suburbanos o que foram e o que são," *Voz de Moçambique* (June 13, 1964): 4.

97. "Eusébio: Um astro no firmament do futebol mundial," *Ídolos do desporto* 6, no. 2 (November 29, 1969).

98. Augusto Matine, interview by author, November 20, 2012.

99. Ernesto Baltazar, interview by author, June 24, 2014.

Chapter 3: Following the Ball, Realizing a Goal

1. Peter Alegi, *African Soccerscapes: How a Continent Changed the World's Game* (Athens: Ohio University Press, 2010), 81.

2. David Goldblatt, *The Ball Is Round: A Global History of Soccer* (New York: Penguin, 2006), 422.

3. João Nuno Coelho, *Portugal—A equipa de todos nós: Nacionalismo, futebol e media* (Porto: Afrontamento, 2001), 105.

4. Ibid.

5. Rahul Mahendra Kumar, *A pureza perdida do desporto: Futebol no Estado Novo* (PhD diss., University of Lisbon, 2014), 283. The Ministry of Education archive in Lisbon houses the letters that constitute the years-long exchange between state and club officials regarding the transfer of players from the colonies to the metropole. Delaying the final ruling that granted permission for these relocations were debates regarding how players officially disengaged from their existing clubs and whether or not transfer rules in place in Portugal and the islands (Madeira and the Azores) also applied to the colonies.

6. Most famously, Guilherme Espírito Santo and Fernando Peyroteo had come from Angola to play in the metropole in the 1930s, the former born in Lisbon but raised in the colonies and the latter the son of Portuguese settlers.

7. Nuno Domingos, "Urban Football Narratives and the Colonial Process in Lourenço Marques," *International Journal of the History of Sport* 28, no. 15 (October 2011): 2159–75.

8. See Alegi, *African Soccerscapes*, 82; Paul Darby, "Out of Africa: The Exodus of Elite African Football Talent to Europe," *WorkingUSA* 10, no. 4 (December 2007): 444.

9. Pierre Lanfranchi and Matthew Taylor, *Moving with the Ball: The Migration of Professional Footballers* (Oxford: Berg, 2001), 180.

10. "Iaúca: A flecha Benfiquista," *Ídolos do desporto* 3, no. 25 (February 17, 1961).

11. Ministry of Education, Oficio no. 2159/47/PC/AN, July 5, 1947.

12. Ministry of Education, Caixa, letter, September 2, 1949.

13. Ministry of Education, Caixa 446, letters, September 2 and 15, 1949.

14. Ministry of Education, Caixa 446, Oficio Lo 3/49 No 4/I-2 (405), October 4, 1949.

15. Kumar, "A pureza perdida do desporto," 284.

16. Ibid.

17. "Encarnados" was the more politically correct term used when referring to Benfica, employed in favor of the term "Vermelhos" (Reds). Personal exchange with Nuno Domingos.

18. Darby, "Out of Africa," 444. According to David Goldblatt, "Guttman brought new levels of sophistication and attention to detail in the club's preparation and organization. He transformed the training regimen of the squad and introduced the team to the tactical and positional innovations of Hungarian football. Where only 'WM' or even more antiquated systems had been the norm, Benfica began to look like a modern football team with a flat back four and attacking midfielders." Goldblatt, *Ball Is Round*, 423.

19. "Águas: 'Esse desconhecido' que veio do Lobit," *Ídolos do desporto*, no. 5 (1956).

20. Mário Wilson, interview by author, October 29, 2010.

21. Hilário da Conceição, interview by author, October 19, 2010.

22. Augusto Matine, interview by author, November 20, 2012.

23. Paola Rolletta, *Finta finta* (Maputo, Mozambique: Texto Editores, 2011), 161.

24. Nuro Americano, interview by author, November 27, 2012.

25. "Bernardo da Velha: O 'Tapa Buracos' do F. Clube do Porto," *Ídolos do desporto* 5, no. 19 (March 23, 1968). The contract was later altered, apparently somewhat underhandedly, and da Velha found that he was beholden to the club—a "prisoner," he later claimed—for three years, rather than one, before eventually moving on and realizing significant success with FC Porto.

26. Gary Armstrong, "The Migration of the Black Panther: An Interview with Eusebio of Mozambique and Portugal," in *Football in Africa: Conflict, Conciliation and Community*, ed. Gary Armstrong and Richard Giulianotti (New York: Palgrave Macmillan, 2004), 255.

27. *Luva*, the Portuguese word for "glove," was also used to describe this type of discreet signing bonus.

28. Mário Coluna, interview by author, November 21, 2012.

29. Rolletta, *Finta finta*, 38. According to Renato Caldeira, Coluna's father was also influenced by the poet Craveirinha, a close friend, who similarly wanted Mário to join the "Eagles" rather than the "Lions," owing to his personal club inclinations. See Caldeira, *Coluna: Monstro sagrado* (Maputo: Sográfica, 2003), 26.

30. Mário Coluna, interview by author, November 21, 2012.

31. Rolletta, *Finta finta*, 38.

32. As will be considered later in this chapter, Sporting Clube de Benguela officials were apparently alarmed to see Pinto in the newspaper playing for the Sporting de Portugal reserve team and consequently filed a formal complaint, suggesting that there were improprieties associated with the player's release and subsequent signing.

33. "Dinis: O Ídolo do Asa que triunfa no Sporting," *Ídolos do desporto* 7, no. 5 (January 1, 1972).

34. Caldeira, *Coluna*, 26.

35. Augusto Matine, interview by author, November 20, 2012.

36. Hilário de Conceição, interview by author, October 19, 2010.

37. Rolletta, *Finta finta*, 97.

38. Paul Hayward, "From Africa to Posterity: How Eusébio Lit Up the World Cup," *Guardian*, June 5, 2010, http://www.theguardian.com/football /2010/jun/06/eusebio-africa-world-cup.

39. Ibid.

40. Eusébio da Silva Ferreira, *My Name Is Eusébio*, trans. Derrik Low (London: Routledge and Kegan Paul, 1967), 17.

41. Legend has it that Elisa deposited the money from her son's initial contract into a bank in Mozambique, with the stipulation that if her son didn't go on to become a great footballer once in Portugal she would pay the money back, because she "had a good heart." Of course, this account is most likely unverifiable, but nevertheless it further feeds the myth of Eusébio and, in particular, the intrigue surrounding his signing. See Hayward, "From Africa to Posterity."

42. Armstrong, "Migration of the Black Panther," 257.

43. Shéu Han, interview by author, July 1, 2014.

44. There is some debate regarding how Benfica rated the player. In one account, club official José Valdivieso, the juniors coach, was in Africa seeking to sign talented players and suggested to the club's directors that Yaúca would be a "valuable resource," while another account suggests that Valdivieso submitted only a lukewarm account of the player's potential. Regardless, Benfica paid for their equivocation, forced to pay out some 2,500 contos in 1963 to pry

Yaúca (who was known as Iaúca by then) away from Belenenses. See "Iaúca: A flecha Benfiquista," *Ídolos do desporto* 3, no. 25 (February 17, 1961).

45. "Yaúca: A pérola negra," *Ídolos do desporto* 2, no. 3 (October 31, 1959).

46. "Carlos Duarte: O extremo-direito que Monteiro da Costa descobriu para o F. C. do Porto," *Ídolos do desporto* 2, no. 49 (January 5, 1957).

47. Ibid. The club apparently promised that Duarte could also continue his studies while playing, but it's unclear if he ever did.

48. Interestingly, Conceição had balked when he was initially approached to play in the metropole. According to the player, who was working in Angola at an air base when Vitória de Setúbal extended this offer, "I was flattered but declined the offer. I had a life that was more or less good, I was near my family and beyond that professional football wasn't that interesting to me." Apparently, though, after writing a letter to his parents to inform them about the offer, they encouraged him to go. He accepted, but with the stipulation that Vitória de Setúbal guarantee him a return trip home in case he didn't make the team, which the club did. He would later indicate that his desire to "get to know the metropole" motivated him to relocate more so than the opportunity to play football. The club also provided him with 10 contos to purchase clothes before he departed, as he was informed that "it would be cold in Portugal." That was, at the time, the most money he'd ever seen. See "Conceição: O 'Grande Capitão' Sadino," *Ídolos do desporto* 6, no. 17 (March 14, 1970).

49. "José Maria: O 'pulmão' do Vitória," *Ídolos do desporto* 6, no. 13 (December 6, 1969).

50. Hilário da Conceição, interview by author, October 19, 2010.

51. "Jacinto João: A 'pérola negra' do Sado," *Ídolos do desporto* 6, no. 3 (December 6, 1969).

52. Ibid.

53. Ibid.

54. Shéu Han, interview by author, July 1, 2014.

55. Rui Rodrigues, interview by author, June 25, 2014. One source indicates that Rodrigues was offered twice as much money by Académica compared to the amount that Benfica was offering. However, this version is difficult to believe, and during our interview he emphasized that the opportunity to study at Coimbra was the decisive factor. Regardless, Rodrigues did eventually make his way to Benfica, signing with the Lisbon club nine years after arriving in Portugal, and for a considerably larger amount of money. See "Rui Rodrigues: Um homem tranquilo a fazer futebol," *Ídolos do desporto* 7, no. 12 (February 19, 1972).

56. "Araújo: O 'Ben Barek' de Sá da Bandeira," *Ídolos do desporto* 2, no. 23 (March 18, 1960).

57. See "Armando: O '115' do Sporting," *Ídolos do desporto* 5, no. 1 (December 30, 1967). Apparently, only Manhiça's fiancée, Adelaide, remained unconvinced, at least for a time.

58. Ernesto Baltazar, interview by author, June 24, 2014. Beginning in 1960, the winner of the top Angolan league played the champion from the top Mozambican league for the right to travel to Portugal to participate in the Taça de Portugal, an annual domestic tournament that Benfica has won twenty-five times to date. Although the colonial clubs had very limited success in the tournament, the inclusion of a squad from the colonies served as further propaganda for the regime as it continued to stress the unity between the empire and the metropole; and, regardless, it did offer the best African players an opportunity to impress metropolitan club officials and hopefully earn a contract. According to Fernando Gomes, a Portuguese who played in Portugal and Angola, when African footballers came to compete in the tournament, "They would often stay [in Portugal] because the club would promise them things . . . and would win them over by talking to them. That was very common, as the Taça de Portugal served as a showcase for these players." Fernando Gomes, interview by author, June 26, 2011.

59. Rolletta, *Finta finta*, 82.

60. Ibid.

61. For example, Augusto Matine left behind Maria Francisca, whom he had married by proxy, when he left Mozambique to play for Benfica in 1966. Two years would pass before he would return to Lourenço Marques over the summer holiday to properly marry her. See Rolletta, *Finta finta*, 156.

62. "Vicente Lucas: O homem que não quis ser 'Matateu II,'" *Ídolos do desporto*, no. 34 (1956).

63. Armstrong, "Migration of the Black Panther," 258.

64. "Carlos Duarte: O extremo-direito que Monteiro da Costa descobriu para o F.C. do Porto," *Ídolos do desporto* 2, no. 49 (January 5, 1957).

65. Fernando Correia, *Matateu: O oitava maravilha* (Lisbon: Sete Caminhos, 2006), 22.

66. "Santana: O 'Molengão' de Catumbela," *Ídolos do desporto* 2, no. 17 (February 5, 1960).

67. Rolletta, *Finta finta*, 119.

68. Ibid., 33.

69. Ibid., 46.

70. "Matateu: Terror dos Guards-Redes," *Ídolos do desporto*, no. 3 (March 17, 1956); Acácio Rosa, *Factos, nomes e números da história do clube de cutebol "Os Belenenses"* (Lisbon: Freitas and Freitas, 1961), 565.

71. Rosa, *Factos, nomes e números*, 565. Both Guilherme Espírito Santo and Fernando Peyroteo had come from Angola to play in the metropole in the 1930s.

72. "Vicente Lucas: O homem que não quis ser 'Matateu II,'" *Ídolos do desporto*, no. 34 (1956); Rolletta, *Finta finta*, 65.

73. Rolletta, *Finta finta*, 105.

74. See "Conceição: O 'Grande Capitão' Sadino," *Ídolos do desporto* 6, no. 17 (March 14, 1970).

75. António Brassard, interview by author, June 19, 2014.

76. "Yaúca: "A pérola negra," *Ídolos do desporto* 2, no. 3 (October 31, 1959).

77. Rolletta, *Finta finta*, 143.

78. Mike Cronin and David Mayall, eds., *Sporting Nationalisms: Identity, Ethnicity, Immigration and Assimilation* (London: Cass, 1998), 7.

79. António Brassard, interview by author, June 19, 2014.

80. Shéu Han, interview by author, July 1, 2014.

81. Augusto Matine, interview by author, November 20, 2012.

82. Ibid.

83. Hilário da Conceição, interview by author, October 19, 2010.

84. António Brassard, interview by author, June 19, 2014.

85. Caldeira, *Coluna*, 31.

86. *Guardian Desportivo* (September 8, 1954): 3.

87. Augusto Matine, interview by author, November 20, 2012.

88. Pierre Lanfranchi and Matthew Taylor, *Moving with the Ball: The Migration of Professional Footballers* (Oxford: Berg, 2001), 179.

89. See, for example, Eusébio, *My Name Is Eusébio*; Armstrong, "Migration of the Black Panther"; and António Simões, *Eusébio: Como nunca se viu* (Alfragide, Portugal: Dom Quixote, 2014).

90. Eusébio, *My Name Is Eusébio*, 28.

91. Armstrong, "Migration of the Black Panther," 258.

92. Ana Santos, *Herois desportivos: Estudo de caso sobre Eusébio, de corpo a ícone da nação* (Lisbon: Instituto do Desporto de Portugal, 2004), 87.

93. Armstrong, "Migration of the Black Panther," 258.

94. Rosa, *Factos, nomes e números*, 565.

Chapter 4: Successes, Setbacks, and Strategies

1. Nuno Domingos, "'Dos subúrbios da Lourenço Marques colonial aos campos de futebol da metrópole,' uma entrevista com Hilário Rosário da Conceição," *Cadernos de Estudos Africanos* 26 (2013): 237.

2. "Vicente Lucas: O homem que não quis ser 'Matateu II,'" *Ídolos do desporto*, no. 34 (1956).

3. Augusto Matine, interview by author, November 20, 2012.

4. "Calado: O 'Papua' de Lourenço Marques," *Ídolos do desporto* 5, no. 9 (February 24, 1968).

5. Eusébio, interview by author, October 28, 2010.

6. "Miguel Arcanjo: O homem duas vezes quase perdido para a futbol," *Ídolos do desporto*, no. 42 (1956).

7. "José Maria: O 'pulmão' do Vitória," *Ídolos do desporto* 6, no. 13 (December 6, 1969).

8. Nuro Americano, interview by author, November 27, 2012.

9. Fernando Gomes, interview by author, June 26, 2011.

10. João Nuno Coelho and Francisco Pinheiro, *A paixão do povo: História do futebol em Portugal* (Porto: Afrontamento, 2002), 516.

11. Ibid.

12. Ruaridh Nicoll, "The Great Escape That Changed Africa's Future," *Guardian*, March 8, 2015.

13. Fernando Gomes, interview by author, June 26, 2011.

14. Nuro Americano, interview by author, November 27, 2012.

15. Augusto Matine, interview by author, November 20, 2012.

16. Paola Rolletta, *Finta finta* (Maputo, Mozambique: Texto Editores, 2011), 155.

17. Gary Armstrong, "The Migration of the Black Panther: An Interview with Eusebio of Mozambique and Portugal," in *Football in Africa: Conflict, Conciliation and Community*, ed. Gary Armstrong and Richard Giulianotti (New York: Palgrave Macmillan, 2004), 259.

18. "A equipa do Sporting Clube de Portugal," *Ídolos do desporto* 2, no. 39 (July 8, 1960).

19. Domingos, "Dos subúrbios da Lourenço Marques," 237.

20. "Jacinto João: A 'pérola negra' do Sado," *Ídolos do desporto* 6, no. 3 (December 6, 1969).

21. Hilário da Conceição, interview by author, October 19, 2010.

22. Renato Caldeira, *Coluna: Monstro sagrado* (Maputo: Sográfica, 2003), 37.

23. Nuno Domingos, "Football in Colonial Lourenço Marques: Bodily Practices and Social Rituals" (PhD diss., University of London, 2008), 213.

24. *Guardian Desportivo* (September 8, 1954), 6. Translation as it appears in Domingos, "Football in Colonial Lourenço Marques," 213.

25. Rolletta, *Finta finta*, 53.

26. Fernando Correia, *Matateu: O oitava maravilha* (Lisbon: Sete Caminhos, 2006), 55.

27. "Santana: O 'Molengão' de Catumbela," *Ídolos do desporto* 2, no. 17 (February 5, 1960).

28. "Mascarenhas: Um Angolano que triunfa no Sporting," *Ídolos do desporto* 3, no. 7 (January 18, 1964).

29. "A equipa do Sporting Clube de Portugal," *Ídolos do desporto* 2, no. 39 (1960).

30. "Hilário: Um herói do 'mundial,'" *Ídolos do desporto* 5, no. 10 (March 2, 1968).

31. Peter Alegi, *African Soccerscapes: How a Continent Changed the World's Game* (Athens: Ohio University Press, 2010), 84.

32. In one instance from 1964 when Eusébio was slated to play for the "Rest of Europe" squad against a Scandinavian all-star squad, certain measures were taken in an attempt to have the Mozambican removed from the "Rest of Europe" team, with race intimated as one of the reasons. Ticket sales were rumored to potentially plummet if this step wasn't taken. Ultimately, Eusébio did play, coming on as a second-half substitute and scoring for his team, 4–2 winners in the affair. See Eusébio da Silva Ferreira, *My Name Is Eusébio*, trans. Derrik Low (London: Routledge and Kegan Paul, 1967), 88.

33. See Lanfranchi and Taylor, *Moving with the Ball*.

34. Marina Tavares Dias, *História do futebol em Lisboa: De 1888 aos grandes estádios* (Coimbra: Quimera Editores, 2000), 236.

35. Domingos, "Football in Colonial Lourenço Marques," 291.

36. Alegi, *African Soccerscapes*, 84.

37. Ibid.

38. Ibid.

39. Lanfranchi and Taylor, *Moving with the Ball*, 176.

40. Caldeira, *Coluna*, 35.

41. Alegi, *African Soccerscapes*, 84.

42. Mário Torres, interview by author, June 22, 2011.

43. "Calado: O "Papua" de Lourenço Marques," *Ídolos do desporto* 5, no. 9 (February 24, 1968).

44. Augusto Matine, interview by author, November 20, 2012.

45. Mário Coluna, interview by author, November 21, 2012.

46. Mário Wilson, interview by author, October 29, 2010.

47. Rui Rodrigues, interview by author, June 25, 2014.

48. Mário Torres, interview by author, June 22, 2011.

49. Acácio Rosa, *Factos, nomes e números da história do clube de futebol "Os Belenenses"* (Lisbon: Freitas and Freitas, 1961), 565.

50. "Águas: 'Esse desconhecido' que veio do Lobito," *Ídolos do desporto*, no. 5 (1956).

51. Shéu Han, interview by author, July 1, 2014.

52. "Bernardo da Velha: O 'Tapa Buracos' do F. Clube do Porto," *Ídolos do desporto* 5, no. 19 (March 23, 1968).

53. See "Iaúca: A flecha Benfiquista," *Ídolos do desporto* 3, no. 25 (February 17, 1961); "Matateu: Um nome que fica na história do futebol," *Ídolos do desporto* 2, no. 72 (February 24, 1961).

54. Hilário da Conceição, interview by author, October 19, 2010.

55. His brothers, Fernando and João, also played in Portugal, with the former also enjoying a brief spell in Spain with Desportivo da Coruña, on loan from his Portuguese side, FC Braga. Unfortunately, frustratingly little biographical information exists related to Mendonça's experiences.

56. Mário Coluna, interview by author, November 21, 2012. Coluna's contract with the French club reportedly dwarfed his Benfica deal, earning him each month roughly what he made annually in Lisbon. In this manner, he approximated his lifelong earnings in Portugal in a single season in France. See Renato Caldeira, *Coluna: Monstro sagrado* (Maputo: Sográfica, 2003), 67.

57. Mário Coluna, interview by author, November 21, 2012.

58. Augusto Matine, interview by author, November 20, 2012.

59. Eusébio, interview by author, October 28, 2010.

60. Ibid.

61. Augusto Matine, interview by author, November 20, 2012.

62. "Rui Rodrigues: Um homem tranquilo a fazer futebol," *Ídolos do desporto* 7, no. 12 (February 19, 1972).

63. Correia, *Matateu*, 56.

64. Rolletta, *Finta finta*, 168.

65. Hilário da Conceição, interview by author, October 19, 2010.

66. Ibid.

67. Eusébio, interview by author, October 28, 2010.

68. Caldeira, *Coluna*, 57.

69. Mário Coluna, interview by author, November 21, 2012.

70. Mário Torres, interview by author, June 22, 2011.

71. Shéu Han, interview by author, July 1, 2014.

72. Hilário da Conceição, interview by author, October 19, 2010.

73. Mário Coluna, interview by author, November 21, 2012.

74. Hilário da Conceição, interview by author, October 19, 2010.

75. Augusto Matine, interview by author, November 20, 2012.

76. "Abel: Chave mestra para abrir defesas," *Ídolos do desporto* 7, no. 6 (January 7, 1972).

77. Eugénio Silva, *Eusébio: Pantera negra* (Lisbon: Meribérica, 1992).

78. António Brassard, interview by author, June 19, 2014.

79. Correia, *Matateu*, 49.

80. Ibid., 50.

81. "Santana: O 'Molengão' de Catumbela," *Ídolos do desporto* 2, no. 17 (February 5, 1960).

82. "Bernardo da Velha: O 'Tapa Buracos' do F. Clube do Porto," *Ídolos do desporto* 5, no. 19 (March 23, 1968).

83. "Calado: O 'Papua' de Lourenço Marques," *Ídolos do desporto* 5, no. 9 (February 24, 1968).

84. "Abel: Chave mestra para abrir defesas," *Ídolos do desporto* 7, no. 6 (January 7, 1972); "Zeca: 'Calma e segurança na zona de perigo,'" *Ídolos do desporto* 7, no. 18 (April 1, 1972).

85. "Mascarenhas: Um Angolano que triunfa no Sporting," *Ídolos do desporto* 3, no. 7 (January 18, 1964); "Bernardo da Velha: O 'Tapa Buracos' do F. Clube do Porto," *Ídolos do desporto* 5, no. 19 (March 23, 1968).

86. Salaries in Portugal were, however, significantly lower than in, for example, Italy and Brazil during this period. Nonetheless, the best-paid African players were earning much more than even the highest-paid public officials.

87. Domingos, "Dos subúrbios da Lourenço Marques," 238.

88. Mário Wilson, interview by author, October 29, 2010.

89. Hilário da Conceição, interview by author, October 19, 2010.

90. Ibid.

91. Correia, *Matateu*, 50. Parenthetical page numbers shown in remainder of text paragraph reference this work.

92. Rolletta, *Finta finta*, 53.

93. *Os 4 gigantes do futebol Português* (Lisbon: Ag. Port. de Revistas, D.L., 1965), 9.

94. Armstrong, "Migration of the Black Panther," 262.

95. Alegi, *African Soccerscapes*, 79.

96. Ibid.

97. "Iaúca: A flecha Benfiquista," *Ídolos do desporto* 3, no. 25 (February 17, 1961).

98. "Dinis: O ídolo do asa que triunfa no Sporting," *Ídolos do desporto* 7, no. 5 (January 1, 1972).

99. "Rui Rodrigues: Um homem tranquilo a fazer futebol," *Ídolos do desporto* 7, no. 12 (February 19, 1972). Rodrigues did, in fact, finish his degree and worked as a pharmacist upon retiring, something I learned when I interviewed him in the small town in central Portugal where he used to work, and still lives.

100. Rui Rodrigues, interview by author, June 25, 2014.

101. Similarly, migrant players from Anglophone and Francophone Africa often traveled to England and France, respectively, only after being offered remunerated employment to complement their soccer exploits.

102. Mário Torres, interview by author, June 22, 2011.

103. If student-footballers abandoned their studies, they were "banished" from the institution and were to return to their former teams. This situation was rare, but the written record reveals a handful of cases in which clubs that lost players to Coimbra demanded that they return due to their alleged lack of attention to their studies. See, for example, Ministry of Education, Caixa 457.

104. Mário Wilson, interview by author, October 29, 2010.

105. Rolletta, *Finta finta*, 46.

106. Mário Wilson, "Uma marca na história," in *Académica: História do futebol*, ed. João Santana and João Mesquita (Coimbra, Portugal: Almedina, 2007), 512.

107. "Araújo: O 'Ben Barek' de Sá da Bandeira," *Ídolos do desporto* 2, no. 23 (March 18, 1960).

108. "Ferreira Pinto: Um médio que dá sempre tudo por tudo," *Ídolos do desporto* 5, no. 13 (March 23, 1968).

109. Pinto moved to the CUF for three years before receiving an irresistible offer to join Benfica. He stayed with the Lisbon club for three years prior to finishing his career at União de Tomar.

110. Mário Wilson, interview by author, October 29, 2010.

111. António Brassard, interview by author, June 19, 2014.

112. Mário Torres, interview by author, June 22, 2011.

113. "Rui Rodrigues: Um homem tranquilo a fazer futebol," *Ídolos do desporto* 7, no. 12 (February 19, 1972). During our interview, he indicated that he pleaded with club directors to release him from his studies while he juggled military duty, football, and schoolwork, but to no avail. Rui Rodrigues, interview by author, June 25, 2014. However, Mário Wilson did convey to me that players enjoyed certain privileges and that teachers would sometimes grant them latitude because "these instructors were big supporters of Académica." Mário Wilson, interview by author, October 29, 2010.

114. "Rui Rodrigues: Um homem tranquilo a fazer futebol," *Ídolos do desporto* 7, no. 12 (February 19, 1972).

115. Lanfranchi and Taylor, *Moving with the Ball*, 181.

116. Fernando Gomes, interview by author, June 26, 2011.

117. Manuel de Oliveira, interview by author, October 26, 2010.

118. "A equipa do Sporting Clube de Portugal," *Ídolos do desporto* 2, no. 39 (1960).

119. Pinto actually played five more seasons, three with Benfica and the next two with União de Tomar.

120. "A equipa do Sporting Clube de Portugal," *Ídolos do desporto* 2, no. 39 (1960).

Chapter 5: Calculated Conciliation

1. For an account of the hijacking written by the Portuguese politician, activist, and ringleader of the operation, see Henrique Galvão, *Santa Maria: My Crusade for Portugal* (London: Weidenfeld and Nicolson, 1961).

2. The Kennedy administration, in particular, in 1961 stressed to Lisbon that it would withdraw its support for Portugal in the UN if the Estado Novo continued to refuse to consider self-determination for the African colonies.

3. Ana Santos, *Herois desportivos: Estudo de caso sobre Eusébio, de corpo a ícone da nação* (Lisbon: Instituto do Desporto de Portugal, 2004), 92.

4. Ibid.

5. Pedro Vasco and Ricardo Galvão, *Monstros sagrados: Benfica anos 60s* (Lisbon: Primebooks, 2011), 8.

6. João Nuno Coelho, *Portugal—A equipa de todos nós: Nacionalismo, futebol e Media* (Porto: Afrontamento, 2001), 112. Nuno Coelho further suggests that the influential paper adopted this increasingly nationalist tone following the 1961 deaths of its more moderate editors (and founders), Cândido de Oliveira and Ribeiro dos Reis. Ibid., 109.

7. Nuno Domingos, "Football in Colonial Lourenço Marques: Bodily Practices and Social Rituals" (PhD diss., University of London, 2008), 95.

8. Coelho, *Portugal*, 109.

9. Ibid.

10. Ibid., 126.

11. Santos, *Herois desportivos*, 89.

12. Ibid., 90.

13. Ibid., 91, 93.

14. João Malheiro, *Eusébio: A biografia autorizado* (Vila do Conde: Quid-Novi, 2012), 113.

15. TT/PIDE/DGS: Folder: PIDE/DGS; 4703-CI (2); N.T. 7366 Sport Lisboa e Benfica.

16. Fátima is the site in central Portugal where, in 1917, apparitions sent from the heavens allegedly appeared. Afterward, a sanctuary was constructed to commemorate the events, and Fátima remains a popular pilgrimage destination for Catholics and, thus, was used by the regime as a symbol for the country's religious devotion.

17. Malheiro, *Eusébio*, 112.

18. Ana Santos, "Narrativas da nação proporcionadas pelas vitórias desportivas e seus heróis," *IV Congresso Português de Sociologia* (April 2000): 6.

19. João Nuno Coelho and Francisco Pinheiro, *A paixão do povo: História do futebol em Portugal* (Porto: Afrontamento, 2002), 482.

20. Ibid.

21. Santos, "Narrativas da nação," 6.

22. Malheiro, *Eusébio*, 112.

23. Santos, *Herois desportivos*, 92.

24. Ibid.; Santos, "Narrativas da nação," 6.

25. Santos, *Herois desportivos*, 94.

26. Eusébio da Silva Ferreira, *My Name Is Eusébio*, trans. Derrik Low (London: Routledge and Kegan Paul, 1967), 158.

27. Santos, "Narrativas da nação," 6.

28. Mário Coluna, interview by author, November 21, 2012.

29. Hilário da Conceição, interview by author, October 19, 2010.

30. António Brassard, interview by author, June 19, 2014.

31. Marcos Cardão, "Um significante instrumental, Eusébio e a banalização lusotropicalismo na década de 1960," in *Esporte, cultura, nação, estado: Brasil e Portugal*, ed. Victor Andrade de Melo, Fabio de Faria Peres, and Maurício Drumond (Rio de Janeiro: 7Letras, 2014), 181.

32. Ibid.

33. Debate continues regarding whether Salazar classified him as a "treasure" or an "asset." See Santos, *Herois desportivos*, 99.

34. A conto is equivalent to one thousand Portuguese escudos. Eventually, due to a poor showing in the 1966 World Cup, the Italian Football Federation banned Italian clubs from employing foreign players, so Eusébio would not have been able to sign for Juventus anyway.

35. Gabrielle Marcotti, "Eusebio: The Agony of '66," *Times* (London), Monday, February 16, 2004.

36. Eusébio indicated to me that at the time of the consecration, only club officials knew that he was in Italy; everyone else assumed he was in Mozambique. Eusébio, interview by author, October 28, 2010.

37. Gary Armstrong, "The Migration of the Black Panther: An Interview with Eusebio of Mozambique and Portugal," in *Football in Africa: Conflict, Conciliation and Community*, ed. Gary Armstrong and Richard Giulianotti (New York: Palgrave Macmillan, 2004), 261.

38. Eusébio, interview by author, October 28, 2010.

39. Divergent from the Lusophone case, in the late 1950s, an important and sizable contingent of Francophone African footballers playing in and for

France fled the country to support the struggle for independence in Algeria. See Pierre Lanfranchi, "Mekloufi, un footballeur français dans la guerre d'Algérie," *Actes de la recherche en sciences sociales* 103, no. 1 (1994): 70–74.

40. Armstrong, "Migration of the Black Panther," 262.

41. "Torres: O 'jogador médico,'" *Ídolos do desporto* 2, no. 6 (November 21, 1959).

42. "Ferreira Pinto: Um médio que dá sempre tudo por tudo," *Ídolos do desporto* 5, no. 13 (March 23, 1968).

43. Eugénio Silva, *Eusébio: Pantera negra* (Lisbon: Meribérica, 1992), 52.

44. Armstrong, "Migration of the Black Panther," 253. Curiously, during the interview, Eusébio actually confused the Black Panthers with the Symbionese Liberation Army, suggesting that the former (rather than the latter) had a "cobra as a symbol and had kidnapped Patricia Hearst."

45. António Simões, *Eusébio: Como nunca se viu* (Alfragide, Portugal: Dom Quixote, 2014), 182. In fact, the 1966 World Cup had already been politicized, as the African and Asian confederations boycotted the tournament owing to FIFA's unwillingness to allocate more spots for their member nations. As such, Eusébio and the other African players on Portugal's squad were, essentially, representing the entire continent at the event.

46. Nuno Domingos, "'Dos subúrbios da Lourenço Marques colonial aos campos de futebol da metrópole,' uma entrevista com Hilário Rosário da Conceição," *Cadernos de Estudos Africanos* 26 (2013): 237.

47. Augusto Matine, interview by author, November 20, 2012.

48. Coelho and Pinheiro, *A paixão do povo*, 516.

49. Mário Wilson, "Uma marca na história," in *Académica: História do futebol*, ed. João Santana and João Mesquita (Coimbra: Almedina, 2011), 512.

50. Mário Wilson, interview by author, October 29, 2010.

51. Wilson, "Uma marca na história," 512.

52. Tomás Medeiros, interview by author, June 30, 2014.

53. Renato Caldeira, *Coluna: Monstro sagrado* (Maputo: Sográfica, 2003), 63.

54. Ibid.

55. António Brassard, interview by author, June 19, 2014.

56. Nuro Americano, interview by author, November 27, 2012.

57. Ibid.

58. Ibid.

59. Paola Rolletta, *Finta finta* (Maputo, Mozambique: Texto Editores, 2011), 161.

60. Ricardo Antunes Martins, dir., *Futebol de causas*, film, written by Ricardo Antunes Martins, 2009.

61. After a split with Neto, Chipenda left the MPLA in the mid-1970s, only to later rejoin the organization in 1992. A full-length biography of this important figure in Angolan history remains to be written.

62. Martins, *Futebol de causas*.

63. Mário Torres, interview by author, June 22, 2011.

64. Wilson, "Uma marca na história," 513.

65. Rolletta, *Finta finta*, 120.

66. Ibid., 48.

67. Martins, *Futebol de causas*.

68. Ibid.

69. Ibid.

70. Coelho and Pinheiro, *A paixão do povo*, 485.

71. Simões, *Eusébio*, 218. Somewhat ironically, Artur Jorge would sign with Benfica only three days after the cup final, rejecting Sporting's overtures.

72. Homero Serpa and Vitor Serpa, *História do futebol em Portugal* (Lisbon: CTT Correios, 2004), 92.

73. Coelho and Pinheiro, *A paixão do povo*, 485.

74. Mário Wilson, interview by author, October 29, 2010.

75. Malheiro, *Eusébio*, 112.

76. For example, at the end of 1965, the Lisbon CEI had almost 600 members, while the Coimbra house had roughly 115. See Cláudia Castelo, "A Casa dos Estudantes do Império: Lugar de memória anticolonial," CIEA7, no. 6: (Counter-)Memories of Colonialism: Remembrance, Resistance and Transference in Anti-colonial African Narratives (2010): 8.

77. The government cut funding for the CEI in 1963, so essentially the entity simply "died a slow death." Moreover, by this time, universities had been established in Angola and Mozambique, so from a purely educational perspective, there was a reduced need to send African students to the metropole for training. See Cláudia Castelo, "Casa dos Estudantes do Império (1944–1965): Uma síntese histórica," *Mensagem: Cinquentenário da fundação da Casa dos Estudantes do Império, 1944–1994* (Lisbon: Associação Casa dos Estudantes do Império, 1997), 28. Apparently, this oppositional reputation traveled with the club, such that during a trip to Guiné as part of a summer tour in 1967, António Brassard, a member of the Académica squad at the time, indicated that the players were instructed not to mix with locals, who might be eager to discuss antiregime politics with these supposedly receptive student-athletes. António Brassard, interview by author, June 19, 2014.

78. During the 1962 student protests and the associated academic crisis, the regime raided the Lisbon branch of the CEI, interrogated members, and

canceled the proposed commemoration of the "Day of the Student." Castelo, "Casa dos Estudantes do Império," 28.

79. Cláudia Castelo, "A Casa dos Estudantes do Império: Lugar de memória anticolonial," CIEA7, no. 6: (Counter-) Memories of Colonialism: Remembrance, Resistance and Transference in Anti-Colonial African Narratives (2010), 15.

80. Most of these future leaders transitioned through the Lisbon CEI. See John Marcum, *The Angolan Revolution*, vol. 1, *The Anatomy of an Explosion (1950–1962)* (Cambridge, MA: MIT Press, 1969), 37.

81. For an account of this courageous and harrowing flight, see Ruaridh Nicoll, "The Great Escape That Changed Africa's Future," *Guardian*, March 8, 2015. Apparently, the Portuguese police had already arrested nine individuals who would eventually flee, erroneously convinced that they had foiled a plan in which an Egyptian submarine was going to pick up these dissident students off Portugal's coast. See Nicoll, "Great Escape."

82. Marcum, *Angolan Revolution*, 37.

83. Augusto Matine, interview by author, November 20, 2012.

84. Rolletta, *Finta finta*, 90.

85. Coluna also found himself under PIDE investigation relating to his Angolan wife's activities and her rumored assistance to the MPLA. In this matter, even Eusébio was not above suspicion given his friendship with Coluna. See TT/PIDE/GS—Relatório Imediato, "Confidencial," September 9, 1969; TT/PIDE/DGS: Letter from the Provincial (MZ) Director of PIDE to the D-G of PIDE in Lisbon, August 8, 1969.

86. Mário Coluna, interview by author, November 21, 2012. FRELIMO was the leftist nationalist party in Mozambique, and the MPLA was the Angolan equivalent.

87. Caldeira, *Coluna*, 55.

88. Ibid.

89. TT/PIDE—March 31, 1961, Processo no. 3767—Delegação de Coimbra da CEI.

90. Cláudia Castelo, "A Casa dos Estudantes," 10.

91. Martins, *Futebol de causas*.

92. Domingos, "Dos subúrbios da Lourenço Marques," 236.

93. See, for example: TT/PIDE/DGS: Folder: PIDE/DGS; SC; 981-SR/61 Eusébio da Silva Ferreira, Report from October 10, 1963: "Assunto: Caso do Rapto do Negro Eusébio, que é Jogador na Equipe Principal de Futebol do Sport Lisboa e Benfica."

94. Armstrong, "Migration of the Black Panther," 253.

Epilogue

1. For an account of these developments, see the first four chapters of Kenneth Maxwell, *The Making of Portuguese Democracy* (New York: Cambridge University Press, 1995).

2. Ricardo Antunes Martins, dir., *Futebol de causas*, film, written by Ricardo Antunes Martins, 2009.

3. Heretofore, exclusively reliant on Portuguese players, including footballers from the colonies, following the revolution Benfica did change its statutes in order to sign foreign players.

4. Peter Alegi, *African Soccerscapes: How a Continent Changed the World's Game* (Athens: Ohio University Press, 2010), 84.

5. He also spent time managing Benfica de Nova Lisboa (Huambo), in Angola, following the revolution. Mário Coluna, interview by author, November 21, 2012.

6. Somewhat ironically, as part of its broader nationalization scheme, Machel's FRELIMO government repossessed a property that Coluna had purchased in Maputo prior to independence and never returned it to him.

7. On June 12, 1975, the city of Vila Pery was renamed Chimoio by the victorious FRELIMO government-in-waiting, which would officially assume power some two weeks later, on June 25, upon the formal independence of Mozambique.

8. Renato Caldeira, *Coluna: Monstro sagrado* (Maputo: Sográfica, 2003), 5.

9. Augusto Matine, interview by author, November 20, 2012.

10. Ibid.

11. As testament to these players' enduring solidarity, following the devastating floods in Mozambique in 2000, António Brassard, Eusébio, Mário Wilson, Shéu Han, Augusto Matine, and Carlos Queiroz formed SOS Mozambique, which raised a considerable amount of money to aid the victims. António Brassard, interview by author, June 19, 2014.

12. Paul Darby, "African Football Labour Migration to Portugal: Colonial and Neo-Colonial Resource," *Soccer and Society* 8, no. 4 (October 2007): 504. Darby explains that similar measures had been implemented in Zaire following Mobutu's ascension.

13. Chiquinho Conde was the first player sanctioned to transfer following the end of the ban, moving from Clube de Desportos da Maxaquene to Belenenses in Portugal.

14. For more on the conflict, see William Finnegan, *A Complicated War: The Harrowing of Mozambique* (Berkeley: University of California Press, 1993).

15. The rescindment of the ban coincided with Mozambican clubs reverting to their original, Portuguese names.

16. Pierre Lanfranchi and Matthew Taylor, *Moving with the Ball: The Migration of Professional Footballers* (Oxford: Berg, 2001), 182.

17. Alegi, *African Soccerscapes*, 89.

18. Darby, "African Football Labour Migration to Portugal," 499.

19. Ibid. Darby also reports that by 2000, "Angola had become the fifth largest exporter of African football labor, accounting for 7.5 percent of all African players in Europe, the majority of whom were based in Portugal." Ibid., 505.

20. Amady Camara's critique comes from the November 8, 1974, edition of the journal *Flama*, in the aftermath of the revolution. The piece appears in João Nuno Coelho and Francisco Pinheiro, *A paixão do povo: História do futebol em Portugal* (Porto: Afrontamento, 2002), 516. For Paul Darby, see, for example, Darby, "The New Scramble for Africa: The African Football Labour Migration to Europe," in *Europe, Sport, World: Shaping Global Societies*, ed. James A. Mangan (London: Cass, 2001), 217–44; and Darby, "Out of Africa: The Exodus of Elite African Football Talent to Europe," *WorkingUSA* 10, no. 4 (December 2007): 443–56.

21. Coelho and Pinheiro, *A paixão do povo*, 516.

22. The match saw the eventual winners fall behind 3–0 after only twenty-four minutes, but four Eusébio goals propelled the Portuguese to victory. Eusébio was also the top scorer of the tournament, with nine total goals.

23. Gabrielle Marcotti, "Eusebio: The Agony of '66," *Times* (London), Monday, February 16, 2004.

24. Ibid.

25. "Eusebio Funeral: Thousands Line Streets to Say Farewell," BBC News, January 6, 2014, http://www.bbc.com/news/world-europe-25621432.

Bibliography

Interviews by Author
Americano, Nuro: November 27, 2012
Baltazar, Ernesto: June 24, 2014
Brassard, António: June 19, 2014
Coluna, Mário: November 21, 2012
Conceição, Hilário da: October 19, 2010
Eusébio: October 28, 2010
Gomes, Fernando: June 26, 2011
Han, Shéu: July 1, 2014
Mataveia: October 20, 2010
Matine, Augusto: November 20, 2012
Medeiros, Tomás: June 30, 2014
Oliveira, Manuel de: October 26, 2010
Rodrigues, Rui: June 25, 2014
Torres, Mário: June 22, 2011
Wilson, Mário: October 29, 2010

Periodicals and Newspapers
A Bola (Portugal)
Diário de Notícias (Portugal)
Guardian (UK)
New York Times (USA)
O Brado Africano (Mozambique)
Tempo (Mozambique)
Times (London)

Archives
Biblioteca Municipal de Coimbra (Coimbra, Portugal)
Portuguese Ministry of Education (Lisbon)
Torre do Tombo: PIDE/DGS archive (Lisbon)

Digital Archives

Casa dos Estudantes do Império, http://disruptiva.net/nodes/view/92

Soccer Politics, Duke University, http://sites.duke.edu/wcwp/research-projects/africa/africa-on-the-field/

WikiSporting, http://www.forumscp.com/wiki/index.php?title=Oct%C3%A1vio_de_S%C3%A1

Ídolos do desporto Pamphlets (Lisbon: Bertrand)

"Abel: Chave mestra para abrir defesas." Series 7, no. 6 (January 7, 1972).

"A equipa de 'Os Belenenses.'" Series 2, no. 51 (September 30, 1960).

"A equipa do Benfica." Series 2, no. 33 (May 27, 1960).

"A equipa do Sporting Clube de Portugal." Series 2, no. 39 (July 8, 1960).

"Águas: 'Esse desconhecido' que veio do Lobito." No. 5 (1956).

"Araújo: O 'Ben Barek' de Sá da Bandeira." Series 2, no. 23 (March 18, 1960).

"Armando: O '115' do Sporting." Series 5, no. 1 (December 30, 1967).

"Bernardo da Velha: O 'Tapa Buracos' do F. Clube do Porto." Series 5, no. 19 (March 23, 1968).

"Calado: O 'Papua' de Lourenço Marques." Series 5, no. 9 (February 24, 1968).

"Carlitos: Um future 'astro' do firmament Leonino." Series 4, no. 14 (March 26, 1966).

"Carlos Duarte: O extremo-direito que Monteiro da Costa descobriu para o F.C. do Porto." Series 2, no. 49 (January 5, 1957).

"Coluna: A locomotiva do Benfica!" Series 2, no. 71 (February 17, 1961).

"Coluna: O homem das 5 Selecções." No. 5 (1956).

"Conceição: O 'Grande Capitão' Sadino." Series 6, no. 17 (March 14, 1970).

"Costa Pereira: O 'goleiro' do Maracanã." No. 5 (1956).

"Dinis: O ídolo do asa que triunfa no Sporting." Series 7, no. 5 (January 1, 1972).

"Eusébio: O 'Pele' da Europa." Series 3, no. 1 (December 7, 1963).

"Eusébio: Um astro no firmament do futebol mundial." Series 6, no. 2 (November 29, 1969).

"Ferreira Pinto: Um médio que dá sempre tudo por tudo." Series 5, no. 13 (March 23, 1968).

"Hilário: O 'rapazinho' do Alto Mahé." Series 2, no. 2 (October 24, 1959).

"Hilário: Um herói do 'mundial.'" Series 5, no. 10 (March 2, 1968).

"Iaúca: A flecha Benfiquista." Series 3, no. 25 (February 17, 1961).

"'Imperador' Eusébio." Series 7, no. 2 (December 11, 1971).

"Jacinto João: A 'pérola negra' do Sado." Series 6, no. 3 (December 6, 1969).

"José Maria: O 'pulmão' do Vitória." Series 6, no. 13 (December 6, 1969).

"Juca: 'O Cabecinha d'Oiro.'" No. 5 (1956).

"Júlio: O 'tigre' que se tornou 'Leão.'" Series 2, no. 62 (December 16, 1960).

"Laurindo: Um dianteiro ágil como um gamo." Series 7, no. 14 (March 4, 1972).
"Mascarenhas: Um Angolano que triunfa no Sporting." Series 3, no. 7 (January 18, 1964).
"Matateu: Terror dos Guards-Redes." No. 3 (March 17, 1956).
"Matateu: Um nome que fica na história do futebol." Series 2, no. 72 (February 24, 1961).
"Miguel Arcanjo: O homem duas vezes quase perdido para a futbol." No. 42 (1956).
"Pérides: O Luso-Grego de Tete." Series 3, no. 14 (March 7, 1964).
"Rui Rodrigues: Um homem tranquilo a fazer futebol." Series 7, no. 12 (February 19, 1972).
"Santana: O 'Molengão' de Catumbela." Series 2, no. 17 (February 5, 1960).
"Torres: O 'jogador médico.'" Series 2, no. 6 (November 21, 1959).
"Vicente Lucas: O homem que não quis ser 'Matateu II.'" No. 34 (1956).
"Vicente: O homem que 'eclipsou' Pelé. Series 3, no. 22 (May 2, 1964).
"Yaúca: 'A pérola negra.'" Series 2, no. 3 (October 31, 1959).
"Zeca: 'Calma e segurança na zona de perigo.'" Series 7, no. 18 (April 1, 1972).

Books and Articles

Aguiar, Mário de. *Coluna: O grande capitão.* Lisbon: Filtro Estúdios Gráficos, 1968.
Alegi, Peter. *African Soccerscapes: How a Continent Changed the World's Game.* Athens: Ohio University Press, 2010.
———. "Football and Apartheid Society: The South African Soccer League, 1960–1966." In Armstrong and Giulianotti, *Football in Africa*, 114–34.
———. *Laduma! Soccer, Politics and Society in South Africa, from Its Origins to 2010.* Scottsville, South Africa: University of KwaZulu-Natal Press, 2010.
Andringa, Diana, dir. *Operação Angola: Fugir para lutar.* Film. 2015.
Armstrong, Gary. "The Migration of the Black Panther: An Interview with Eusebio of Mozambique and Portugal." In Armstrong and Giulianotti, *Football in Africa*, 247–68.
Armstrong, Gary, and Richard Giulianotti, eds. *Football in Africa: Conflict, Conciliation and Community.* New York: Palgrave Macmillan, 2004.
Bale, John, and Joe Sang. *Kenyan Running: Movement Culture, Geography and Global Change.* London: Cass, 1996.
Bender, Gerald J. *Angola under the Portuguese: The Myth and the Reality.* Berkeley: University of California Press, 1978.
Billig, Michael. *Banal Nationalism.* London: Sage, 1995.
Bittencourt, Marcelo. "Jogando no campo do inimigo: Futebol e luta política em Angola." Lisbon: Seventh Congress on African Studies, 2010.
———. "Moral e política: A vigilância colonial sobre o esporte angolano." In Nascimento et al., *Esporte e lazer na África*, 155–78.

Boer, Wiebe. "A Story of Heroes, of Epics: The Rise of Football in Nigeria." In Armstrong and Giulianotti, *Football in Africa*, 59–79.

Booth, Douglas. "Hitting Apartheid for Six? The Politics of the South African Sports Boycott." *Journal of Contemporary History* 38, no. 3 (2003): 477–93.

Borgal, Clément, and Fernando Garcia. *15 histórias de futebol*. Viseu, Portugal: Tipografia Guerra, 1980.

Caldeira, Renato. *Coluna: Monstro sagrado*. Maputo: Sográfica, 2003.

Cardão, Marcos. "Peregrinações exemplars: As embaixadas patrióticas dos clubes metropolitanos ao 'ultramar português.'" In Nascimento et al., *Esporte e lazer na África*, 109–28.

———. "Um significante instrumental, Eusébio e a banalização lusotropicalismo na década de 1960." In Melo, Peres, and Drumond, *Esporte, cultura, nação, estado*, 172–88.

Carney, Judith A. *Black Rice: The African Origins of Rice Cultivation in the Americas*. Cambridge, MA: Harvard University Press, 2001.

Carvalho, Guido de. *Matateu: O "gigante" de Alto Mahé; Festa de homenagem*. September 21, 1960.

Cashman, Richard. "Cricket and Colonialism: Colonial Hegemony and Indigenous Subversion?" In *Pleasure, Profit, Proselytism: British Culture and Sport at Home and Abroad, 1700–1914*, edited by James A. Mangan, 258–72. London: Cass, 1988.

Castelo, Cláudia. "A Casa dos Estudantes do Império: Lugar de memória anticolonial." CIEA7, no. 6: (Counter-) Memories of Colonialism: Remembrance, Resistance and Transference in Anti-Colonial African Narratives (2010): 1–18.

———. "Casa dos Estudantes do Império (1944–1965): Uma síntese histórica." In *Mensagem: Cinquentenário da fundação da Casa dos Estudantes do Império, 1944–1994*, 25–31. Lisbon: Associação Casa dos Estudantes do Império, 1997.

Cleveland, Todd. *Diamonds in the Rough: Corporate Paternalism and African Professionalism on the Mines of Colonial Angola, 1917–1975*. Athens: Ohio University Press, 2015.

Clignet, Rémi, and Maureen Stark. "Modernisation and Football in Cameroun." *Journal of Modern African Studies* 12, no. 3 (September 1974): 409–21.

Coelho, João Nuno. *Portugal—A equipa de todos nós: Nacionalismo, futebol e media*. Porto: Afrontamento, 2001.

Coelho, João Nuno, and Francisco Pinheiro. *A paixão do povo: História do futebol em Portugal*. Porto: Afrontamento, 2002.

Correia, Fernando. *Matateu: O oitava maravilha*. Lisbon: Sete Caminhos, 2006.

Cronin, Mike, and David Mayall, eds. *Sporting Nationalisms: Identity, Ethnicity, Immigration and Assimilation.* London: Cass, 1998.

Darby, Paul. *Africa, Football and FIFA: Politics, Colonialism and Resistance.* London: Cass, 2002.

———. "African Football Labour Migration to Portugal: Colonial and Neo-Colonial Resource." *Soccer and Society* 8, no. 4 (October 2007): 495–509.

———. "'Go Outside': The History, Economics and Geography of Ghanaian Football Labour Migration." *African Historical Review* 42, no. 1 (2010): 19–41.

———. "The New Scramble for Africa: The African Football Labour Migration to Europe." In *Europe, Sport, World: Shaping Global Societies,* edited by James A. Mangan, 217–44. London: Cass, 2001.

———. "Out of Africa: The Exodus of Elite African Football Talent to Europe." *WorkingUSA* 10, no. 4 (December 2007): 443–56.

Dias, Manuel, and Carlos Pinhão. *Benfica: O voo da aguia, álbum 88/89.* Lisbon: Edições, 1992.

Dias, Marina Tavares. *História do futebol em Lisboa: De 1888 aos grandes estádios.* Coimbra: Quimera, 2000.

Dietschy, Paul. "Making Football Global? FIFA, Europe, and the Non-European Football World, 1912–74." *Journal of Global History* 8, no. 2 (July 2013): 279–98.

Domingos, Nuno. "A circulação de um esquema táctico: O exemplo do WM em Inglaterra, Portugal e Moçambique." *Esporte e Sociedade* 5, no. 14 (March–June 2010): 1–32.

———. "'Dos subúrbios da Lourenço Marques colonial aos campos de futebol da metrópole,' uma entrevista com Hilário Rosário da Conceição." *Cadernos de Estudos Africanos* 26 (2013): 225–45.

———. "Football and Colonialism, Domination and Appropriation: The Mozambican Case." *Soccer and Society* 8, no. 4 (October 2007): 478–94.

———. "Football in Colonial Lourenço Marques: Bodily Practices and Social Rituals." PhD diss., University of London, 2008.

———. *Futebol e colonialismo: Corpo e cultura popular em Moçambique.* Lisbon: Imprensa de Ciências Sociais, 2012.

———. "O campo de desportivização imperial português." In Nascimento et al., *Esporte e lazer na África,* 81–108.

———. "O desporte e o Império Português." In *Uma história do desporto em Portugal.* Vol. 2, *Nação, império e globalização,* edited by José Neves and Nuno Domingos, 51–107. Lisbon: QuidNovi, 2011.

———. "Urban Football Narratives and the Colonial Process in Lourenço Marques." *International Journal of the History of Sport* 28, no. 15 (October 2011): 2159–75.

Fair, Laura. "Kickin' It: Leisure, Politics and Football in Colonial Zanzibar, 1900s–1950s." *Africa* 67, no. 2 (1997): 224–51.

——. "Ngoma Reverberations: Swahili Music Culture and the Making of Football Aesthetics in Early Twentieth-Century Zanzibar." In Armstrong and Giulianotti, *Football in Africa*, 103–13.

——. *Pastimes and Politics: Culture, Community, and Identity in Post-Abolition Urban Zanzibar, 1890–1945*. Athens: Ohio University Press, 2001.

Fanon, Frantz. *Black Skin, White Masks*. New York: Grove Press, 1967.

Fates, Youseff. "Football in Algeria: Between Violence and Politics." In Armstrong and Giulianotti, *Football in Africa*, 41–58.

Ferreira, Eusébio da Silva. *My Name Is Eusébio*. Translated by Derrik Low. London: Routledge and Kegan Paul, 1967.

Finnegan, William. *A Complicated War: The Harrowing of Mozambique*. Berkeley: University of California Press, 1993.

Freyre, Gilberto. *Casa-Grande e Senzala*. Rio de Janeiro: Global Editora, 1933.

Galvão, Henrique. *Santa Maria: My Crusade for Portugal*. London: Weidenfeld and Nicolson, 1961.

Gengenbach, Heidi. "'What My Heart Wanted': Gendered Stories of Early Colonial Encounters in Southern Mozambique." In *Women in African Colonial Histories*, edited by Jean Allman, Susan Geiger, and Nakanyike Musisi, 19–47. Bloomington: Indiana University Press, 2002.

Giulianotti, Richard. "Between Colonialism, Independence and Globalization: Football in Zimbabwe." In Armstrong and Giulianotti, *Football in Africa*, 80–102.

Goldblatt, David. *The Ball Is Round: A Global History of Soccer*. New York: Penguin, 2006.

Gomez, Michael A. *Exchanging Our Country Marks: The Transformation of African Identities in the Colonial and Antebellum South*. Chapel Hill: University of North Carolina Press, 1998.

Guttmann, Allen. *Games and Empires: Modern Sports and Cultural Imperialism*. New York: Columbia University Press, 1996.

Harries, Patrick. *Work, Culture, and Identity: Migrant Laborers in Mozambique and South Africa, c. 1860–1910*. Portsmouth, NH: Heinemann, 1994.

Henriques, Isabel Castro. "Africans in Portuguese Society: Classification Ambiguities and Colonial Realities." In *Imperial Migrations: Colonial Communities and Diaspora in the Portuguese World*, edited by Eric Morier-Genoud and Michel Cahen, 72–103. New York: Palgrave Macmillan, 2012.

Hinds, Rodney. *Black Lions: A History of Black Players in English Football*. London: Sportsbooks, 2006.

Hine, Darlene Clark, Trica Danielle Keaton, and Stephen Small, eds. *Black Europe and the African Diaspora*. Urbana: University of Illinois Press, 2009.

História e figuras do campeonato nacional de futebol da 1.ª divisão 1955–1956. Lisbon: Edição da Agência de Revistas, 1956.

James, C. L. R. *Beyond a Boundary*. London: Yellow Jersey Press, 2005.

Knight, Frederick C. *Working the Diaspora: The Impact of African Labor on the Anglo-American World, 1650–1850*. New York: New York University Press, 2010.

Kumar, Rahul Mahendra. "A pureza perdida do desporto: Futebol no Estado Novo." PhD diss., University of Lisbon, 2014.

Lanfranchi, Pierre. "Mekloufi, un footballeur français dans la guerre d'Algérie." *Actes de la recherche en sciences sociales* 103, no. 1 (1994): 70–74.

Lanfranchi, Pierre, and Matthew Taylor. *Moving with the Ball: The Migration of Professional Footballers*. Oxford: Berg, 2001.

Lanfranchi, Pierre, and Alfred Wahl. "The Immigrant as Hero: Kopa, Mekloufi and French Football." In *European Heroes: Myth, Identity, Sport*, edited by Richard Holt, James A. Mangan, and Pierre Lanfranchi, 114–27. London: Cass, 1996.

Last, Alex. "Containment and Counter-Attack: A History of Eritrean Football." In Armstrong and Giulianotii, *Football in Africa*, 27–40.

Lawrence, Benjamin N., Emily Lynn Osborn, and Richard L. Roberts, eds. *Intermediaries, Interpreters, and Clerks: African Employees in the Making of Colonial Africa*. Madison: University of Wisconsin Press, 2006.

Magalhães, Álvaro, and Manuel Dias. *F.C. Porto: 100 anos de história, 1893–1993*. Porto: Edições Asa, 1995.

Magode, José. *Pouvoir et reseaux sociaux au Mozambique: Appartenances, interactivité du social et du politique, 1933–1994*. Paris: Connaissances et Savoirs, 2005.

Malheiro, João. *Eusébio: A biografia autorizado*. Vila do Conde: QuidNovi, 2012.

Mangan, James A., ed. *The Cultural Bond: Sport, Empire, Society*. London: Cass, 1992.

Marcum, John. *The Angolan Revolution*. Vol. 1, *The Anatomy of an Explosion (1950–1962)*. Cambridge, MA: MIT Press, 1969.

Martin, Phyllis M. "Colonialism, Youth and Football in French Equatorial Africa." *International Journal of the History of Sport* 8, no. 1 (1991): 56–71.

———. *Leisure and Society in Colonial Brazzaville*. Cambridge: Cambridge University Press, 1995.

Martins, Ricardo Antunes, dir. *Futebol de causas*. Film, written by Ricardo Antunes Martins. 2009.

Marzano, Andrea. "Nem todas as batalhas eram de flores: Cotidiano, lazer e conflitos sociais em Luanda." In Nascimento et al., *Esporte e lazer na África*, 13–36.

Maxwell, Kenneth. *The Making of Portuguese Democracy*. New York: Cambridge University Press, 1995.

Melo, Victor Andrade de. "(Des)mobilização para a luta: O esporte como estratégia nos conflitos de Guiné Portuguesa (décadas de 1950 e 1960)." In Melo, Peres, and Drumond, *Esporte, cultura, nação, estado*, 68–82.

———. "Pequenas-grandes representações do império portuguêes: A série postal 'modalidades desportivas' (1962)." In Nascimento et al., *Esporte e lazer na África*, 129–54.

Melo, Victor Andrade de, Fabio de Faria Peres, and Maurício Drumond, eds. *Esporte, cultura, nação, estado: Brasil e Portugal*. Rio de Janeiro: 7Letras, 2014.

Mills, James. "Football in Goa: Sport, Politics and the Portuguese in India." In *Soccer in South Asia: Empire, Nation, Diaspora*, edited by Paul Dimeo and James Mills, 75–88. London: Routledge, 2001.

Moorman, Marissa J. *Intonations: A Social History of Music and Nation in Luanda, Angola, from 1945 to Recent Times*. Athens: Ohio University Press, 2008.

Morais, António Manuel, Carlos Perdigão, João Loureiro, and José de Oliveira Santos. *Benfica: 90 anos de glória, 1904–1994*. Lisbon: Sogapal, 1996.

Moyd, Michelle R. *Violent Intermediaries: African Soldiers, Conquest, and Everyday Colonialism in German East Africa*. Athens: Ohio University Press, 2014.

Mustafa, Fahad. "Cricket and Globalization: Global Processes and the Imperial Game." *Journal of Global History* 8, no. 2 (2013): 318–41.

Nascimento, Augusto, Marcelo Bittencourt, Nuno Domingos, and Victor Andrade de Melo, eds. *Esporte e lazer na África: Novos olhares*. Rio de Janeiro: 7Letras, 2013.

N'Diaye, Boubacar. "Ivory Coast's Civilian Control Strategies 1961–1998: A Critical Assessment." *Journal of Political and Military Sociology* 28, no. 2 (2000): 246–70.

Oliveira, Angelo. *Isto de futebóis*. Maputo, Mozambique: Ndjira, 1998.

Os 4 gigantes do futebol Português. Lisbon: Ag. Port. de Revistas, D.L., 1965.

Os 50 anos da Federação Portuguesa de Futebol. Lisbon: Orbis, 1964.

Parsons, Timothy H. *The African Rank-and-File: Social Implications of Colonial Military Service in the King's African Rifles, 1902–1964*. Portsmouth, NH: Heinemann, 1999.

Pereira, Barros. *Sporting Clube de Braga, 1921–1985*. Braga: Correo do Minho, 1986.

Pereira, Matheus Serva. "Beiço a mais, miolos a menos . . .': Representação, repressão e lazer dos grupos africanos subalternos nas páginas da imprensa de Lourenço Marques (1890–1910)." In Nascimento et al., *Esporte e lazer na África*, 37–62.

Pinto, Fernando. *50 anos de Selecções Nacionais Futebol*. Viseu: Edições Fama, 1972.

Poli, Raffaele. "Explaining the 'Muscle Drain' of African Football Players: World-System Theory and Beyond." BAB Working Paper No. 1, presented at the Basler Afrika Bibliographien, Basel, Switzerland, 2008.

———. "Migrations and Trade of African Football Players: Histories, Geographical and Cultural Aspects." *Africa Spectrum* 41, no. 3 (2006): 393–414.

Portugal-Rússia: O jogo que nos deu o 3.° lugar. 1966.

Rocha, Aurélio. "Associativismo e nativismo em Moçambique: O grémio Africano de Lourenço Marques, 1908–1938." PhD diss., Universidade Nova de Lisboa, 1991.

Rodrigues, Perfeito. *Recordando . . . algumas velhas glórias do futebol Português*. Coimbra: Gráfica de Coimbra, 1980.

Rolletta, Paola. *Finta finta*. Maputo, Mozambique: Texto Editores, 2011.

Rosa, Acácio. *Factos, nomes e números da história do clube de futebol "Os Belenenses."* Lisbon: Freitas and Freitas, 1961.

Rosenhaft, Eve, and Robbie Aitken, eds. *Africa in Europe: Studies in Transnational Practice in the Long Twentieth Century*. Liverpool: Liverpool University Press, 2013.

Rukanshagiza, Joseph B. "African Armies: Understanding the Origin and Continuation of Their Non-Professionalism." PhD diss., State University of New York, Albany, 1995.

Santos, Ana. *Herois desportivos: Estudo de caso sobre Eusébio, de corpo a ícone da nação*. Lisbon: Instituto do Desporto de Portugal, 2004.

———. "Narrativas da nação proporcionadas pelas vitórias desportivas e seus heróis." *IV Congresso Português de Sociologia* (April 2000): 1–12.

Serpa, Homero, and Vitor Serpa. *História do futebol em Portugal*. Lisbon: CTT Correios, 2004.

Silva, Eugénio. *Eusébio: Pantera negra*. Lisbon: Meribérica, 1992.

Simões, António. *Eusébio: Como nunca se viu*. Alfragide, Portugal: Dom Quixote, 2014.

Sousa, Manuel de. *História do futebol: Origens, nomes, números e factos*. Mem-Martins, Portugal: SporPress, 1997.

Stoddart, Brian. "Sport, Cultural Imperialism, and Colonial Response in the British Empire." *Comparative Studies in Society and History* 30, no. 4 (1988): 649–73.

Tapada, Joaquim. *Futebol: Dicionário onomástico dos internacionais séniores portugueses de 1921 a 1980*. Braga: Oficinas Gráficas da Livraria Editora Pax, 1981.

Taylor, Matthew. "Editorial—Sort, Transnationalism, and Global History." *Journal of Global History* 8, no. 2 (July 2013): 199–208.

Tovar, Rui. *Grandes equipas portuguesas de futebol.* Lisbon: Amigos do Livro, 1980.

Tovar, Rui, and Joaquim Tapada. *A selecção nacional de futebol.* 2 vols. Lisbon: Amigos do Livro, 1980.

Vasco, Pedro, and Ricardo Galvão. *Monstros sagrados: Benfica anos 60s.* Lisbon: Primebooks, 2011.

Vasili, Phil. *Colouring over the White Line: The History of Black Footballers in Britain.* Edinburgh: Mainstream, 2000.

———. *The First Black Footballer—Arthur Wharton, 1865–1930: An Absence of Memory.* London: Cass, 1998.

Veloso, Jacinto. *Memories at Low Altitude: The Autobiography of a Mozambican Security Chief.* Cape Town: Zebra Press, 2012.

Vidacs, Bea. "Through the Prism of Sports: Why Should Africanists Study Sports?" *Afrika Spectrum* 41, no. 3 (2006): 331–49.

Wilson, Jonathan. *Inverting the Pyramid: The History of Soccer Tactics.* New York: Nation Books, 2013.

Wilson, Mário. "Uma marca na história." In *Académica: História do futebol,* edited by João Santana and João Mesquita. Coimbra, Portugal: Almedina, 2007.

Zimmerman, Andrew. "Africa in Imperial and Transnational History: Multi-Sited Historiography and the Necessity of Theory." *Journal of African History* 54, no. 3 (2013): 331–40.

Index

147, 149, 178–79, 185–88, 197, 201
Santana, João, 54, 115, 138, 160, 176, 193, 197
Santo, Guilherme Espírito ("Pérola Negra"), 231n6, 223n35
Santos, 148
Santos, Marcelino dos, 192–93, 201, 204
São Tomé and Príncipe, 2, 24, 192
saudades, 113, 118–21, 127–29, 146, 154
scouting, 19, 44, 57–58, 67, 78–79, 82, 85, 93–99, 107, 110, 124, 168, 187, 229n57
selecção, 73, 88, 97, 100, 111, 144, 180, 230n74.
    See also Portugal: National Team
Sentrensa, 131
Setúbal, 108, 117, 135
signing, 4, 19, 32, 44, 66, 74, 78, 80, 82, 85–88, 90–116, 123, 131, 147–49, 159, 165, 170, 187, 208, 210, 214, 232n27, 233n41. *See also* contracts
Silva, Ângelo Gomes da, 36, 39
Silva, Domingos António da ("Mascarenhas"), 138–39, 155, 161
Silva, Manuel António Vassalo e, 42
Soares da Cunha, Francisco, 105
Sousa, João de, 38–39
South Africa, 7, 35, 41, 44, 61, 68, 134, 213, 225n39. *See also* Johannesburg African Football Association; Johannesburg's All-Blacks Football Club; Transvaal African Football Association (TAFA)
South America, 44, 90, 148. *See also* individual countries
Soviet Union (USSR), 87, 182, 186
Spain, 67, 88, 145, 149, 172, 181, 201, 224n21
Sport Clube da Catumbela, 54, 71
Sport Clube Estrela de Portalegre, 149
Sporting. *See* Sporting Clube de Portugal
Sporting Clube de Benguela, 66, 91, 101
Sporting Clube de Bissau, 66
Sporting Clube de Espinho and Leixões, 147
Sporting Clube de Luanda, 67, 90–91
Sporting Clube de Portugal (Sporting), 1, 8, 15–16, 22, 30, 36–37, 40, 52, 54, 66, 71, 79–80, 84, 90–92, 94–95, 98, 100–105, 109–11, 115, 117, 123–24, 126, 128, 131, 134,

136, 139, 145, 147–48, 154, 161–62, 165, 168, 170–73, 176, 189, 192, 197–99, 208
Sporting da Beira, 140
Sporting de Lourenço Marques, 66, 77–81, 84, 91, 94, 100–101, 103–4, 124, 230n89
Sporting de Vila Nova, 36
Sporting do Huambo, 36
Sporting Lisbon. *See* Sporting Clube de Portugal
Sport Luanda e Benfica. *See* Benfica de Luanda
"stacking," 134, 140–42
Stadium, 33
stadiums, 45, 73, 98, 105, 115, 117, 137, 140, 145, 151, 153, 159, 161, 198–99, 216
Sweden, 56

Taça de Portugal (Portuguese Cup), 22, 112, 131, 199, 211, 235n58
Taça Latina, 224n21
tactics. *See* game tactics
teammates, 4, 6–7, 11, 14, 18, 58, 65, 74–75, 107–8, 119, 129–30, 134–35, 137–38, 141, 151, 153–54, 158–60, 172, 174, 188, 191, 193–95, 198, 200, 205, 209
teams. *See selecção; individual teams*
Tête, 139
Textáfrica da Cidade de Vila Pery, 211
Tirsense, 138
Tomás, Américo, 184, 199
Toronto Metros-Croatia, 210
Torres, Mário, 36, 143, 145, 157, 168–71, 189, 195–97, 213
training, 14–15, 64, 68–70, 82, 96–97, 115, 117–18, 120–22, 127, 134–36, 149, 151–54, 195, 198, 216, 232n18
Transvaal African Football Association (TAFA), 61
Travassos, José, 37

UEFA Cup Winners' Cup, 139
União de Tomar, 129, 189, 210
United Kingdom, 33
United Nations, 29
United States, 27, 87, 172, 178, 189–90, 210